CHANGING TEACHERS' WORK

CHANGING EDUCATION

Series Editors:
Professor Andy Hargreaves, Ontario Institute for Studies in Education
Professor Ivor Goodson, University of East Anglia

This authoritative series addresses the key issues raised by the unprecedented levels of educational change now facing schools and societies throughout the world.

The different directions of change can seem conflicting and are often contested. Decentralized systems of school self-management are accompanied by centralized systems of curriculum and assessment control. Moves to develop more authentic assessments are paralleled by the tightened imposition of standardized tests. Curriculum integration is being advocated in some places, more specialization and subject departmentalization in others.

These complex and contradictory cross-currents pose real challenges to theoretical and practical interpretation in many fields of education and constitute an important and intriguing agenda for educational change. *Changing Education* brings together leading international scholars who address these vital issues with authority and accessibility in areas where they are noted specialists. The series will commission books from all parts of the world in an attempt to cover the global and interlinked nature of current changes.

CHANGING TEACHERS' WORK

The 'reform' of secondary schooling

GILL HELSBY

OPEN UNIVERSITY PRESS
Buckingham · Philadelphia

For Denis, Katie and Beth

Open University Press
Celtic Court
22 Ballmoor
Buckingham
MK18 1XW

email: enquiries@openup.co.uk
world wide web: http://www.openup.co.uk

and

325 Chestnut Street
Philadelphia, PA 19106, USA

First Published 1999

A catalogue record of this book is available from the British Library

ISBN   0 335 19938 0 (pbk)   0 335 19939 9 (hbk)

Library of Congress Cataloging-in-Publication Data
Helsby, Gill
    Changing teachers' work : the reform of secondary schooling / Gill Helsby.
       p.   cm. — (Changing education)
    Includes bibliographical references and index.
    ISBN 0-335-19939-9 (hbk) ISBN 0-335-19938-0 (pbk)
    1. Education. Secondary—Great Britain.   2. High school teaching—Great Britain.   3. School management and organization—Great Britain.
4. Educational change—Great Britain.   I. Title.   II. Series.
LA635.H375   1999
373.41—dc21   98-44937   CIP

Typeset by Type Study, Scarborough
Printed in Great Britain by Biddles Limited, Guildford and Kings Lynn

CONTENTS

SERIES EDITORS' PREFACE

Around the world, schools, and the societies of which they are a part, are confronting the most profound changes, the like of which have not been seen since the last great global movement of economic and educational restructuring more than a century ago. The fundamental forms of public education that were designed for an age of heavy manufacturing and mechanical industry are under challenge and fading fast as we move into a world of high technology, flexible workforces, more diverse school populations, downsized administrations and declining resources.

What is to follow is uncertain and unclear. The different directions of change can seem conflicting and are often contested. Decentralized systems of school self-management are accompanied by centralized systems of curriculum and assessment control. Moves to develop more authentic assessments are paralleled by the tightened imposition of standardized tests. Curriculum integration is being advocated in some places, more specialization and subject departmentalization in others.

These complex and contradictory cross-currents pose real challenges to theoretical and practical interpretation in many fields of education, and constitute an important and intriguing agenda for educational change – and for this series, which is intended to meet a deep-seated need among researchers and practitioners. International, social and technological changes require a profound and rapid response from the educational community. By establishing and interpreting the nature and scope of educational change, *Changing Teachers' Work* will make a significant contribution to meeting this challenge.

Gill Helsby has spent the last decade and more investigating the nature and fate of teachers and teaching in times of dramatic change and reform.

The combination of quantitative and qualitative methods she has used throughout her research, make her findings both dependable and insightful. By investigating how teachers responded to a complex set of technical and vocational innovations, then how the secondary school teaching force in England and Wales has been profoundly reshaped by the high-profile National Curriculum, Helsby portrays a profession that has been pushed, pulled, moulded, twisted and sometimes broken by a collection of reforms, whose scope and force have been unparalleled in recent educational history.

Helsby documents with power and sensitivity, how an era of reform has impacted on teachers' competence and also slowly eroded their professional confidence. From her extensive basis of evidence, she shows how teachers have gained some new skills because of the reform movement in classroom assessment and collaborating with colleagues, for example. But they have also lost a great deal in the process in terms of status, confidence, time, energy and opportunities for professional development.

Changing Teachers' Work is not an ideological battering-ram of a book; but a sober, sustained and highly readable assessment of how teaching has changed and continues to change in England's educational reform climate. It bears witness, along with other books on English educational reform, on how this reform movement, like others, has been built on the backs of teachers, reducing the capacity of many to meet childrens' needs in the process. It is important reading for reformers, school leaders and teachers themselves who design, implement or deal with the consequences of educational reform. From its pages, we can perhaps build a stronger, more optimistic and trusting vision of how to design educational reforms that really benefit pupils, in ways that involve and engage the professionalism of those teachers who will ultimately have to ensure the success of these reforms in the classroom.

PREFACE AND ACKNOWLEDGEMENTS

Educational reform or restructuring has occurred in many westernized nations in recent years, with remarkable similarities between developments in different countries. The decentralization of educational administration, a strengthening of accountability mechanisms, the development or refinement of national curricula and an increasing focus upon quantifying and measuring the outcomes of schooling are all key features of reforms, as national governments look increasingly towards their education systems to solve economic problems created by globalization. Despite the similarities, the way in which these reforms are promoted varies considerably according to the historical, cultural and social context. Some countries have chosen a gradual approach, conferring widely and appealing to teachers' sense of 'professionalism' to help develop and implement the reforms. In England, however, the changes have been introduced in a particularly aggressive way, with minimal consultation, high levels of central prescription, constant criticism of teachers and draconian systems of surveillance. This stands in marked contrast with the distinctively English notion of teacher professionalism based upon a strong tradition of curriculum autonomy, leading many commentators to suggest that teachers' work is now being deskilled.

In many ways the introduction of the Technical and Vocational Education Initiative, a major, nationally funded curriculum development project, into English and Welsh secondary schools in 1983 marked the first stage of the current educational reforms. By accident and good luck, the beginning of my own career in educational research coincided with the launch of TVEI, and I have since spent a considerable proportion of my working life visiting schools involved in this and other curriculum reform projects and talking to teachers about the impact of these reforms upon themselves, their students and their schools. Much of the work has been commissioned evaluative research of particular initiatives but, over the years, data have been accumulated which point towards the enormous changes which have been taking place in teachers' working lives, especially as a result of the multiple educational reforms introduced by politicians. This book will draw upon those data to present a picture of the complex ways in which teachers respond to constant innovation and themselves play a crucial part in shaping not only its outcomes but also their own role within it.

My thanks are due to the many people who have helped me over the years of research covered by this book. I am very grateful for the ongoing support and friendship of colleagues in the Centre for the Study of Education and Training and Department of Educational Research at Lancaster University, particularly to Oliver Fulton for encouraging me to write this book and to Peter Knight for reading and making such incisive comments on the manuscript. My thinking about teachers' work has been greatly helped and stimulated by members of the international Professional Actions and Cultures of Teaching research network, directed by Ivor Goodson and Andy Hargreaves, and also by colleagues in the Lancaster TVEI Evaluation Programme and in the 30-month research project funded by the Economic and Social Research Council on 'The Professional Culture of Teachers and the Secondary School Curriculum' (RO00234738), Peter Knight, Gary McCulloch, Murray Saunders and Terry Warburton. Last, but certainly not least, I owe a huge debt of gratitude to the many teachers and other educationalists who have given freely of their time and shared their experiences over the years, despite the pressures created by recent educational reforms. Without their help, this book could not have been written.

ABBREVIATIONS

CATE	Council for the Accreditation of Teacher Education
DES	Department of Education and Science
DfE	Department for Education
DfEE	Department for Education and Employment
ERO	Education Review Office
GCSE	General Certificate of Secondary Education
GEST	Grants for Educational Support and Training
HMI	Her Majesty's Inspectorate
INSET	in-service education and training
ITE	initial teacher education
JSA	Joint Support Activities
LEA	local education authority
LMS	local management of schools
MSC	Manpower Services Commission
OECD	Organization for Economic Cooperation and Development
Ofsted	Office for Standards in Education
PE	physical education
SAT	standard assessment task
SCAA	School Curriculum and Assessment Authority
SMT	senior management team
TEC	Training and Enterprise Council
TTA	Teacher Training Agency
TVEI	Technical and Vocational Education Initiative

one

CHANGING DISCOURSES
FOR NEW TIMES

Introduction

Teachers' work is undoubtedly changing. Across the westernized world, new responsibilities, new demands and new terms and conditions of service are being imposed with increasing frequency as education is 'reformed' and schooling 'restructured' to meet the perceived needs of the twenty-first century. Suddenly 'education' and 'schooling' are important topics in the media, occupying a vast acreage of newspaper columns and countless hours of television and radio broadcasts. The general public are constantly invited to participate in the general concern over 'falling standards' and 'nations at risk', to become angry about 'failing teachers' or 'failing schools' and to admire the determination of governments to improve the 'quality' of education (albeit whilst simultaneously continuing to reduce public expenditure in this area).

Despite some clear differences of emphasis between nations, the general pattern of reforms is remarkably consistent. The dismantling of large educational bureaucracies, the introduction of new and devolved forms of governance, school-based financial management and school–business–community partnerships are rapidly becoming commonplace as former public monopoly schools are subjected to the discipline of the market. At the same time, central control is tightened through goal-steering devices such as the development or recasting of a prescribed national curriculum, an increased emphasis upon learning outcomes and associated assessment, more stringent and more overt accountability requirements and/or increased surveillance of classroom practice. Meanwhile, teachers themselves are given more onerous and more diverse responsibilities, are increasingly exhorted to collaborate with their colleagues over the means (although not the ends) of education and are subject to greater managerial control by school leaders. Finally, a closer specification of duties and changes in terms and conditions of service point towards a transition from a body of state professionals to a more flexible and differentiated workforce (Lawn 1995).

These changes can be seen as symptomatic of a wider set of economic, social, cultural and political realignments that transcend national boundaries and are currently transforming late twentieth-century society. The globalization of capital, the restructuring of world economies and the growth of deregulated, international markets all create profound political uncertainties, whilst the gradual emergence of a new world order is accompanied by the simultaneous proclamation of a 'new work order' (Gee *et al.* 1996) of flattened hierarchies, corporate visions, flexible labour markets, customer responsiveness and the inexorability of continuous quality improvement to gain competitive edge. In the wider social context, the information explosion and the failure of technical rationalism to solve society's problems have led to considerable distrust in professional expertise and widespread uncertainty about the best way of dealing with the changes. At the level of the individual, uncertainty is exacerbated by the increasing lack of stability in family life, in employment and in geographical location, whilst many experience additional stress because of the compression of time and space (Hargreaves 1994) brought about by the speed of technological advances, increased mobility and more rapid communications.

Individual nation states, faced with a triple crisis of accumulation, of social unrest and of legitimacy, have inevitably looked anew at the role of their education systems in producing the compliant citizenry and the skilled, flexible and differentiated workforce deemed necessary to ensure social stability and economic success in the future. Consequently, the aims of education have been subjected to close scrutiny and to a variety of attempts to realign them more closely with the perceived needs of the labour market. Since the education of young people lies at the very heart of teachers' work, changes to the former inevitably impact fundamentally upon the latter. At the same time, the widespread dismantling of the Keynesian welfare state in favour of monetarist and managerialist approaches and the general marketization of public services have profound implications for the work of all public sector employees, including teachers. Finally, the fact that teaching is a form of paid employment means that teachers, like other workers, may be subject to the effects of changing beliefs about the organization of work. Of particular note in recent times has been the gradual transition in organizational theory from the certainties of F.W. Taylor's scientific management to the more open-ended and responsive prescriptions of today's popular management gurus.

Discourses and the social construction of reality

Whatever the theories of change – whether social, economic, political or organizational – the realities are complex and contested, since they generally involve altered relationships between people and shifts in the locus of power and control. Major change does not normally occur spontaneously but rather as a result of an ongoing struggle over the definition of meanings and the adoption of particular social identities. These struggles do not take place in a vacuum, but rather within a given social discourse which both shapes and is shaped by the actions of individuals and groups. Gee *et al.* (1996: 10), drawing upon the work of Bourdieu and Foucault, argue that a discourse is a set of related social practices which 'is composed of ways of talking, listening, reading, writing, acting, interacting, believing, valuing, and using tools and objects, in particular settings and at specific times, so as to display or to recognise a particular social identity'. They cite the case of the American legal system and the way in which the discourse of the typical law school socializes its students into the concepts, values and ways of interacting that are appropriate to the legal domain. In this way those who are successful learn and are disciplined to think, speak and act in the distinctive mode of a lawyer.

Discourses are powerful because they construct, and invite people to participate in, particular versions of reality, of social authority and of desirable behaviour. Within any specific discourse at any given time some people and some views are privileged and others marginalized – as Ball (1994: 21) puts it: 'Discourses are about what can be said, and thought, but also about who can speak, when, where and with what authority'. Ball (1990a: 18) gives the example of the educational 'discourses of derision' of the New Right, which devalue words such as 'progressivism' and 'comprehensivism' whilst at the same time undermining the authority of professionals within the 'educational establishment' who would defend them.

Thus discourses are not neutral descriptions of reality but rather examples of attempts by those with some degree of authority to impose their views and interpretations upon others. Many different discourses may exist at the same time, although some become dominant at particular periods. Two discourses that are in ascendancy in these times of global economic change are those of the 'new work order' and of the 'new public management', and it is to these that we now turn.

From Fordism to post-Fordism: the discourse of the new work order

As indicated above, educational reform and restructuring coincide with the movement towards economic globalization and with the accompanying changes in the organization of work. These changes are frequently described in terms of a shift from 'Fordism' to 'post-Fordism', or from capitalism to 'new', 'late' or 'post-capitalism' (see Drucker 1993). Whatever the terminology, these are profound changes that impact significantly not only at the macro-economic level but also at the level of organizations and of individual workers. A particular version of this reality is portrayed in a series of popular management texts (among them Peters 1988; 1992; Senge 1991; Drucker 1993; Champy 1995) which both describe and project a vision of a 'new work order'.

Economic level

The characteristic Fordist system of mass production of standardized products for mass markets was dominant in the middle years of the twentieth century, particularly in the United States where post-war prosperity created a large and stable market for consumer goods. Over time, however, techniques of mass production gradually spread to other countries, where lower labour costs meant that goods could be produced more cheaply. This, coupled with improved communications and transport and technological advances, resulted in increased competition as traditional markets became flooded with consumer goods. When protectionist measures failed to safeguard home markets, manufacturers were forced not only to seek alternative markets but also to try to produce even better goods at lower prices in order to secure sales. As competition continued to escalate, the notion of standardized production for mass markets began to give way, at least in westernized societies, to identifying and supplying increasingly specialized and personalized goods for particular niche markets. In terms of labour requirements, there was also a general shift of emphasis away from products and towards the provision of personal services, accompanied by an increasing differentiation within the workforce. Distinctions can now be made between the 'rising one-fifth', an elite minority capable of commanding the highest salaries, and the 'falling four-fifths', composed of a significant middle group destined to perform more routine and less well-remunerated tasks and a growing underclass experiencing periods of unemployment and very low-paid part-time or temporary work (Reich 1993; Hutton 1996).

At the same time it has been claimed that national economic borders have been effectively dismantled by the progressive globalization of capital. This has been facilitated by the development of deregulated, international financial markets, and by the transformation of large, national corporations into multinational conglomerates which now dominate the world economy. The latter tend to operate as global webs, drawing capital, expertise and labour from across the world in different combinations at different times in order to serve constantly changing and increasingly fragmented global markets. As

Reich (1993) has argued, national prosperity is now dependent upon the proportion of citizens who are sufficiently skilled to be able to add value to global enterprises: the notion of a national economy that can be managed and controlled is rapidly becoming an outdated illusion.

Organizational level

Rooted in modernist beliefs in the power of rational planning to achieve the perfect system, the old Fordist model of mass production was based upon Taylorist principles of scientific management and relied upon large, bureaucratic structures and a hierarchical division of labour. In more recent times the perceived need for businesses to respond rapidly to changing markets, to innovate constantly and to raise quality whilst reducing costs has led to changed prescriptions and beliefs about the organization of work. According to the popular and influential management texts of the 'new work order', the need for flexibility, customer awareness and rapid response rates demands the dismantling of slow-moving and cumbersome bureaucracies in favour of smaller, self-managing units that take decision-making 'closer to the customer'. The accelerating speed of change requires lightweight structures, with fewer permanent buildings and plant, 'just in time' stock-keeping, changing personnel, a smaller core workforce and the use of home-based working and flexible hours. Whilst technological advances and a surplus supply of manual workers combine to reduce reliance upon, and lower the value of, labour power 'from the neck down', there is a new emphasis upon the importance of specialist 'knowledge workers', capable of high value-added problem-solving (Blackler 1995).

With the proposed flattening of the old hierarchies, the weakening of traditional chains of command and the loss of secure career structures, there is a need both to motivate the workforce and to find less overt forms of worker control. Here the prescribed solution is a cultural one, whereby the individual worker is invited to become 'empowered' by accepting responsibility for the means of achieving the organizational mission or vision. The vision itself, however, is pre-specified and is not open to debate. Corporate mono-culturism, evident in such popular initiatives as the 'excellence' or 'total quality management' models, represents an attempt to extend managerial control by colonizing the affective domain (Wilmott 1993). Such emotional commitment is deemed necessary to stimulate creativity and initiative which, according to popular management texts, have now replaced conformity and routine task completion as desired characteristics of today's workforce. It has the additional advantage of displacing responsibility for any hardship or misfortune on to the individual worker.

In order to gain and retain competitive edge in an increasingly tight market-place, the ubiquitous mantra of continuous quality improvement demands that organizations 'thrive on chaos' (Peters 1988), constantly embracing new ideas, new procedures, new relationships and new ways of operating. There is also an increased emphasis upon the importance of team-work, as changing groups of workers come together to solve particular problems or to achieve particular goals. This has the added benefit of dispersing knowledge and skills across a number of people rather than within a single individual, who might take that expertise to another employer (Gee *et al.* 1996).

Individual worker level

This idealization of desirable organizational behaviour necessitates the creation of a new kind of worker, one who will readily accept and 'buy into' the 'new work order' and invest fully in achieving its aims. As well as commitment, it is claimed that the ideal worker will have to acquire a range of skills and capacities that are very different from those required under the old Fordist system. According to popular management texts, the dismantling of bureaucracies means that the majority of lower-level workers will need to become more knowledgeable and proactive. The devolution of decision-making in order to take it 'closer to customers' requires workers 'who can learn and adapt quickly, think for themselves, take responsibility, make decisions, and communicate what they need and know to leaders who coach, supply, and inspire them' (Gee *et al.* 1996: 19). They also need to be good teamworkers and to be able to use information and other technologies. At the same time an elite minority of higher-level workers – what Reich (1993) calls 'symbolic analysts' – are required to add value to organizations through their specialized 'knowledge work' (Blackler 1995). This leads to a growing differentiation within the workforce, which is continuing to widen the gap between Reich's (1993) 'rising one-fifth', endowed with the most sought-after skills and capacities and consequently able to command ever higher remuneration, and the 'falling four-fifths', whose earning capacity is constantly eroded by comparison. Accordingly the majority must be socialized to accept personal responsibility for their own limited success or failure within the workplace, rather than blaming it upon (and possibly challenging) the system.

Perhaps the most obvious changes actually experienced in recent times by many in this majority group have been an intensification of working life, a sharp increase in casual and part-time work and a rise in job insecurity. The latter is perhaps inevitable, given the changes in the supply and demand of workers and the consequent shift in the balance of power away from organized labour and towards capital. The much-vaunted need for an unregulated and flexible labour market has, in reality, operated in the interests of employers to facilitate more temporary and part-time appointments, lack of career structures and progression and less favourable conditions of service for many workers, albeit more favourable ones for a minority (Merson 1996). At the same time global corporations, unfettered by national constraints, have been free to open, close or relocate their businesses at will. Accordingly, continuity of employment is no longer the norm, unemployment has risen and many of those currently in employment know that they face the ever-present risk of redeployment or redundancy.

Workloads for most people have also increased as a result of coping with constant changes, attending more frequent team meetings, satisfying more extensive accountability, reporting and quality assurance requirements and meeting targets for continuing increases in productivity. Job insecurity tends to enhance compliance, as people work longer hours in order to meet work demands, which increasingly impinge upon their private life. The seductive rhetoric of 'empowerment' rings somewhat hollow for many as excessive responsibilities, imposed by others, force them towards corner-cutting and survival strategies and reduce scope for meaningful reflection and creative thinking. Whilst rapid technological advances have frequently obliged people in employment to acquire new capabilities, continuing changes to work practices have the effect of repeatedly deskilling many, whilst persistent calls for 'upskilling' are often based upon a demoralizing view of the presumed deficiencies of the workforce.

Many of the elements of post-Fordism described above can already be observed in current economic and business practice, most particularly in terms of increased competitiveness, greater customer orientation and a more flexible and differentiated workforce. However, it is important to remember that the seductive images of flattened hierarchies, collaborative learning organizations and worker empowerment which are portrayed as part of the 'new work order' of popular management books are not *faits accomplis*. Rather than offering a description of current reality, the array of 'fast capitalist texts' (Gee *et al.* 1996) represents a prescriptive discourse, a version of the new capitalism in whose realization the reader is invited to participate. In so far as the readers are often senior managers and in a position to affect business practice, it is potentially very influential.

In recent years this potential influence has been further widened by the growing incursion of business practices and business thinking into the management of public services. Confronted with the dilemma of an increasing demand for services that is not matched by increasing revenues, many governments have sought to reduce their direct involvement in the administration of such services whilst seeking to increase both efficiency and central control. A key strategy in achieving this end has been the deployment of the beliefs and practices of a particularly powerful discourse, that of the 'new public management'.

From the Keynesian welfare state to the discourse of the new public management

The post-war consensus on the desirability of building a better and more equal society and the consequent widespread assumption of state responsibility for the security and welfare of its citizens had led to a rapid expansion of public sector services in many westernized nations and the concomitant growth of large, professional bureaucracies. However, the notion of the universal welfare state came under increasing threat in the 1970s and 1980s, firstly because of the escalating economic difficulties confronting national governments, especially in the wake of the oil crisis of 1973, and secondly because of a spate of ideological attacks from the New Right. In the USA, for example, a decline both in public confidence in government sector activity and in commitments to the public interest was accompanied by persistent calls for regulation through private enterprise and consumer choice (Murphy 1998). In Britain there were repeated claims from the Institute of Economic Affairs, an influential right-wing think tank, that the welfare state had failed, and that the solution was to dismantle its bureaucracies and to subject it to the discipline of market choice and competition. Meanwhile in New Zealand a decade of prolonged economic crisis and declining profits persuaded the Labour government that the time had come to follow the example of Britain and America in rolling back the welfare state and introducing a competitive market economy (Court 1997a). Starting with calls for greater efficiency and more targeted resourcing within the public services, over time the 'welfare consensus' was gradually broken and replaced by a fundamentally different approach operating within 'a new frame of reference – individualist rather than collectivist, stressing the values of self-help and enterprise rather than those of community and social concern' (Jones 1994: 189).

The 'new public management' (Hood 1991; Bottery 1996), which is closely linked to many aspects of current business thinking within the 'new work order', has become increasingly prevalent in many westernized nations. Underpinned by a form of economic rationalism that sees human beings as motivated primarily by self-interest, it denigrates notions of the 'public interest' as special pleading and depicts workers within the public sector as motivated by extrinsic, rather than intrinsic, rewards. This new form of organization is based upon, and supported by, the twin strategies of the marketization of public services and the growth of managerialism, both of which have had profound effects upon the work of public sector employees.

Marketization

The marketization of the public sector has generally been accompanied by the recurrent rhetoric of an escape from 'producer capture' and a shift from a producer to a consumer culture (see, for example, Ball 1990a; Bichard 1995; Grace 1995), as public service bureaucracies have been dismantled or disempowered and responsibility for resource management passed to smaller, local units which, freed from bureaucratic restraints, are expected to compete for business in a newly created market-place. In this discourse the erstwhile clients of public services are transformed into would-be 'consumers', in need of simple information on the comparative performance of competing service providers in order to inform their purchasing 'choices'. Neo-liberal ideology claims that the expansion of consumer choice will increase competition amongst service providers and consequently improve both the quality and the cost-effectiveness of services, as the 'better' providers are rewarded with increased business and resources and the 'poorer' providers are squeezed out. As a 'natural' order becomes established, the need for central regulation and planning will largely disappear, and the state will be able to adopt a much lower profile within the social policy arena as decision-making passes into the hands of consumers (Jones 1994).

The marketization of welfare services is taken a step further by the enforced extension of purchasing power to public contracting authorities and institutions. Compulsory competitive tendering has been introduced in many areas in an attempt both to subject state monopolies to competition from alternative suppliers and to encourage 'value for money' and 'efficiency savings' amongst competing service providers, thereby driving down public spending. At the same time the practice of independent fund-holding has been keenly promoted in order further to weaken local public monopolies, to stimulate greater entrepreneurialism in the provision of services and to make welfare practitioners more aware of the financial implications of their professional judgements.

In practice, there have been severe constraints upon the effective operation of a free market within the public services. Whilst competition between providers has undoubtedly increased, it can never be universal: for example, there will always be sparsely populated geographical areas which will only support a single provider, whilst the lack of potential profitability in many aspects of welfare provision ensures the continuation of public service monopoly (Pfeffer and Coote 1991). The concept of consumer choice is equally problematic in relation to public services, not least because of the lack of adequate knowledge or purchasing power amongst those most in need of welfare services (Jones 1994), but also because of the limited possibilities for individuals to effectively employ strategies of either 'exit' or 'voice' (Hirschman 1970) when they are dissatisfied with the services on offer. Moreover, success in attracting more customers, which generally leads to increased profitability in the private sector, can place severe additional burdens upon the providers of welfare services, sometimes forcing them to limit access by substituting choice *by* consumers with institutional choice *of* consumers (Ball 1990b). Finally, continued government involvement and intervention constantly interfere with the ability of public service providers to operate freely within the market-place. As part of its strategy to relinquish the more costly aspects of public administration and to transfer responsibility for any failures to either consumers or providers, the government must ensure a reasonable degree of transparency in the operation of the public sector (Dale 1992). This, coupled with pressures to curb social unrest and constantly to reduce public expenditure, necessitates some form of central control or steerage. Such control is facilitated by the promotion of managerialism.

Managerialism

The recent transformation of public services has been marked both by an increasing use of management discourses and techniques from the private sector and by the appointment and elevation of a new class of 'professional managers', charged with overseeing the activities of welfare professionals within their institution (Pfeffer and Coote 1991; Bottery 1996). In addition to this, some have identified a more profound change: a 'deeper ideological process of managerialization which is transforming relationships of power, culture, control and accountability' (Clarke *et al*. 1994a: 3).

These changes can be seen as part of a general political strategy to regain central control over public services. As population growth and escalating demands brought into question the notion of universal entitlement that had underpinned the development of the welfare state in many countries, governments, beset by economic difficulties, sought to move towards more targeted provision and to control and reduce public expenditure. This implied the generation of better information about service needs and provision, a reordering of priorities, greater accountability and, most importantly, more efficient and effective management. In the private sector, the need for reorganization and 'downsizing' in recent years had led to the emergence of more macho styles of management and the reassertion of the 'managerial prerogative' (Ozga 1995; Menter *et al*. 1997), as the bargaining power of organized labour steadily declined. Images of strong control led many in government to favour the importation of business models of management into the public sector, previously characterized by a more collective and democratic approach to decision-making. Accordingly, the notion of strong management was constantly portrayed as the key way to improve public services and was encouraged by structural changes and by government-sponsored programmes of management training. It was also supported by the new market requirements for comparative information for consumers which, as Menter *et al*. (1997) point out, coincidentally provide powerful managerial imperatives and greatly enhance management control.

At the same time as encouraging strong management, theorists of the New Right argued that there was a need to curb the power of public service professionals, who were portrayed as 'vested interests', likely to oppose any radical reform to the *status quo* of 'producer capture'. Accordingly, government discourses consistently affirmed the importance of the trained manager over that of conventional public service professionals whilst government policies encouraged the development of a more 'hands-on' approach to public sector management at the expense of the tradition of autonomous professional judgements. This attempt to diminish professional control is reflected in a variety of initiatives in different service sectors. In England, for example, Bottery (1996) cites the imposition of a National Curriculum upon teachers, the drawing up of key policing objectives by the Home Office and the specification of areas of treatment by district health authorities. At the same time a series of 'Citizens' Charters' set minimum standards for public services and affirmed the rights of service consumers at the expense of those of service providers. In New Zealand, the Public Finance Act of 1989 shifted the funding basis of public services away from a concern with 'inputs' and towards an emphasis upon specified 'outputs', facilitated through the use of contracts between government and providers and of third-party auditing of service delivery. Other pieces of legislation reduced the power of unions and left public sector workers much more exposed to the control of local managers (Robertson 1998).

The slow dismantling of large public sector bureaucracies removes a potential power base for providers, who must now develop roles within smaller and more fragmented operating units. Within these units a new emphasis upon managerial scrutiny of staff performance and of outcomes places further constraints upon professional autonomy. All of these factors combine to suggest that the kind of bureaucratized professionalism which had developed so strongly within the welfare state is being systematically undermined (Ozga 1996; Menter *et al.* 1997).

The changes do not simply reflect a shift of power away from professionals and towards managers, they also encourage the incursion of new discourses and new sets of values into the public services. As organizations strive to become more businesslike and start to focus upon target setting, financial planning, human resource management, quality assurance and performance indicators, there is a danger that the public sector will begin to move away from the 'culture of welfare' and towards the 'culture of profit and production' (Ball 1994). Traditional notions of 'entitlement' and 'equity' risk being displaced by the ubiquitous three Es of government policy: economy, efficiency and effectiveness. As pressures grow for everything to be measured and costed and financial discourses proliferate, it becomes increasingly difficult to argue for alternative diagnoses or remedies. Instead, those working in the public services are invited to 'buy in' to the new pervasive vision of entrepreneurial and competitive individualism within a framework of tight fiscal control.

This new dominant discourse threatens to shape the actions and roles not only of traditional public sector professionals but also of the new managers. Whilst the latter may be given greater status and jurisdiction over the former, nonetheless they too are subject to wider disciplines which make them responsible for the achievement of centrally prescribed outcomes. Targets for improvement in such areas as school leaving qualifications, crime prevention or detection, hospital waiting lists or community care are routinely set by government ministers with little evidence of prior consultation or appropriate resourcing. Good management is then equated with the ability to ensure staff compliance in achieving these targets, a goal which becomes increasingly difficult to meet in the context of the continuous quest for 'value for money' and efficiency savings. Attempts are made to ensure that ultimate control is increasingly vested at the centre, where targets are set, rather than with the new public sector managers: devolution of responsibility is not to be confused with devolution of power.

As with the 'new work order', managerialism is a discourse which combines description of *what is* with prescription of *what should be*. Accordingly, the extent to which it has already restructured public services in its own image is open to interpretation and can be described as 'unfinished business' rather than 'mission accomplished' (Clarke *et al.* 1994b).

Competing discourses, education and teachers' work

Enduring faith in the ability of public education systems to create a better society, coupled with differing notions of what such a society might look like, has meant that educational aims have long been the subject of intense debate and disagreement. Whilst some have seen schools as having a key role in ensuring social stability by preparing young people to become compliant citizens and obedient workers within the existing hierarchy, others have argued that their task should be to develop critical thinking capacities and initiative in their students in order that they may play a full and active part within a democratic society. Similarly, public perceptions of the proper role of teachers have varied between a belief in their importance as key professionals, entrusted to make crucial decisions about educational practice in the best interests of their students, and a view of them as low-level functionaries, in need of instruction, regulation and control.

Currently dominant discourses, such as those of the 'new work order' and the 'new public management', create particular images of schooling and of the role of teachers and teacher managers within it. As indicated above, such discourses are not neutral but involve the exercise of power, as people are disciplined into particular ways of seeing, thinking and behaving. Analysing the deployment of post-Fordist discourses within the field of education and training in Britain, Edwards (1993: 185) argues that, by 'making the contingent appear unchallengeable', such discourses can

> normalize a view of the future of work – based in structural unemployment and underemployment – as not only inevitable, but also preferable. As a result . . . persons will be disciplined into certain forms of behaviour and more readily managed within a social formation of structural inequality.

Despite the enormous influence of this discourse, however, such outcomes remain possibilities rather than foregone conclusions since discourses are never fixed but rather open to challenge, both from within the discourse itself and from other, competing discourses. For example, education is the subject of professional and social-democratic discourses which, although weakened in recent years, continue to be asserted from time to time, especially from within the educational establishment. Meanwhile, changing government policies on education tend to succeed each other in cycles, as different views become fashionable and different interest groups gain or lose influence. At the same time institutional practice evolves only gradually, as teachers attempt to reconcile calls for change with existing approaches (Tyack and Cuban 1995). The following chapter will look in more detail at the way in which public educational systems in general, and the work of teachers in particular, are shaped by the interplay of imposed structural changes with the active agency of teachers in accommodating, ignoring or adapting such changes within particular contexts and cultures of schooling.

two

CHANGING TEACHERS' WORK: STRUCTURE, CULTURE AND AGENCY

Whilst the previous chapter considered some of the broader changes emanating from the attempts to establish both a 'new work order' and a 'new public management' through the importation of business thinking and business practice into public service provision, this chapter will focus in more detail upon the effects of these developments on schooling and more particularly on the work of teachers.

Teachers are trebly affected by changing patterns in the organization of work:

- Firstly, as employees themselves, teachers may be subjected to the same increasing demands and constraints as other sections of the workforce.
- Secondly, the importation of current business thinking and business practice into the management of all public services and the consequent restructuring of the education service fundamentally change the frameworks within which teachers operate, subjecting their work efforts to the forces of marketization and managerialization. In particular, the emphasis within the 'new public management' upon extrinsic rewards ignores and belittles the psychic and intrinsic rewards which many teachers value, with potentially adverse effects upon teacher motivation.
- Thirdly, the discourses of global economic change place new and more pressing requirements upon schools to prepare their students for the fast-moving and very different workplace of the twenty-first century. Thus the very heart of teachers' work, the education of young people, is itself being subjected to contestation and redefinition as coalitions of state and industrial interests seek in various ways and to varying degrees to develop policies that will align the educational system more closely with the perceived requirements of the labour market.

Despite the remarkable commonality of developments across nations, however, it would be unwise to assume that this kind of description of the structural changes that are currently taking place offers an adequate account of reality. Both in work generally, and in schooling in particular, external imperatives are constantly mediated and moderated through human agency and are incorporated to a greater or lesser extent into existing practice. In this way the nature of any change to teachers' work is never predetermined, but instead results from actions and choices that are made at different stages in the long process from the initial production of central educational policy texts through to day-to-day policy realization in the classroom.

Whilst structure and agency may be complementary facets of the social construction of educational reality, the nature and relative strength of agency is profoundly affected by the cultural context within which people – whether central policy-makers, educational managers or teachers – live and work. Accordingly, any consideration of changes to teachers' work must take account not only of the social and political context within which educational policies are developed but also of the range of cultures (for example, occupational, professional, subject, institutional or departmental) which profoundly shape teachers' responses to these and to other external demands.

To begin with, this chapter will look at two kinds of relationship – between education and work, and between education and the state – both of which have frequently been said to account for structural changes to public education systems and therefore to the work of teachers. In both cases, it will be argued that such functional views offer an incomplete and often misleading explanation of educational developments. On the one hand, they falsely suggest an uncontentious interpretation of 'work', a unified and unproblematic view of labour market needs and a simplistic conception of the state as a single entity. On the other hand, they ignore the complexities of how political intentions are realized in practice.

Education and work

Much of the literature on education and work not only equates work with paid employment but generally associates it with particular and hierarchical forms of employment prevalent within capitalist economies. Even the more recent writing related to the 'new work order' and the supposed need to create 'empowered' workers for the 'collaborative' and 'democratic' workplaces of the future masks the growing polarization of core and peripheral workers and the accompanying increases in social differentiation (Green 1994) with the consequent need to prepare young people to accept future inequalities. Only a small number of commentators draw attention to alternative and more empowering conceptions of work. John Dewey, for example, defined work as purposeful activity, which could take place both in and out of paid employment, and involved service to others, moral engagement and personal growth. Such distinctions have profound implications for teachers' work, in terms both of dictating the nature and purpose of their teaching and of defining the labour process in which they are engaged. On the one hand, schooling could be conceived as the necessary socialization of young people into an acceptance of their future status and of the inevitable involvement of many in 'useless toil'; on the other hand, it could be seen as empowering students by developing critical capacities and asserting their autonomy through engagement in practice (Quicke 1996). Similarly, the work of teachers could be viewed either as routine labour, undertaken for financial reward, or as a moral enterprise involving the pursuit of intrinsic goods and the exercise of 'virtue' (MacIntyre 1981). As already indicated, however, the dominant discourse on 'education and work' defines work as paid employment, and it is this definition that will be used in the rest of this section.

In so far as schooling is about preparing young people for adult life, and formal employment is still an important part of adult life for the majority, there will always and inevitably be links of one kind or another between education and paid work. These 'bonds' may involve schools in processes of selection, socialization, orientation or preparation of young people for work (Watts 1983), though the latter could well be broad and generic rather than explicitly vocational. There is, however, considerable disagreement over the extent to which education is in practice influenced by – or indeed contributes to – economic development. In terms of explicit purposes, some have seen education as primarily serving the needs of capitalism, particularly in the USA in the first half of the twentieth century (Reich 1993), and accordingly advocated a Fordist conception and organization of schooling (see Cubberly 1934) which mirrored the system of mass production. At the other end of the spectrum, proponents of a liberal perspective on education such as John Dewey have emphasized the primacy of developing the individual student over more functionalist approaches and argued that any ensuing benefits for capitalism are, and should be, entirely coincidental. As long as the relationship between education and economic requirements remains open to contestation, it is inconceivable, despite the apparent wishes of some industrialists and politicians, that formal structures could successfully be introduced that would render the aims of schooling completely subservient to the needs of commerce and industry.

Even a *reorientation* of schooling towards a more functionalist view of economic development is often problematic. In England, for example, a strong liberal-humanist tradition, characterized by a belief in the intrinsic, non-instrumental value of education, a distrust of vocational studies and an antipathy towards technical education, proved particularly resistant to successive attempts to promote an alternative approach. Even when the economic crises of the 1960s and, most particularly, of 1973–75 stimulated a renewed political determination to overhaul the education system and make it more responsive to the needs of industry (DES 1977), early efforts to implement this goal continued to rely predominantly upon persuasion and exhortation. The newly elected Conservative government of 1979 promised more concerted action, but was beset by disagreements as to whether a more highly skilled workforce would best be produced through a work-related curriculum or through teaching traditional academic subjects. The former was promoted through the introduction in 1983 of the Technical and Vocational Education Initiative (TVEI), a voluntary scheme which sought to pilot new approaches to general, technical and vocational education for 14–18-year-olds. Only five years later, however, the Education Reform Act of 1988 introduced a compulsory National Curriculum for all state schools which was based upon a collection of traditional subjects. Once again disagreements over the desirability of direct preparation for work in schools allowed space for contestation, whilst both initiatives, as we shall see later, have had only limited impact upon either the composition of the workforce or upon economic growth.

With regard to the actual practices of schooling, there is little evidence of the widespread development amongst students of specific technical and vocational skills needed in employment, even during the brief period of TVEI developments. This may reflect both the continuing influence over the curriculum of educationalists, steeped in the liberal-humanist tradition, and the implicit acceptance by successive governments of human capital theory, which sees economic value in raising the general level of education of the workforce, irrespective of content. Attempts in the 1980s to make the curriculum more directly relevant to the needs of industry ran into the problem of lack of agreement or clarity about the exact nature of those needs. In the absence of a coherent or united voice from employers, the Manpower Services Commission (MSC) developed a theoretical model of training needs, drawn from labour market analyses and based upon a behavioural objectives approach to learning. However, their lack of authority to impose this model upon schools left TVEI teachers free to develop an alternative model, in which the development of skills for industry was linked with the deployment of progressive pedagogical *processes*, rather than with the achievement of pre-defined *objectives* (Holly 1987; Moore 1990). As Stenhouse (1975) has argued, it is the processes, rather than the outcomes, of education over which teachers can exercise control. Within TVEI, this ability to focus upon the development of pedagogical processes meant that committed teachers became active agents in transforming it from a potentially narrow and functionalist scheme of vocational training into a broad educational initiative aimed at developing generic and interpersonal skills in young people. The extent to which this actually coincided with employers' requirements remains, at best, open to question.

An alternative view of the links between education and work which gained prominence in the 1970s dismisses the importance of the *content* of what is taught in favour of the socializing effects of the basic processes of schooling. In particular, Bowles and Gintis (1976) claimed strong 'correspondence' between the social relationships of the school and of the workplace. The way in which schools are organized and run, they argued, encourages perseverance and passivity in students, along with an acceptance of hierarchy. At the same time the fragmentation of knowledge and of learning into separate subjects militates against overall understanding and prepares young people for their future roles within a fragmented workforce which is alienating and relies upon extrinsic, rather than intrinsic, rewards.

Whilst at first sight this argument appears persuasive, it fails to take into account a number of factors and offers only a partial version of reality. Firstly, the claim of a close correspondence between the practices of schooling and of the economy, and therefore to a form of economic determinism, ignores a number of historical disjunctions – for example, the long delay in Britain between the industrial revolution and the growth of a national education system (Hickox 1982; Green 1990) or the notable educational transformations in France at a time when the mode of production remained stable (Archer and Vaughan 1971). Secondly, the theory fails to take account of the 'relative autonomy' (Giroux 1984) of the education system from the economic infrastructure or of the composition of the teaching force, including as it does a proportion of radical idealists (Reynolds 1984) who would be unlikely to sacrifice the individual development and empowerment of their students to the functional needs of capitalism. Most importantly, the ideas of Bowles and Gintis would need to be reviewed in the light of the decline in employment opportunities since they first published their book, the supposed changes in the requirements of employers for a more creative, innovative and entrepreneurial workforce and the extent to which schools had or had not adapted their practices as a result. Indeed, several writers have highlighted the contradictions between post-Fordist and postmodernist society and the tenaciously modernist structures of schooling (see, for example, Hargreaves 1994; Hartley 1997a).

Further contradictions arise between notions of appropriate schooling to meet the claimed needs of the 'new work order' and certain aspects of current educational restructuring. For example, whilst the former calls for information handling skills, the ability to work co-operatively in teams and the development of extended personal and social skills, the latter is often characterized by an emphasis upon knowledge memorization, competitive individualism and the importance of going 'back to basics'. Similarly, whilst the rhetoric of popular management texts speaks constantly of personal empowerment, a combination of standardized curricula and national testing are symptomatic of an increasing central control over both the content and the method of teaching and learning, thereby reducing the scope for either student or teacher autonomy. Finally, the apparent need for investment in education in order to produce the value-adding knowledge workers of the future is constantly displaced by concerns for control of – and even reductions in – public spending in this area. Reich (1993) quotes the example of George Bush's presidential campaign, in which he styled himself the future 'education president' yet showed himself unwilling to spend further federal money on schools.

Thus, it would seem overall that, despite claims to the contrary, education is not *directly* or *inevitably* influenced by changing employment requirements and that any 'correspondence' between education and work practices is far from automatic. This does not, however, prevent such correspondences occurring, nor does it preclude indirect influences upon the school system. However, such structural linkages are complex and subject to change over time, as interest groups such as the 'industrial trainers' or 'old humanists' (Williams 1961; Ball 1990a) gain or lose influence over the formation of educational policy. To a large extent the form and strength of the linkages between education and work depend upon the agency of groups of educational decision-makers: 'Education has the characteristics it does because of the goals pursued by those who control it . . . Change occurs because new educational goals are pursued by those who have power to modify previous practices' (Archer 1979: 2). Such groups include not only educational managers and policy-makers but also teachers who, in their day-to-day practices, may or may not choose to make links between what they are teaching and the 'world of work'. However, all such groups inevitably operate within particular structures, and outcomes in terms of the relationship between education and work are ultimately determined by a complex interplay between structure and agency within a specific social and political context.

Education and the state

If the case for simple economic determinism remains unproven within the field of educational change, some have claimed that the role of the state is a more significant factor. Although 'the state' is a complex entity, embracing a variety of bodies and interests, it is clear that a particular embodiment of the state bears ultimate responsibility for the development and maintenance of any national education system as an 'ideological state apparatus' (Althusser 1971). In his comparative study of the rise of education systems in England, continental Europe and America, Green (1990) concludes that the key determinants of such educational development are the nature of the state and the process of state formation or 'nation-building'. He also identifies three historical factors that have been especially associated with an accelerated process of nation-building: military threat or territorial conflicts; major internal transformations (for example the French Revolution or the American struggle for independence); and national efforts to counteract relative economic underdevelopment (Green 1990: 310).

It is not difficult to identify modern-day equivalents to these historical factors arising from the pervasive processes of globalization. Instead of military threat or territorial conflicts, many countries now face a relative loss of independence and economic control because of the domination of world markets by huge, international conglomerates. At the same time national identity and traditional forms of authority are being seriously challenged by a combination of widespread economic, social and political changes which threaten the very basis of the nation state and necessitate major reformulation and reconstruction. Finally, concerns over relatively poor economic performance currently dominate a great deal of political planning and policy-making, as countries seek to improve their competitive edge and either secure or restore economic prosperity.

If we accept the appropriateness of Green's original three causes of nation-building and therefore of educational development, perhaps we should not be surprised when the emergence of broadly comparable factors is accompanied by the restructuring of schooling, and by the consequent transformation of teachers' work, in so many westernized nations. Furthermore, the current prevalence of 'policy borrowing' between nations, supported both by improved communications and by the growing political influence of international organizations such as the OECD and the World Bank, has led to a degree of convergence in many aspects of restructuring. Indeed, there has been much international interest in the so-called New Zealand experiment as a 'globalized localism', which appears to prove that social democracy is no barrier to the introduction of deregulatory policies (Dale 1998) and, significantly, the former head of the New Zealand Education Department is now working for the World Bank and advising other countries on strategies for liberalization.

Many aspects of current educational restructuring have been related by some commentators to attempts by individual capitalist states to find solutions to the changed core problems – of accumulation, of social control and of legitimation – created by economic decline and its effects upon the role and functions of the state (Ball 1994; Gewirtz 1997). The intractability of these core problems means that the solutions introduced by the state are often contradictory. Certainly, recent government policies have reflected the dominance of New Right discourses and their inherent tensions between a neo-liberal emphasis upon 'market values', and a consequent minimization of the role of the state, and the neo-conservative attachment to 'traditional values', and therefore to a stronger state role in promoting them (Apple 1996). Thus there is a widespread tendency towards both greater state control of, and at the same time diminished state involvement in, the national education system. This is typically achieved through central prescription and goal setting accompanied by devolution of responsibility for goal achievement through a system of school-based management. At the same time there has been a gradual shift in the control of education from bureaucratic forms towards approaches based upon managerial technology (Dale 1989), whereby an emphasis upon rule following and political persuasion has been replaced by positive planning and outcome-based accountability systems.

Some have argued that it is the changing relationship between teachers and the state that lies at the heart of these educational reforms. As Grace (1987: 197) reminds us, teachers have long been regarded as 'crucial agents in the structuring of popular consciousness' and therefore able to support or threaten the existing social order. Drawing upon the work of Gramsci, Green (1990: 98) also highlights 'the dualistic nature of education . . . which can be at once an instrument of social control and a force for liberation'.

State concerns, therefore, are not limited to the requirements of capital accumulation but extend to issues of social authority and the legitimation of the *status quo* and its existing divisions and hierarchies. Accordingly, control of the teaching force has always been seen as an important state objective, although this has been achieved in different ways over time, including both direct control, as in nineteenth-century England through a system of 'payment by results', and a form of 'indirect rule' (Lawn 1987a; 1996). As with colonial rule, this approach combined an apparent decentralization of power with strategic co-ordination from the centre through such means as the use of local agents, the allocation of grants and the issuing of 'advice' or 'guidance'. Under this strategy teachers were won over by appeals to their 'professionalism' and by the granting of a degree of independence over their day-to-day work and thus were gradually co-opted into achieving state purposes.

It has been suggested that the strategies adopted by the state to control the teaching force alternate cyclically between direct rule, leading to militancy and resistance, and indirect rule, leading to increased professionalization and autonomy (Ozga 1996; Menter *et al.* 1997). Certainly it is possible to identify a historical period of 'indirect rule' in England from about 1925 to 1980 (Lawn 1996) which was both preceded and followed by periods of more direct control of the education system. At the same time the current variations in approach to educational restructuring between countries would seem to suggest differential use of such strategies in particular national or social contexts. For example, whilst countries such as Sweden and some key states in the USA have conferred widely over reforms and appealed to teachers' sense of 'professionalism' to help develop and implement the changes, other governments have adopted a much more aggressive stance, involving minimal consultation, strong central prescription, constant criticism of teachers and draconian systems of surveillance and accountability. Thus the relationship between teachers and the state, and the extent of their licence and autonomy, is constructed differently according to the particular historical or social-cultural context in which they work.

It is also important to remember that the state is not a single entity. Although the government of the day is perhaps the most visible and active part of it, the state also consists of a number of 'state apparatuses'. These include not only government departments but also public agencies (for example, the police, the military and the judiciary) and local government bureaucracies. Despite a degree of public accountability and the common task of dealing with the core problems confronting the state, each of these state apparatuses enjoys 'significant margins for discretionary action in the fulfilment of [its] tasks' (Mayntz 1979: 633) and has developed its own approaches and traditions over time. Tensions frequently arise both between and within different state apparatuses, as they emphasize different aspects of the core or other problems and adopt different approaches to their solution. These tensions may be exacerbated in those areas of state activity, such as education, which are reliant upon a group of professional workers to use their discretion in dealing with problems that lack any standard solution.

Thus the 'management' of the education system by 'the state' is neither straightforward nor pre-ordained but is based instead upon a contested and dynamic process of struggle between competing interests and changing priorities. Following Gramsci, Green (1990: 99) locates this contestation within a wider frame based upon the potential of education to act as either a coercive or emancipatory force: 'Education is a weapon in the struggle for hegemony, the school is a vital agency in the process of state formation. But the process is ever contested and the results of the struggle are never decided in advance.' In the course of this conflict, control and influence will accrue to different parts of the education state apparatus at different times, with the balance of power constantly shifting – for example, between ministers and bureaucrats, between central and local government and between teachers and 'the state'. Whilst the structure and traditions of the education system place some constraints upon the actions of those involved, nonetheless an element of choice remains, and the accumulation of choices and alternative actions taken by different people at different levels may serve to transform the structures over time. Thus the place and role of teachers within the state system remains open to contestation and to change.

Educational policy-making

Educational policies provide one of the frameworks within which the nature and scope of teachers' work is constructed. Such policies, whether developed at national, regional, school or departmental level, may serve to confirm particular ways of working or to suggest ways in which practices might be changed. Given the ambiguous and often contradictory aims of education and the degree of disagreement and contestation operating at different levels both within and outside of the education state apparatus, it is hardly surprising that policy-making is rarely a simple process.

Firstly, educational policy-making is not a one-off event that happens in a particular place or time. The traditional and linear view of policies being developed rationally within the circles of government administration and then transported for automatic implementation in schools bears little relation to reality. Instead, policy-making is a cyclical and iterative process that occurs in different contexts. Tyack and Cuban (1995), for example, distinguish between problem diagnosis and the advocacy of solutions (*policy talk*); decision-making and formal adoption of policies (*policy action*); and the slow process whereby policy plans are translated to varying degrees into practice (*implementation*). Similarly, Bowe *et al.* (1992) identify the *context of influence*, in which policies are initiated, policy discourse constructed and key policy concepts established; the *context of policy text production*, where policy is represented through texts, public pronouncements and commentaries; and the *context of practice*, in which policy is subject to reinterpretation and recreation. All three contexts are sites of contestation and struggle, and what happens in any one context can and does influence what happens in the other two. Indeed, educational policy has been described as 'the provisional outcome of a continuous socio-political struggle' (CCCS Education Group 1981; Grace 1987: 195).

At the level of the central state, educational policy-making must take into account the ambiguity of educational goals, the intractability of the problems which it confronts and the need to balance the conflicting interests of different stakeholders. Before a written policy is produced, representations are made about the nature of the problems to be addressed and about the possible solutions. In the policy discourse which develops, some individuals and groups gain more influence than others, and so different sets of interests predominate at different times, with important consequences for the direction of educational policy, and potentially profound effects upon fundamental aspects of teachers' work. The school curriculum, for example, was a particular site of ideological struggle in England in the 1980s: the initial ascendancy of the 'industrial trainers', which led to the introduction and development of the TVEI, was soon overtaken by the growing influence of the 'cultural restorationists' of the New Right (Ball 1990a) and the legislative imposition of an increasingly traditional academic curriculum.

Policy discourses are affected not only by the variable influence of different interest groups but also by the personal preferences, political persuasions and relative strength of key players within both the education and wider state apparatus. Education ministers may adopt a high or low profile in policy-making; the education department may be seen as a political backwater or (increasingly in recent times) as a site of high strategic importance; key civil servants may see their role as leading or following ministerial decision-making; the local state may be weak or powerful; the teaching force may be highly organized and influential or fragmented and excluded from state-level policy-making. As power and influence ebb and flow amongst the different groups, what is valued and what is discussed will change over time and the development of policy by the state, rather than being scientific and rational as policy-makers would claim, is the untidy outcome of contestation and accommodation between different options:

> the State itself is an arena of conflict. It is a site in which groups with decidedly different interests struggle over policies, goals, procedures and personnel. Thus, state policy is always the result of multiple levels of conflicts and compromises that stem from and lead to contradictory outcomes.
>
> (Apple 1989: 13)

Despite its inherent arbitrariness and irrationality, the policy discourse must gain some degree of public acceptance and state policy-makers need to create an appropriate public climate for their preferred policies. Most notable in recent years has been the deliberate generation in several countries of a strong sense of crisis about education as a forerunner to government intervention (Reich 1993). This has been fuelled by repeated but unsubstantiated assertions by politicians and others that 'standards are falling' and that high levels of educational achievement are essential to economic and social well-being. In the USA, the image generated by the National Commission on Excellence in Education (1983) of 'a nation at risk' helped to pave the way for successive waves of educational reform, whilst in England a constant battery of 'discourses of derision' (Ball 1990a) created a sense of general unease about the state of teaching and justified subsequent government attempts to reconstruct teachers' work and notions of the 'good teacher'. These discourses can be seen as an exercise in power, whereby definitions of 'reality' are constructed through language by those with authority to speak in the public domain and policy is presented as rationality rather than ideology (Ball 1990a). Thus policy-making becomes a cultural and political process which shapes 'common-sense' understandings, especially through the repeated and exclusive use of key words and concepts such as 'curriculum delivery', 'target setting' and 'performance measurement'. Such terms are not neutral but act as powerful disciplinary mechanisms to transform both teachers and their work (Gewirtz 1997). The renewed and repeated emphasis upon the need for accountability in teaching is a case in point: 'the term accountability has been used by successive governments to establish a discursive consensus which constructs teachers as being in need of external regulation' (Poulson 1996: 585).

The ability of state policy-makers to direct and manipulate public consciousness in this way is not, however, infallible. Occasionally, alternative views gain ascendancy and preferred policies are withdrawn or amended, as in the case of the 1993 proposal by John Patten, then Secretary of State for Education, to introduce a 'mum's army' of untrained classroom assistants into English primary schools.

This protracted contestation between different views and different interest groups means that the policy texts which finally emerge from the process are inevitably based upon a series of compromises and trade-offs and incorporate incomplete specifications for action (Ball 1994). In addition, the distance of policy-makers from schools, and their lack of adequate knowledge of the realities of classroom practice, mean that their policy texts can reasonably be regarded as 'hypotheses', inevitably subject to alteration in the context of a real school (Tyack and Cuban 1995). Finally, successive policy texts are not necessarily cumulative or consistent with each other (Merson 1992), but instead may suggest policy lurches or even reversals, as priorities shift, governments or ministers come and go, the public climate changes or different interest groups gain or lose influence over the policy-making process.

Public contestation continues once a policy document is issued, as ministers and other officials offer explanations and verbal and written commentaries on the proposals, which may be reported and discussed in the media. Interpretation and commentary also take place at local level: indeed, many teachers never read formal policy texts, but instead rely upon the summaries of others to gain an understanding of what is expected of them. Thus policy texts merely present a framework within which teachers are expected to work: 'Policies do not normally tell you what to do, they create circumstances in which the range of options available in deciding what to do are narrowed or changed, or particular goals or outcomes are set' (Ball 1994: 19).

Clearly, some policy texts and related documents place greater constraints upon teachers' work than others: legislation associated with the English National Curriculum, for example, specified in some detail what teachers should teach and introduced systems of national inspection and national testing to ensure compliance. Even here, however, limitations on the powers of state policy-makers to change educational practice in radical ways soon became apparent. Some teachers chose to treat National Curriculum policies as 'writerly' texts (Barthes in Bowe *et al.* 1992), open to creative interpretation, whilst others simply absorbed the new demands into existing practice.

The impossibility of achieving top-down control of teachers' work can be attributed to a number of factors. Some relate to the lack of a clear knowledge base for teaching, making it hard to draw up and enforce bureaucratic rules that teachers must follow in their classroom practice, others to the inherently contradictory nature of educational goals, which makes it difficult to achieve technical control by agreeing and measuring progress against fixed and pre-defined outcomes (Dale 1989). Thus teachers tend to operate as 'street-level bureaucrats' (Lipsky 1980), developing their own means of reconciling the conflicting demands made upon them. Furthermore, the fact that these conflicting demands come not only from outside the classroom, in the form of various social imperatives and policy mandates, but also from within it, in terms of the differential and competing needs of the young people in their care, means that 'teaching is impossible . . . [and] makes greater demands than any individual can possibly fulfill' (Shulman, 1983: 497). Similarly, Connell argues that, since the amorphous nature of teaching is effectively 'a labour process without an object' (1985: 70), then there is 'no logical limit to the expansion of an individual teachers' work' (1985: 72).

In such circumstances, with multiple and competing demands and no single agreed pathway through them, the educational system remains reliant upon individual teachers to balance these demands in relation to the needs of their particular students and to make a succession of practical choices within their day-to-day work. The accumulation of these choices shapes teachers' work and is an important basis of their relative but enduring autonomy. This autonomy is further assured by the practical impossibility of inspecting or monitoring teachers' classroom work on a regular basis, thereby guaranteeing a degree of freedom and control over their day-to-day practice. This freedom is not, however, total but operates within a formal policy context: 'The autonomy of the teacher is . . . constrained and made responsible by the particular configuration of policies operating during a particular period' (Shulman 1983: 501).

Furthermore, teachers are tied by the 'practicality ethic' (Doyle and Ponder 1977): what they choose to do must work practically with their students in their classrooms and in their schools. They must also build upon existing practice and relationships: as Tyack and Cuban (1995: 82) point out, '[p]olicymakers may ignore the "pedagogical past," but teachers and students cannot'. Indeed teachers interviewed by McLaughlin (1993: 81–2) see their students as the key referent of their work, with the greatest influence upon classroom practices being 'the cultural diversity of students in their classes and . . . the demands, difficulties, and pressures associated with today's students'.

Institutional priorities may place additional constraints upon teachers' autonomy: working in a school which emphasizes the personal and social development of students and encourages teacher initiative and innovation will be very different from working in a school which stresses examination success and rewards conformity to traditional teaching practices. Moreover, teachers' personal attitudes are also relevant, since autonomy can only be realized through its exercise in practice. Whilst some teachers may be active agents in continuously constructing their own versions of educational practice, others may simply replicate traditional classroom routines in an unthinking way and so be more amenable to direction from outside.

Thus policy-making in practice is a complex balance of competing forces and conflicting considerations, the outcome of which is never pre-ordained but is resolved in different ways in different contexts. For many years a degree of equilibrium was achieved between the various constituencies, but in recent times it is possible to identify an increase in activity by the state in terms of 'policy talk' and 'policy action' in many countries. In England, for example, the post-war tradition of consensual and incremental policy-making in education was characterized by high levels of neutrality and low levels of initiative by either the secretary of state or the Department of Education and Science (DES). However, from about the mid-1970s a series of ideological attacks on teachers began to change the balance of power within the education system and the traditional notion of 'partnership' between central government, local government and teachers was increasingly replaced by the dominant metaphor of 'accountability' (Chitty 1989: 136). Over time a series of increasingly aggressive state initiatives in education have involved 'a steady reassertion of central and visible control over state schooling', accompanied by bureaucratic imperatives from the DES as it 'has moved strongly towards an interventionist policy on curriculum matters' (Grace 1987: 217–18). The escalating pace of change and ever more frantic attempts by the state to find new solutions to educational problems have led to a form of 'policy hysteria' (Stronach and Morris 1994), with overlapping waves of reform, multiple innovation, frequent changes in policy and a growing emphasis upon rhetoric and presentation rather than substance. The effects of this complex of policies and rapid policy changes upon teachers have been profound: 'Together these changes assert a massive and complex technology of control over teachers' work in all its aspects' (Ball 1994: 12). It is not just the content of the reforms which puts pressure on teachers but also: 'the sheer cumulative impact of multiple, complex, non-negotiable innovations on teachers' time, energy, motivation, opportunities to reflect, and their very capacity to cope' (Hargreaves 1994: 6).

However, despite both the pace and extent of the reforms and their centralizing tendencies teachers still retain the potential for some control over their working lives. Even the abrasive Chris Woodhead, Her Majesty's Chief

Inspector of Schools in England and Wales, was forced to concede 'the limits of legislation': 'Government cannot legislate to raise educational standards: it is, though some of us outside of schools tend to forget this, only teachers in classrooms who can really make the difference' (Woodhead 1995: 14). In some cases the inability of state legislators to provide adequate specification of requirements makes them reliant upon 'professional experience and "teacherly knowledge" ' (Jenkins 1997: 126) to turn nebulous policy into concrete practice. In other cases the gaps, ambiguities and contradictions within policy texts leave teachers 'spaces for manoeuvre' (Bowe *et al.* 1992) within which they can assert their own priorities and beliefs. In this way the individual choices made by teachers in their classrooms may allow them to mediate educational policy in creative ways, whilst the cumulative effect of their decisions can transform them into 'policy-makers in practice' (Croll *et al.* 1994; Osborn 1997). Just as in the USA in the early decades of this century, the language of business efficiency and control used by policy-makers did not necessarily translate into classroom practice: 'Schools were not factories and children were not passive raw materials. Like their students, teachers were active agents, not docile workers on a pedagogical assembly line' (Tyack and Cuban 1995: 115).

As indicated above, however, the potential for teachers to act as active agents in constructing educational policy does not necessarily guarantee that they will do so. Lack of inclination to be proactive, low levels of 'professional confidence' (Helsby 1995), increasing isolation or simply exhaustion, stress or 'burnout' from the plethora of new initiatives have led many teachers to take the line of least resistance and adopt a relatively passive stance towards the demands of educational reformers. The extent to which teachers adopt either an active or passive approach to educational policy-making is heavily influenced by the professional and work cultures within which they operate. In particular, high degrees of collegiality and strong commitments to fundamental principles within a group make it more likely that teachers will resist external direction and be active in constructing their own versions of educational practice (Helsby 1996a; Helsby and McCulloch 1997).

Structure, culture and agency

As can be seen from the above, the relationship between educational reform and the contested emergence of a 'new work order' is highly complex. Clearly education systems are affected in important ways by the effects of globalization and consequent changes in the perceived needs of labour markets, but there is no automatic correspondence. Whilst the vision and values of 'fast capitalist texts' have 'deeply informed contemporary calls for [educational] reform' (Gee *et al.* 1996: 25), resulting in 'a growing alignment between the business world in the new capitalism and various non-business spheres of interest, including schools and academic disciplines promoting school reform efforts' (1996: 49), nonetheless their hegemony is far from total. At each stage in the complex process of policy development and implementation, the idealized prescriptions of the new capitalism are contested, mediated and transformed through a series of interpretations, choices and decisions taken at different levels within individual nation states and their national education systems.

Educational policy-making at the level of the central state takes place within a particular framework of structural constraints – for example, those imposed by public spending targets, by current government priorities or by public expectations – but is also dependent upon the convictions, strength of purpose and actions of key policy-makers. At this level, the discourse of the 'new work order' vies for attention with other discourses, for example those relating to the maintenance of social order, to more traditional, social-democratic notions of educational aims or to new conceptions of the role of the state. As individuals and groups seek with varying degrees of success to advance their own interests in the ensuing policy debate, certain views and options begin to gain prominence and to influence the choices of political decision-makers. As these choices become clearer, politicians and others may use some form of public consultation to gain general acceptance for their ideas or to identify necessary modifications before formally adopting particular courses of action (although the extent of, and importance attached to, such consultation seems to have diminished significantly in recent years). What finally emerges from this contestation is a set of policy texts and directives which indicate a preferred direction for educational change and provide a framework for its development.

As indicated above, policy texts represent only one stage in the process of policy development and remain dependent upon teachers to translate them into practice. However, many of the policy texts which have emerged recently have led to the enactment of notable changes to the basic structures of schooling that have been largely outside of teacher control. In particular, the enforced dismantling of large educational bureaucracies and related changes to the funding and governance of education have been features of the reforms in many countries, as school-based management has become the dominant mode of organization and former public monopoly schools have been exposed to the discipline of the market. At the same time a widespread increase in central control over teachers' work has been achieved through a combination of curriculum prescription or more general goal steering, an emphasis upon comparative national testing, increased surveillance of classroom practice and more stringent accountability requirements.

Whilst the extension of central control is ubiquitous, the means by which this is realized varies between countries, ranging from aggressive forms of 'direct rule' to the more subtle use of 'indirect rule' based upon persuasion and encouragement. The now well-documented failure of past educational reforms to produce significant changes in classroom practices has led many to the realization that 'you can't mandate what matters' (Fullan 1993: 21) and that there are distinct limits to what can be achieved through structural, as opposed to cultural, changes: 'Changing formal structures is not the same as changing norms, habits, skills and beliefs' (1993: 49). Accordingly, some national governments have begun to place more emphasis upon 'reculturing', through growth and professional development, rather than upon formal 'restructuring': an ostensibly bottom-up strategy of improving schools from within rather than a top-down approach to reforming them from without (Hargreaves 1994: 255). Thus there has been considerable emphasis upon improving in-service teacher development – for example, through the spread of professional development schools, of professional networks and of work-time agreements to enable teachers to engage in joint planning. This second strategy is much more in line with the precepts of the 'new work order', which advocates the replacement of traditional, hierarchical chains of command with the development of a corporate culture which 'empowers' workers to take responsibility for the achievement of pre-specified organizational goals.

Whether governments approach the reform of schooling primarily through 'restructuring' or 'reculturing', the two are often interlinked. For example, structural changes in England to the funding and governance of education have led to the development of a new culture in many schools in which fund-raising, marketing, the maximization of examination results and student recruitment may be given priority over broader educational aims or compensatory teaching. Similarly, the plethora of new requirements placed upon teachers has resulted in an intensification of working life that has severely reduced the opportunities to develop or sustain collegial or collaborative cultures both within and between schools. As Hargreaves (1994: 256) points out, 'cultures do not operate in a vacuum' but 'are formed within and framed by particular structures'. Thus it may be necessary to change existing school structures in order to establish more productive school cultures.

Ultimately, however, both structural and cultural changes to schooling will do little to improve schooling unless they take into account the importance of the active agency of teachers in constructing the reality of educational practice on a day-to-day basis in their schools and in their classrooms. Whilst teachers are constrained to varying degrees by external imperatives, the inevitability of their relative autonomy means that they retain the capacity to make an infinite number of (often minor) choices which, cumulatively, shape the outcomes of any educational reform initiatives and may well subvert the

intentions of state policy-makers. As indicated above, however, their autonomy is only *relative* and, like other players in the education system, their
choices are always limited by a range of external structural and cultural factors.

Any area of organized human activity, but particularly a value-laden and
contested area such as educational reform, displays what Giddens (1981;
1984) calls the 'duality of structure', whereby social actions both create, and
are constrained by, social structures. By their actions, human agents may
either transform or reproduce such structures: indeed, Ball (1994: 21) argues
that any analysis of policy requires 'an understanding that is based not on
constraint *or* agency but on the changing relationships between constraint
and agency and their inter-penetration'. The degree to which either structures act as constraints upon human agency or agency transforms structures
is heavily dependent upon the context and culture within which people operate. Relevant aspects of culture include not only the set of beliefs, values and
norms of behaviour developed within a particular group but also the habit-
ual patterns of relationship and forms of association within that group – the
'content' and 'form' of culture (Hargreaves 1992). Through immersion in a
specific culture, its members both create and accept a distinctive social identity and are thereby disciplined into accepted ways of thinking, speaking and
behaving within a given context. Drawing upon research in an English primary school in the early years of National Curriculum implementation,
Acker (1997: 47) emphasizes the importance of the interplay between structure, culture and human agency in determining the outcomes of educational
reforms:

> We learn that school cultures cannot survive untouched by imposed
> change, but that material realities and school cultures influence the
> form taken by innovation. We have, in effect, a case study of the intri-
> cate and changing relationships of agency, culture and structure.

As already suggested, however, this interplay not only takes place as educational reforms reach schools, but also at the various levels of policy discussion, development, text production, interpretation and change which
both precede and follow that stage. For this reason the nature of education
in general, and of teachers' work in particular, is never stable over space or
time but is constantly open to contestation, redefinition and reconstruction.
To study changes to teachers' work, therefore, is to look at general trends in
particular places at particular times: the complexity and provisionality of
developments means that it can never offer a full account of reality.

three

CHANGING FRAMEWORKS, CHANGING SYSTEMS

Whilst acknowledging that educational change is the outcome of a complex and recurrent interplay between structure, culture and agency, it is clear that, in recent years, teachers' work has been significantly affected by a conspicuous tightening of the structural frameworks initiated or imposed by the central state. Across the westernized world, educational reform legislation has mushroomed, as governments have sought to keep pace with burgeoning beliefs that the restructuring of schooling will lead to the promised land of economic success. Woods *et al.* (1997: 23) have described the impact of these changes upon teachers' work as a diminution of choice, as the inevitable 'dilemmas' of teaching multiply and intensify, becoming less amenable to 'creative resolution'. As a result, teachers may begin to experience these dilemmas as 'tensions', as choice becomes more limited, or as 'constraints', when they are forced in a particular direction against their better judgement. Whilst acknowledging that the situation is not static, Woods *et al.* (1997: 22) perceive that 'in general . . . teaching has become more tension-ridden and constrained and less dilemmatic'.

This chapter will explore some of the recent attempts being made to restructure teachers' work by radically changing the systems and frameworks within which they operate. Whilst some aspects of the reforms accord well with the precepts of the 'new work order' – for example, the breaking up of large bureaucracies, the devolution of management to smaller units and the encouragement of flexibility and choice – some of the less subtle manifestations of central control appear more in tune with the 'old work order' of Fordism and scientific management. Amongst the latter may be mentioned highly prescriptive forms of national curriculum and national testing and those forms of teacher inspection which encourage conformity with a centrally preferred model of teaching. To some extent these differences mirror the tensions within the dominant New Right coalition between neo-liberal and neo-conservative ideologies which have led to compromises and inconsistencies in policy-making. They also reflect the fact that the ideology of the 'new work order' is itself full of contradictions, gaps and silences (Gee *et al.* 1996) and is far from having achieved hegemony even in the world of business, and certainly not in the world of government and politics or in the world of education.

The 'new' work order of schools

This section will examine those aspects of restructuring that appear to accord more closely with the prescriptions of the 'new work order'. This will include the widespread devolution of management to the local and institutional level; a variety of initiatives intended to open schooling to the discipline of market forces, thereby increasing competition and driving down costs; attempts to reculture both schools and teachers either by making them more 'businesslike' or through appeals to professionalism and collegiality; and finally, the series of structural changes to teachers' terms and conditions of service designed to create a more flexible and differentiated workforce.

Devolved management

At first glance, the most obvious overlap between the practices advocated in popular management texts and current educational reforms arises from the apparently widespread application of the 'fast capitalist' blueprint for dismantling large bureaucracies in favour of smaller, self-managing units. Decentralization and the devolution of various decision-making powers to local or institutional level have been widely advocated as a means of improving educational quality (see OECD 1987) and increasingly have become characteristic features of educational administration in both developed and developing countries (Bullock and Thomas 1997).

Despite the increasing prevalence of decentralization, the reasons for its introduction may vary from country to country according to different economic and political circumstances (Fowler *et al.* 1993; Levačić 1995). For example, whilst some countries may introduce school-based management as part of a strategy to create a quasi-market in education, others may emphasize local decision-making as the key to motivating teachers and thereby enhancing their performance. On the other hand, some developing countries or former communist states of eastern Europe may simply lack the resources either to develop or to maintain strong central bureaucracies.

Where decentralization is deliberately planned, rather than occurring through default, there are still considerable variations in the focus of local decision-making. Levačić (1995: 5) suggests five domains of school-based management:

- budget
- physical resources
- staffing
- student recruitment
- curriculum.

Bullock and Thomas (1997) offer a very similar categorization, although with 'assessment' added to 'curriculum' and the term 'access' used instead of 'student recruitment'. They also draw attention to the extraordinary polarization between those countries which have devolved considerable decision-making powers over 'curriculum' to the institutional level (albeit within a framework of general principles) and those which have moved curriculum control firmly towards the centre, whilst delegating responsibilities for resource management to schools. There are also variations in the exact location of local decision-making, with differential powers granted in different countries to parents, to teachers, to headteachers, to community representatives (for example, school governors in England, school councils in various American and Australian states or boards of trustees in New Zealand) or to municipalities (for example, in the Scandinavian countries).

Despite disparities in the purpose, focus and location of decentralization between countries, there are also some commonalities, especially in terms of the effects upon schools and upon the work of teachers. Firstly, it seems clear that the degree of autonomy granted to the local level is always relative and set within particular limits:

> Governments throughout the world seem intent on increasing the autonomy of schools. Yet it can be argued that the terms 'self-managing' or 'self-determining' schools rarely mean unlimited autonomy without regard to system-wide policy parameters and agreed national standards.
>
> (Chitty and Lawn 1995: 141)

Given the national importance and public funding of education systems, it is perhaps inevitable that moves towards local or school-based management should be accompanied by new systems of accountability. In practice, many of these involve making teachers or local representatives responsible for achieving certain pre-specified goals or meeting particular standards. This is entirely in line with the 'new work order' precepts of such gurus as Peters and Waterman (1982) who argue that managers should not be told how to manage but should be held accountable for achieving particular objectives. In the USA, for example, President Bush linked local licence directly with accountability by calling for the decentralization of authority and decision-making responsibility to the school site, so that educators are empowered to determine the means for accomplishing the goals and to be held accountable for accomplishing them.

(*New York Times*, 1 October 1989, quoted in Tyack and Cuban 1995: 81)

Similarly. in New Zealand, the delegation of school management to elected boards of trustees was accompanied by measures to make them directly responsible to the minister through a form of contract or school charter, many aspects of which were centrally prescribed (Court 1997a; Robertson 1998). Considering the impact of recent reforms in Australia, Smyth (1995: 195) concluded that the development of various national statements, standards and benchmarks indicated that the promotion of decentralization masked a quite different agenda:

Like other parts of the world, Australia is gripped by an irresistible urge towards recentralisation of control over education, while at the same time trying to give the appearance of doing the reverse.

Whilst Codd (1996: 7) identified a definite diminution of overall local control in New Zealand schools:

the effect of decentralisation of certain areas of decision-making in education has been greater overall centralisation of control.

Similarly, in the Edmonton Public School District of Canada, Levačić (1992: 82) found that

decentralisation can be used to secure more effective control by headquarter's management than a highly centralised system of direct control of resources and processes in the schools.

Again control was achieved by making schools accountable for results, whilst devolving responsibility for managing resources and processes to the school level. This separation of authority over *means* and *ends* appears typical of decentralized systems in many countries (Hartley 1994; 1997b), although there are variations in the degree of prescriptiveness inherent in the latter.

Another common feature of school-based management is the changed relationship between teachers and managers and, in particular, the very strong emphasis upon the pivotal role of the headteacher or principal. Despite the fact that some countries have stressed the 'professional' role of teachers within school reforms (see, for example, Finn and Rebarber 1992; Carlgren 1996), the new importance attached to managing schools locally has inevitably led to a widespread redefinition of the roles of both teachers and teacher managers, with a marked trend in many countries towards redistributing authority to the latter. Thus Robertson (1996: 39) has talked of 'the reassertion of managerial power' and Menter *et al.* (1997: 53) of the reaffirmation of 'the managerial prerogative', whilst Power *et al.* (1997: 350), in their review of 'new' education management in five countries, have concluded that, in many cases 'the devolution of decision-making to the school has resulted in a concentration of power "at the top" '.

As well as creating divisions between 'managers' and 'managed' (Evetts 1994a; 1994b; van Zanten 1995; Webb and Vulliamy 1996), the new tasks placed upon headteachers and principals have often had a profound influence upon the nature of their work, as they have been forced into the role of 'managing director' (Menter *et al.* 1995) or 'chief executive' (Ball 1990a) within a new business-oriented organization of schooling. Primary headteachers in Northern Ireland interviewed by McHugh and McMullan (1995: 27) felt that they were 'tied to the office much more' and that they had 'lost touch' with the 'real school world'. In her studies of the reconstruction of the New Zealand principal, Court identified 'shifts from professional forms of leadership to an increased hierarchical managerialism' (1997a: 2) in a new managerial/market context which 'is masculinist in its rationale and practice' (Court 1997b: 6). Within the new technicist discourse, value is attached to efficiency, productivity, cost-effectiveness, ambition, competition and scientific rationality, thereby dislodging traditional feminine qualities such as caring, nurturing, loyalty and co-operation (Inglis 1989; Evetts 1994b; Acker 1999).

Local management inevitably involves the devolution of new and additional management tasks, with consequent increases in the workload of both teachers and teacher managers. Whilst headteachers and principals take on the extra duties of resource allocation, budget management, planning, reporting, marketing, public relations and negotiation with governors, schools councils or other community representatives, heavy demands are also placed upon teachers not only to translate changed central curriculum requirements into practice and to maximize the realization of pre-specified learning outcomes, but also to keep careful account of their work through extensive form-filling, record-keeping or other kinds of data collection. Indeed, despite the rhetoric of the 'new work order' it would seem that the local management of schools (LMS) is generating an increase in bureaucratic requirements: 'our research suggests that far from releasing people from the burdens of bureaucracy LMS may well increase the internal administrative load' (Bowe and Ball 1992: 51).

Another common feature of devolved management which is affecting the work of teachers is the increased use of school development planning, which brings together processes of administrative and educational target-setting, evaluation and resource allocation. As Grundy and Bonser (1997: 23) point out, the power to plan could be devolved hierarchically to school managers or democratically to all members of the school community, although their evidence from Australian schools suggest that the extent and quality of such democratic involvement is questionable. Ball (1994: 61) concludes that it is non-existent: 'The [school development plan] signifies and celebrates the exclusion and subjection of the teacher. Not only does the teacher lose control over classroom planning decisions, but will be monitored, judged and compared by criteria set elsewhere.'

However, whilst headteachers and principals may have gained some new authority over teachers, they have not been empowered politically to take major strategic decisions about the management of their schools. A combination of strong external imperatives and the limited financial flexibility available in handling a cash-limited budget with high staffing costs suggests that what has been devolved is administrative responsibility rather than managerial power: 'Planning is predominantly about managing the statutory requirements, within the financial limitations' (Wallace 1992: 2). Moreover, school managers are themselves subject to external appraisal of their performance: 'headteachers and principals are increasingly forced into a position in which they have to demonstrate performance along centrally prescribed criteria in a context over which they often have diminishing control' (Power *et al.* 1997: 358). Thus, as Codd (1996: 9) argues, the move towards local or school-based management has in practice tended to produce 'centrally determined and controlled policies associated with devolved responsibility for operations' and 'a structure in which managerial decisions are more effectively controlled'. Given the ubiquitousness of overall reductions in educational spending, local school management has also been described as a means of devolving to schools both the blame for cutbacks (Angus 1994: 89) and the responsibility for hard decisions about competing educational priorities (Blackmore *et al.* 1996: 215).

A further effect of the introduction of local or school-based management in many countries has been a significant reduction in the power, influence and support capacity of the district office or local education authority (LEA) (Murphy 1992; Grace 1995). At the same time there has been a strengthening of the role of smaller, school-level bodies representing community interests, whether in the form of governing bodies, school councils or school boards. This latter development could be seen as potentially threatening professional control by encouraging lay participation in the running of schools. However, as Deem (1994) points out, such involvement can have quite diverse effects and support either democratic or neo-liberal, market-driven ends. Indeed, evidence suggests that school governors, far from acting as 'government agents' (Court 1997a), often make alliances with teachers to oppose national policies (McGovern 1992; Munn 1992). Once again, the structural framework created by government policies does not guarantee particular outcomes in practice: 'Devolution can only set the scene. It is the performance of the key actors which determines the results' (Sharpe 1996: 7).

Market forces

Murphy (1998), in his review of the 'new consumerism' in education, has distinguished between two clusters of strategies, the first relating to consumer control through changes to school governance (where the appeal to market forces may be relatively weak) and the second strengthening the role of consumers through a more direct exercise of market structures. The latter is premised upon the key concepts of choice and competition, and includes developments such as open enrolment, vouchers, and the creation of contract, charter or, in England, grant-maintained schools. The marketization of education, whilst less widespread than decentralization, is making significant inroads in several countries and accords well with the precepts of the 'new work order', which glorify competition as a means of reducing unit costs and promoting excellence. For governments imbued with a belief in the inefficiency, undesirability and unacceptable costs of traditional welfarist organization of public services, the allocative mechanisms and disciplines of the market offer an attractive alternative approach.

Whilst devolved school management has helped to fragment local bureaucracies and to create the independent units needed to compete in the market-place, governments need to take further measures to produce market-governed behaviour (Hatcher 1994). The introduction or promotion of parental choice, often accompanied by the diversification of the kinds of school from which they can choose, has been a hallmark of neoliberal approaches in many countries, whilst the linking of resourcing to recruitment through student-related funding has concentrated the minds of school managers anxious to maximize income at a time of economic cutbacks. According to Chubb and Moe, arch advocates of educational marketization in the USA, the combination of increased institutional autonomy and financial incentives offers the best means of improving educational standards: 'The key to better schools . . . is a new system of public education that eliminates most political and bureaucratic control over the schools and relies instead on indirect control through markets and parental choice' (Chubb and Moe 1992a: 37). For them, democratic control results in gross inefficiencies, whilst 'choice' and 'competition' can promote desirable forms of school organization, release 'the productive potential already present in schools and in their personnel' (1992a: 38) and thereby raise student achievement. Poor schools, they claim, will lose support and be weeded out in favour of more successful institutions: 'This process of natural selection complements the incentives of the marketplace in propelling and supporting a population of autonomous, effectively organized schools' (1992a: 40).

In those countries which have already subjected their schools to market forces, the outcomes in practice have been far from universally beneficial. Certainly there have been 'winners' and 'losers' amongst school: in many cases, however, the 'losers' have not closed down, but have continued to operate in extremely difficult circumstances and with reduced budgets, often to the detriment of the educational provision offered to their students and with consequent increases in inequality of opportunities (Grace 1995; Apple 1996; Blackmore *et al.* 1996).

Moreover, the marketization of education has also had other significant effects upon both schools and teachers, almost regardless of the degree of 'market success' that they have enjoyed. As Grace (1995) points out, the creation of a free market demands the destruction of alternative forms of regulation, including professional autonomy and organized teacher unions (see also Gewirtz 1997). In countries such as New Zealand and England and in some Australian states, consultation with teachers over educational reforms has become increasingly perfunctory, and consistent efforts have been made to undermine the power of teacher unions by abandoning collective bargaining in favour of locally negotiated settlements (Ozga 1995; Smyth 1995; Robertson 1998).

The decision to cast parents in the role of 'consumers' in the new educational market-place and the consequent need to provide information on which they can base their purchasing choices has created additional work for teachers in terms of producing reports, statistics and other forms of aggregable performance data (Blackmore *et al.* 1996). Where funding is tied to levels of enrolment, schools are often driven to concentrate their efforts on maximizing those 'measurable' outcomes that are valued in the official forms of comparison between schools, such as the league tables of assessment results in England. In the process other educational outcomes valued by teachers may be marginalized, as market forces take precedence over professional judgements. In New Zealand, as reported by Court (1997a), this is an explicit aim of government policy: 'The bottom line for a manager of a business is profit and staying in business. The bottom line for a principal is roll numbers and keeping the school viable' (Education Review Office (ERO) 1996: 9). This need to 'keep the school viable' also pushes teachers to direct growing amounts of effort, energy and resources into marketing their school (McKeown and Byrne 1996), despite the fact that this is usually 'a zero sum game [which] creates no extra pupils' (Hesketh and Knight 1998: 21). Moreover, the whole process of marketization frequently places contradictory demands upon teachers and principals, who may increasingly have to choose between investing their energies in 'image management' in response to external demands or in meeting the educational and social needs of their students (Ball 1994; Blackmore *et al.* 1996).

Another key characteristic of marketization is the increase in competition both between and within schools. This was promoted particularly strongly by the policies of the Conservative government in England after its third successive electoral victory in 1987. According to Warnock (1988: 173) competition based upon self-interest had by then become 'the central Thatcherite concept', and it was subsequently transported to other countries. In the USA, Chubb and Moe (1990; 1992b) were soon advocating its adoption, whilst schools in Victoria were required 'to compete against one another for students and resources' (Smyth 1995: 192). In many cases this enforced competition reduced the amount of contact between schools and inhibited traditional forms of collaboration. Principals interviewed by Blackmore *et al.* (1996: 208) believed that there was 'little sharing of information or trust between principals as each sought to maintain or gain market advantage'. In some cases, however, there was evidence of deliberate attempts to maintain collaborative activity despite the unfavourable political climate (Bridges and Husbands 1996; Wallace 1998).

One of the side-effects of financial cutbacks and institutional budget management has been the introduction of internal systems of competitive bidding for resources and increased rivalry between faculties and subject departments and between academic and pastoral provision. Reay (1998: 190) has identified the emergence in English secondary schools of 'a culture of winners and losers in which competition between departments is exacerbated'. In England, Australia and New Zealand, new teacher career structures have been based not upon incremental progression and reward for good teaching but rather upon the tenets of competitive individualism. Although, as Tyack and Cuban (1995: 127) point out, such measures have rarely succeeded because they are 'out of alignment with the values and practices of teachers', they are only one part of a wider strategy. League tables of student assessment results and formal appraisals and inspections of teachers have also been used to encourage competition amongst staff, whilst in some cases headteachers and principals have adopted a 'divide and rule' strategy to ensure compliance with school policies: 'An increasingly competitive climate both across and within schools and heightened forms of surveillance mean that teachers feel under growing pressure to perform and conform' (Gewirtz 1997: 224). Thus the competition engendered is not that of a free market but rather of a quasi-market which is 'steered by the government, which sets the rules of exchange . . . [and] decide[s] the nature of the product' (Hartley 1997a: 138).

Despite the rhetoric of autonomy and enterprise and the promise of 'choice and diversity' (DfE and Welsh Office 1992), the marketization of education has more frequently been associated with convergence of practice and with 'defensive strategies' (Hesketh and Knight 1998: 34). According to Codd (1996: 14) this helps to foster a 'culture of compliance' and to ensure that schools remain 'conservative institutions, manifesting a commitment to the *status quo*'. Far from being 'empowered' within the market-place, many teachers have experienced decreased confidence and increased insecurity.

School reculturing

The long history of failure of earlier attempts at educational reform has led some policy-makers to a realization of the inadequacy of purely structural changes to schooling. For example, Timar and Kirp's study of the implementation of American state reforms in the 1980s concluded that excellence could not be coerced by top-down regulation (reported in Tyack and Cuban 1995), whilst the slogan 'you can't mandate what matters' (Fullan 1993) began to be used with increasing frequency both in the USA and beyond. The alternative approach involves attempts to go beyond the structural level and to bring about changes in the culture of schools and of teachers. This is certainly in line with a key tenet the 'new work order' which suggests that, in the absence of traditional, hierarchical chains of command, control is best assured through the manipulation of organizational cultures and the colonization of the 'hearts and minds' of individual employees (Wilmott 1993).

Within current attempts at educational restructuring it is possible to identify two quite distinct forms of reculturing:

- the attempted imposition of a new technical-rational, business-oriented culture upon schools
- the promotion of a culture of change and improvement based upon appeals to teacher autonomy and teacher professionalism.

These very different approaches can be seen as examples of alternating government strategies of 'direct rule', involving standardization and deprofessionalization, and 'indirect rule', based upon appeals to teacher professionalism and involving diversity of practice (Lawn 1996; Ozga 1996; Menter *et al.* 1997). In some countries elements of both strategies are apparently being adopted at the same time, although one is generally dominant.

In countries such as England, New Zealand and Australia which have vigorously pursued policies of marketization, there is strong evidence of attempts to commodify schooling in order to make it more amenable to technical-rational aspects of business management. Thus complex educational processes can be virtually ignored in favour of quantifiable 'inputs' and 'outputs', 'targets' can be set and 'performance indicators' developed, whilst the curriculum becomes a product that is 'delivered', parents become 'consumers' and staff become 'human resources' who need to be 'managed'. As Gewirtz (1997: 219) points out, these terms are not neutral but form part of discourses which 'function as powerful disciplinary mechanisms for transforming teacher subjectivities and the culture and values of classroom practice'. In this process, teachers 'can be discursively repositioned as non-experts' (Robertson 1996: 30), whilst institutional power and authority flow to headteachers and principals. They in turn are encouraged by particular forms of technical-rational management training to adopt and impose new sets of values which emphasize efficiency, accountability and the reduction of complex educational problems to technically resolvable management issues (Angus 1994). In what Ball (1994: 138) has identified as 'the assertion of *technocratic managerialism* over and above what might be termed *ethical professionalism*', the views of classroom teachers are marginalized, any debate on educational values is repressed and 'severe constraints' placed upon 'the realisation of democratic ideals in schooling' (Rizvi 1989: 56). According to Harris (1994: 4), teachers are reoriented 'away from the broader concerns of determining curricula, formulating educational goals and promoting social reconstruction and towards the realm of efficient school management within an educational marketplace'.

In contrast to these overt attempts to engineer a culture of top-down business management within schools, considerable efforts have been made elsewhere to promote an ostensibly more empowering and bottom-up cultural change by appealing to notions of teacher professionalism. In the USA, for example, the failure of the 'first wave' of structural reforms of the early and mid-1980s led to an alternative 'second wave', underpinned by the belief that the key to improving educational provision lay in 'empowering teachers to work more effectively with their students' (Murphy 1992: 6). According to McLaughlin (1995: 15), the new reform era has involved a 'transfer of authority and voice to the profession', and restructuring in the USA has been described as 'a professional process which implies a re-establishment of control over work by teachers' (Lawn 1995: 348). In Scandinavia in the late 1980s and in some of the German *Länder* teachers were invited to extend their professionalism through involvement in curriculum development within a loose framework of general principles (Carlgren 1993; Bullock and Thomas 1997; Klette 1998). This has not been without cost in terms of increased workload, and some have been offered additional non-teaching time, career rewards or the promise of professional dignity in return for changing their work practices and/or accepting additional responsibilities such as mentoring, subject co-ordination and curriculum planning. Various reform initiatives have sought to change the traditionally individualistic culture of teaching by pressing teachers towards collaboration and collegiality (Little and McLaughlin 1993).

As Hargreaves (1994: 248) points out, however, collaboration can be 'helpful or harmful': 'what is really important is who controls it, who is involved in it, what are its purposes'. On the one hand, genuine and open-ended collaboration can facilitate the development of professional confidence and autonomy through exposure to diverse points of view in a supportive context. An example of this is the National Schools Network in Australia, which 'promotes and supports collaborative research and collegial reflective practices using critical action research methodologies' (Sachs 1997: 12). This has allowed teachers an opportunity to 'reclaim their professionalism' despite an unfavourable political climate. On the other hand, teacher collaboration may take the form of 'contrived collegiality' (Hargreaves and Dawe 1990; Hargreaves 1992; 1994) in which teachers are brought together by managers for a limited amount of time in order to work together upon pre-specified tasks of restricted scope. Such processes may result in 'a lack of ownership in the planned work' (Pollard *et al.* 1994: 93) or in reductionist and disempowering 'groupthink' (Fullan 1993) in which divergent views are discouraged in favour of uncritical task completion and the acceptance of core institutional values.

Terms and conditions of service

The demands of the 'new work order' for flexibility and responsiveness at ever lower cost are premised upon the establishment of a 'lean and mean' and differentiated workforce that can be deployed at will when opportunities arise and just as easily dispersed at times of over-production or over-provision of services. This is the antithesis of traditional forms of bureaucratic organization that rewarded loyalty to the firm with individual security of employment and steady career advancement. Despite differences of emphasis between countries, recent attempts to restructure education have been accompanied by a variety of changes to teachers' terms and conditions of service which, whilst not altogether overturning traditional practices, have gone a long way towards increasing flexibility and differentiation within the educational workforce.

A striking feature of many restructuring efforts has been a change in teachers' career and promotion structures away from long-established collective agreements and towards more locally determined and flexible arrangements. Devolved management structures have frequently involved increases in the power of school management bodies over the employment of teachers and over their terms and conditions of service. Thus teachers in New Zealand have become employees of their school's board of trustees through an individual employment contract which specifies their duties and responsibilities (Jesson 1995). Similarly, school governing bodies in England, which must by law include business people and other non-educationalists, are now responsible for appointing, disciplining and dismissing staff, whilst governors of grant-maintained schools – or school boards of charter schools in some American states – employ teachers directly (Deem 1994; Hartley 1997a). In the Australian state of Victoria, responsibility for staffing and industrial issues has moved from the Directorate of School Education to school principals (Smyth 1995). This localization of control over staffing increases organizational flexibility and allows schools to reward forms of middle management outside of the traditional leadership of subject departments: Hargreaves (1994) gives examples from the Cincinnati Public Schools District and from Australia's National Schools Project. However, the dominance of the cash-limited school budget also encourages the 'economy of teacher employment' (Grace 1995: 148) and, in some cases, has led to delays in filling vacancies and to an increased tendency to appoint less experienced and therefore less expensive teachers.

Coupled with more locally controlled employment practices is a shift in career structures away from progressive development along common salary scales and towards a much greater use of differentiated rewards for additional duties or approved performance in particular areas. The use of 'performance management systems of bonuses and appraisal' (Blackmore *et al.* 1996: 201), 'accelerated incremental progression' and 'discretionary payments' (Lawn 1995: 353) has proliferated, all premised upon the supposed benefits of stimulating competitive individualism amongst teachers and all encouraging conformity and compliance with managerial priorities in order to secure career advancement. As status and pay differentials have widened between main-grade and 'rewarded' teachers, further divisions have been created within the workforce by the marked increase in the appointment of classroom assistants, technicians and other non-teaching staff, suggesting an expansion of a periphery of cheaper, semi-skilled labour and a numerical decrease in a central core of trained teachers (Busher and Saran 1995; Robertson 1996).

Core teachers have in turn been subjected to a tightened specification of their duties, often through the imposition of new legislative requirements and/or formal contracts. These include new 'work-time agreements' in Norway, with compulsory elements of organized collaborative work (Klette 1998) and the introduction of scheduled preparation time in elementary schools in Ontario (Hargreaves 1993). In England the statutory employment contract imposed upon teachers in 1987 specified minimum hours of work per year and a range of non-teaching duties, including the management of teaching support staff. It also lengthened the working year by the addition of five days' compulsory school-based training. In some countries organized teacher unions have been marginalized as collective bargaining has been abandoned, and even in countries like the USA, where they are incorporated as partners in restructuring, they tread a difficult line between protecting members' interests and lending spurious legitimacy to managerial reforms (Lawn 1995).

This shift in the balance of power away from organized labour and towards management has left teachers exposed to more exploitative practices, and in most countries there is evidence of an expansion of non-teaching duties and a general intensification of working life. It has also produced greater insecurity of employment, with increases in the numbers of part-time and temporary staff (Busher and Saran 1995) and more teacher redundancies.

The 'old' work order of schools

The changes described so far are in many ways in accord with the canons of the 'new work order', which advocate devolved management, the pursuit of competitive edge, the manipulation of culture to motivate staff and the establishment of a flexible labour market. As can be seen from the above, these developments often operate to the advantage of the system rather than of the individual, and the seductive promises of 'empowerment' that they embody may all too easily contribute to forms of control and exploitation (Helsby *et al.* 1998) if teachers are not able to seize the initiative and impose their own interpretations upon the situation. There are, however, some aspects of current educational reforms that simply do not adopt the empowering language of 'fast capitalist texts' and are more reminiscent of the authoritarian discourses of the 'old' work order. These initiatives have not been taken up universally or have not been implemented to the same extent in all contexts, and are predominant in those countries which have adopted a more aggressive approach towards teachers in their restructuring efforts.

National curricula and national testing

Faced with the advance of globalization and consequent threats to national identity, many governments have introduced or strengthened a national curriculum for schools (Goodson 1994). This does not in itself pose a threat to professional autonomy: indeed, many countries have long since developed such curricula in pursuit of equal educational opportunities for all students. However, in some recent cases a highly prescriptive and centralized curriculum model, coupled with an aggressive disregard for the views of educationalists, has led to a profound sense of deprofessionalization amongst teachers. This has been particularly true in England, where a strong tradition of teacher control of the curriculum was abruptly overturned in 1988 by the legislative imposition of a National Curriculum which specified in considerable detail, through prescribed attainment targets and programmes of study, what students should know and be able to do at various 'key stages' from age 5 to 16. In most other countries the national curriculum has taken the form of a 'framework' curriculum, with scope for local interpretation, although the 1980 version in Sweden marked a shift away from earlier progressivism (Englund 1996) whilst the 1997 Norwegian national curriculum was more prescriptive than its predecessor and included detailed instructions about teaching and learning at each stage (Klette 1998).

More common than the imposition of detailed national curricula is the specification of national standards and the development of various forms of national testing. In Australia there are national curriculum statements and profiles and national outcomes statements for students, whilst state-wide testing is either in place or under discussion. In Sweden and Finland there are national tests and test banks with national marking criteria, whilst in Canada there is benchmarking. In Hong Kong student learning outcomes are identified through a Target Oriented Curriculum and in the USA the federal Goals 2000 programme established a framework to measure student progress towards 'world-class' academic standards. In England national attainment targets and standard assessment tasks (SATs) have been developed, whilst the results of national assessment are published in the media in the form of school league tables.

The importance currently attached to these external and outcome-based assessments of student learning places significant constraints upon teachers' classroom work, as they feel compelled increasingly to 'teach to the test' and to direct their energies towards achieving what are often fairly limited and easily measurable learning outcomes (Gipps 1993). Scope for innovation or for responding to students' needs is reduced in favour of covering the prescribed content or coaching in particular skills, and 'teaching' risks being reduced to standardized routines.

Audit and inspection

In some countries innovative practice and a sense of professional autonomy are further discouraged by standardized audit and inspection procedures which encourage conformity to a particular model of the 'good teacher'. The most notable examples of this are the establishment of the Office for Standards in Education (Ofsted) in England and the Education Review Office (ERO) in New Zealand. The audit and inspection work of these two bodies offers 'a powerful set of techniques for reshaping the work of teachers in schools' (Robertson 1998: 7). Both require the extensive production of documentation that details professional practice in terms of technical-rational conceptions of effective and efficient management of learning and both use limited classroom observation with judgements based upon a pre-defined list of desirable behaviours. According to Codd (1996: 10), the ERO has been 'the dominant technocratic force within the New Zealand education system' whilst Hartley (1997a) points out that Ofsted's concern with standards imposes a bureaucratic framing of good practice that invites conformity.

There is a growing body of evidence that the experience of inspection increases teachers' workloads and can be very stressful, although the teachers interviewed by Woods *et al.* (1997) showed quite varied reactions, reminding us that constraints can sometimes be changed into opportunities. However, the process itself implies a lack of trust in the professionalism of teachers and as such fits well with the 'discourses of derision' (Ball 1990a) which have been deployed in some countries to encourage a lack of confidence in 'failing' schools and 'failing' teachers and to justify government intervention. This is clearly the antithesis of the vision of the 'new work order' which promises to motivate staff and to unleash their capacity to be innovative and entrepreneurial in responding to customer needs, rather than to chain them to conformist rule-following.

Conclusions

Whatever the similarities or dissimilarities of various reform efforts to the precepts of the 'new work order', there is an overall tendency towards both the intensification of teaching and an increase in central control over teachers' work. Ball (1990a: 98) has argued that it is not any one policy that is achieving this transformation but rather

> a massive, inter-connected policy ensemble, a complex of projects, initiatives, schemes, agencies, imperatives and legislation, which is pushing education in new directions and affecting the way teachers work, the way schools are run and organised and the nature and delivery of the school curriculum.

Moreover, most of the current reform initiatives fly in the face of what we know about implementing change and improving education:

> Contractual compliance may ensure that minimal levels of performance are maintained and managerial competence can improve efficiency, but educational excellence derives from personal initiative and professional autonomy.
>
> (Codd 1996: 14)

Despite all of this, however, the role of the teacher remains crucial in shaping the reality both of policy-in-practice and of educational outcomes. Having considered some of the policy structures that have been introduced in educational reform efforts in recent years, the following chapters will examine the empirical evidence of how some of these developments have changed teachers' work in England.

four

CHANGING WHAT
TEACHERS TEACH

The school curriculum is absolutely central to the organization of teachers' work: indeed Connell (1985: 87) argues that it actually constitutes 'a definition of teachers' work' and that 'the way it is organised, and the social practices that surround it, have profound consequences for teachers'. The term 'curriculum' is often used loosely to mean simply the collection of subjects that is taught in school, although in fact there are several aspects of curriculum that are highly significant in shaping teachers' work:

- *curriculum content* specifies what should be taught to young people;
- *curriculum form* refers to the way in which the teaching is organized (for example, in subject-specific modules, in longer blocks of time or on a short and regular 'drip-feed' basis);
- *curriculum method* reflects how it is taught (the pedagogy);
- *curriculum assessment* indicates what aspects of learning are formally tested and valued.

Since a curriculum represents a particular selection from a range of possible choices, and since educational goals and practices are always contentious, the social construction of a school curriculum involves political and ideological contestation and the exercise of power at different levels within the system (Goodson 1994). Such contestation, especially that over curriculum content and curriculum assessment, has often been discernible in many of the recent attempts to restructure education.

This chapter will focus on the recent struggles in England over curriculum *content* and *assessment*, and in particular on the attempts by the government to reassert central control in this area, initially through the introduction of a broad curriculum framework for 14–18-year-olds and subsequently through the detailed prescription of what should be taught and assessed in state schools at different stages throughout the period of compulsory schooling. Like subsequent chapters, it will draw upon extensive data-sets gathered over the last 15 years[1] which relate to the two major curriculum initiatives of that period, namely TVEI and the National Curriculum. TVEI was initially introduced for the 14–18 age group on a voluntary basis in 1983, and the National Curriculum was made compulsory through the Education Reform Act of 1988. Whilst both initiatives were virulently attacked at their inception on the grounds of unwarranted state interference in professional matters, in practice their effects and their impact upon teachers' work have been profoundly different.

Background

The introduction of central curriculum initiatives in England was particularly contentious because of the unusually strong, post-war tradition of curriculum autonomy that had long been associated in public consciousness with notions of teacher 'professionalism'. For almost four decades it was widely assumed that teachers, as professionals, enjoyed almost total freedom to develop whatever courses they judged appropriate for their students. The fact that a combination of inertia, cultural expectations and the requirements of public examinations meant that this assumed freedom frequently lay dormant, rather than being actively exploited in practice, did little to diminish the symbolic importance of this tradition, which has been a distinctive feature of the modern English education system.

This association between the notions of 'teacher professionalism' and 'curriculum autonomy' can best be understood in its historic context as part of an implicit and relatively long-lasting settlement in the frequently contested relationship between teachers and the state (Grace 1987). As Green (1990) points out in his comparative study of education and state formation in England, France and the USA, England was relatively late in developing a national education system, and remnants of nineteenth-century *laissez-faire* approaches ensured that what eventually emerged was both fragmented and weakly co-ordinated. Nonetheless, a dilemma arose in the 1920s over the control of schooling, as teachers' growing aspirations to professional status and to better terms and conditions of service coincided with the need for reductions in public spending and fears that an alienated teaching force might act as a subversive social influence. This latter fear was particularly alarming in the wake of the recent socialist revolution in Russia and in the context of growing public unrest and dissension in England. Rather than adopting a hard, dictatorial line, the government of the time, and in particular the President of the Board of Education, Lord Eustace Percy, chose a strategy of co-option and indirect rule (Lawn and Ozga 1986; Grace 1987). This involved the tactical use of a degree of educational deregulation (Lawn 1987a; 1996) and the strategic employment of the ideology of professionalism to discourage teachers from militancy and to encourage instead loyalty to the state and responsible behaviour (Ozga 1992; 1996; Menter *et al.* 1997). This led to the development of a form of 'legitimated professionalism' based upon

> an understanding that organised teachers would keep to their proper sphere of activity within the classroom and the educational system and the state, for its part, would grant them a measure of trust, a measure of material reward and occupational security, and a measure of professional dignity.
>
> (Grace 1987: 208)

The trust accorded to teachers by this settlement concerned primarily their discretion over the content and methods of the school curriculum. The abandonment of the Elementary Code in 1926 and of the Secondary Regulations after 1944 in favour of 'professional judgement' was part of a process whereby the notion of teachers' right to curriculum autonomy became firmly established in educational understanding. Thus, in his 1957 survey of the modern English education system, Lester Smith (1966: 161–2) could conclude that:

> No freedom that teachers in this country possess is so important as that of determining the curriculum and methods of teaching. Neither the Minister nor the Local Education Authority exercises authority over the curriculum of any school beyond that of agreeing the general educational character of the school and its place in the local education system . . . in practice the curriculum is settled by the head in co-operation with the assistant staff.

In reality, the curriculum autonomy of teachers was always relative. On the one hand, it was largely limited to what took place within their individual classrooms, and they exercised little control over the context of their work (Hoyle 1974), in terms either of its organization or of the whole school curriculum. On the other hand, teachers have always been subject to external influences over what they teach because of their role in preparing students for progression to a subsequent stage. In particular, the need for most secondary students to gain nationally recognized qualifications has meant that the requirements of university-based examining boards have placed significant constraints upon classroom autonomy. Moreover, because of a combination of inertia, lack of time and lack of incentive, few teachers actually exploited what freedom of action that they did enjoy, preferring to fall back upon their own experiences and to replicate traditional practice.

Despite the fragility of claims to curriculum autonomy as a distinctive feature of teacher professionalism in England, the symbolic power of the concept was profound. Over time, it took on the characteristics of a 'myth' (Lawn 1996; McCulloch 1997a; 1997b), a social construct that shaped understanding of reality and fuelled expectations of what could or could not be done by either teachers or the state. Thus the Conservative Education Minister, David Eccles, could complain in a 1960 House of Commons debate that the school curriculum was a 'secret garden' into which Parliament dare not tread. Subsequent efforts to infiltrate the forbidden territory through the establishment of a Curriculum Study Group within the DES were met with such fierce opposition from educationalists that the group was soon disbanded and replaced by the teacher-dominated Schools Council for the Curriculum and Examinations. This body continued to support the principle of teacher autonomy in curriculum matters, and the myth remained largely unchallenged throughout the 1960s and early 1970s (Chitty 1989).

Set against a background of deepening economic crisis and growing political unease about state schools, the 1976 Ruskin College speech by the then Prime Minister, James Callaghan, is often cited as the turning point in the struggle for control of the school curriculum. His explicit questioning of teacher autonomy and his call for a public debate on education clearly suggested an imminent reduction of teacher influence and a period of proactivity by the state. However, central initiatives in the years immediately following this speech consisted largely of a number of publications on a possible 'common' or 'core' curriculum by the DES and by Her Majesty's Inspectorate (HMI), both of which continued the tradition of respecting professional autonomy and working through persuasion and exhortation. Indeed, Batteson (1997) has offered an alternative view of 1976 as a 'missed moment' for the Labour government, which became increasingly preoccupied with comprehensive reorganization, leaving the processes of schooling to the discretion of teachers.

TVEI and the National Curriculum

With the advent of a new Conservative administration in 1979, determination to reassert central control of the school curriculum grew steadily, against a background of repeated claims that its traditional academic emphasis had created an anti-industry and anti-technology culture that had contributed significantly to national economic decline. In November 1982, Margaret Thatcher made a surprise announcement in the House of Commons of a new Technical and Vocational Education Initiative for 14–18-year-olds, which was to be piloted from September 1983. The declared aims of this initiative were to stimulate technical and vocational education, to help young people prepare for the world of work and to develop their adaptability and willingness to learn in the face of fast-changing occupational requirements. The scheme was to be managed through a new process of 'categorical funding', whereby schools and LEAs were invited to bid for funding in accordance with certain pre-specified criteria: if they were successful, pilot schemes would subsequently be evaluated for compliance with the initial proposals. Controversially, TVEI was to be administered not by the DES but by the MSC, a semi-autonomous unit within the Department of Employment.

An immediate response from many educationalists to this announcement was one of outrage at the perceived intrusion of the state in professional matters. However, the broadness of the criteria that emerged and, most particularly, the prospect of additional funding for curriculum development at a time of financial stringency offered considerable incentive for involvement. By early 1983, 66 LEAs had submitted bids for inclusion in the scheme and 14 of them were selected to run pilot schemes from the autumn term. Subsequent bidding rounds over the next four years meant that by 1987 all LEAs were piloting TVEI with some of their students in some of their schools and, in July of that year, an announcement was made that it would be extended from a pilot scheme to embrace all 14–18-year-olds in all state schools and colleges. At a cost of over £1 billion, TVEI was by far the most expensive curriculum initiative ever undertaken in the UK. However, the lack of a clear curriculum blueprint and the consequent reliance upon educational professionals to develop schemes in accordance with very broad and general criteria meant that the reality of TVEI did not necessarily match government intentions, leading to widespread claims that the scheme had been 'hijacked' by teachers (Harland 1987; Helsby 1989).

In the meantime the Education Secretary, Kenneth Baker, had announced at the end of 1986 his intention of introducing an extensive programme of educational reform which would include the establishment of a national core curriculum. The subsequent consultation document (DES 1987) presented a hastily conceived curriculum defined in terms of a collection of nine traditional subjects (plus a modern foreign language in secondary schools) to be taken by all 5–16-year-olds in compulsory state education (private schools were exempt from its requirements). Curriculum content was to be prescribed through the development of detailed programmes of study for each subject, and attainment targets were to be set, initially in the three core subjects of English, maths and science, for 7-, 11-, 14- and 16-year-olds. Nationally prescribed tests were also to be introduced to supplement teachers' assessments.

The consultation document was notable not only for the degree of curricular prescription that it contained and its emphasis upon assessable outcomes, but also for its almost total disregard of TVEI. Despite the virtually simultaneous announcement of its extension, TVEI merited only two brief mentions in this document, both of which portrayed it as relatively inconsequential and very much subservient to the academic subject-based National Curriculum. The proposals also showed little relationship to other developments in curriculum thinking which had preceded it, for example the Schools Council's curriculum projects or the work of HMI on a common culture curriculum, based upon the notion of student entitlement in key areas of experience. Instead, schools were presented with a somewhat arbitrary and unjustified collection of subject titles that were to occupy 80–90 per cent of curriculum time and whose centrally prescribed content was to be subject to national testing. Unlike TVEI, where participation had been voluntary, 'delivery' of the National Curriculum was to become a legal requirement. The views of teachers and other educationalists were not, apparently, a major consideration, a fact underlined by the timing of the consultation period which coincided with the school summer holidays. Despite some compromises along the way, progress was rapid and the passing of the Education Reform Act of 1988 made the National Curriculum legally enforceable in all state schools.

Implications for teachers' work

Both TVEI and the National Curriculum were notable for the lack of consultation with teachers before their formal announcement, for the degree of professional antagonism provoked in the initial stages and, in spite of this, for the speed of their implementation. Both could be seen as clear attempts by state policy-makers to restrict the autonomy of teachers and to regain control of the school curriculum, thereby undermining and starkly redefining the notion of 'legitimated professionalism'. However, as indicated in Chapter 2, government intentions are not the same as outcomes in practice and imposed structures do not necessarily produce mechanistic responses. Accordingly, it is necessary to look at the impact of these two initiatives in practice in order to understand how the interaction of structure, agency and culture affected and continues to affect teachers' working lives.

Impact of TVEI

Whilst the initial announcements of TVEI had suggested a very directive and centralist approach to its development, the structural framework which actually emerged was notable for its breadth and relative open-endedness. It seems likely that the government's desire to achieve rapid results persuaded it to modify some of its original intentions. For example, the controversial idea of setting up special TVEI schools, independent of LEA control, was abandoned in favour of the easier and quicker solution of working through existing educational structures. This meant, however, that a number of concessions had to be made to encourage participation, including an agreement that the MSC, charged with the task of administration, would work in conjunction with LEAs to develop the scheme. Furthermore, the National Steering Group, which was rapidly appointed to oversee and advise on the project, was dominated by educationalists and the criteria which the group drew up for TVEI projects were reasonably 'teacher-friendly'. For example, they emphasized the importance of general education alongside technical and vocational elements; they reflected a broad view of vocational education, with an emphasis upon generic aims such as students' personal and social development and the promotion of equal opportunities; they specified that TVEI should be targeted at students across the ability range; and they again confirmed LEA responsibility for organizing and managing individual programmes within existing provision (MSC 1984).

The importance of piloting new and innovative approaches was constantly underlined in early documents and speeches relating to TVEI. This was accompanied by a stress upon, and celebration of, flexibility, experimentation and diversity in pilot projects, which contrasted starkly with earlier fears of central prescription and control. Although there was talk of stringent monitoring and evaluation in the official documentation, a factor reflected in the amount of money and effort expended in this area, in reality this posed few constraints upon development. Early monitoring by local MSC officials (who were not educationalists) focused almost exclusively upon accurate budget preparation, whilst the more evaluative studies commissioned at both national and local levels were primarily formative, and offered little scope for holding local projects accountable for educational outcomes. Thus TVEI in its early stages could be seen as an opportunity to gain substantial resources for curriculum development and innovation within a fairly broad framework of requirements. Accordingly it offered enormous potential for teachers to take control of the school curriculum.

The open-endedness of TVEI curricular aims was very apparent to some of the teachers involved in the early pilot schemes:

> Nobody has ever sat down and gone through the aims of TVEI, you were just asked to submit a budget and suggest what you wanted to do.
> (Teacher interview, 1987)

> No one knew what TVEI was about, except knowing that it was about change. We saw ourselves as taking part in an experiment where we didn't know what the end product would be.
> (Teacher interview, 1989)

However, enjoying the potential for curriculum autonomy is not the same as exercising it, as shown in the 1950s and 1960s, during the so-called 'golden age of teacher control (or non-control) of the curriculum' (Lawton 1980: 22). Teachers must take active steps to transform this latent freedom into reality by developing the curriculum in accordance with their own professional judgements. For those who already had a clear sense of curricular direction, TVEI resources were used to facilitate developments.

> It allowed us to do the things that we wanted to do because of the funding.
>
> (Headteacher interview, 1991)

> It was like pulling a cork out of a bottle, with people wanting to move in that direction and being given the resources to do it.
>
> (Teacher interview, 1989)

Many, however, did not have a pre-conceived plan for change. Some of these welcomed the general prompt for internal review:

> It's generated discussion about the curriculum and the way we are delivering it.
>
> (Teacher interview, 1991)

Some found that TVEI offered a useful sense of direction:

> TVEI encouraged an emphasis in learning on students taking more responsibility.
>
> (Teacher interview, 1991)

In many instances, however, teachers experienced considerable feelings of anxiety about the open-endedness of the scheme and had to draw very much upon their own resources in order to transform a general sense of direction into educational practice, as shown by these quotations from interviews in 1987:

> I spent a lot of time wondering whether I was doing the right thing and fulfilling TVEI aims – I was very fuzzy about them for the first year.

> . . . we were thrown in at the deep end and left to swim on our own.

The commonest solution to this dilemma was to collaborate with other colleagues involved in TVEI, both informally and through funded preparation time, when staff met together to plan, to share experiences and to solve problems:

> [TVEI] welded people together . . . there was so much INSET and cross-talk of ideas and worries. That level of communication wouldn't have happened without TVEI.
>
> (Headteacher interview, 1989)

The combination of a broad impetus to innovate, a degree of uncertainty about appropriate strategies and funded non-contact time meant that collaboration soon became a major characteristic of TVEI development (Bridgwood 1989; 1996; Saunders *et al.* 1991). This aspect of TVEI culture, which was a crucial factor in supporting and encouraging the active agency of teachers in curriculum development, will be dealt with more fully in Chapter 6.

In terms of curriculum content, the centrally devised criteria for TVEI were, as already indicated, extremely broad. Whilst they specified that the four-year programmes to be developed for 14–18-year-olds should include general, technical and vocational elements throughout, they also said that the balance between these elements 'should vary according to students' individual needs and the stage of the course' (MSC 1984: 25). There were no lists of subjects to be taught and no indications of preferred content. Instead, the courses were to have 'clear objectives', including 'encouraging initiative, problem-solving abilities, and other aspects of personal development', and they were to be designed 'to prepare the student for particular aspects of employment and for adult life in a society liable to rapid change' (1984: 25). Which aspects of employment or adult life were to be addressed and how students were to be prepared for them (both highly contentious issues) were left entirely to local discretion. The only specific requirements in terms of curriculum content were that there should be a period of planned work experience for students aged over 15 and 'good careers and educational counselling'. The courses were also to lead to nationally recognized qualifications, whether academic or vocational, and student attainments in this and other areas were to be documented in a 'record of achievement'.

Thus the question of *what* was to be taught was, within these very broad guidelines, left wide open. Curriculum change was demanded, but the precise direction of that change, and the means of getting there, were largely left to the professional judgement of teachers. In practice, the typical pattern of provision that emerged for 14–16-year-olds, at least as far as assessed courses were concerned, comprised an unchanged core of traditional school subjects, occupying some 60–70 per cent of curriculum time and typically covering aspects of mathematics, English, science, humanities and modern languages, alongside a range of newly developed TVEI courses. Initially, most of these courses grew out of existing practical and vocational subjects, although this involved considerable transformations in the process. Thus, for example, teachers from different craft areas often worked together to develop integrated, design-oriented courses in craft, design and technology or new 'high-tech' or applied options in such areas as pneumatics, control technology, food industries or textiles. At the same time, commerce teachers became involved in devising broad programmes of business studies whilst art and drama teachers designed new courses in graphics, communication arts or media studies. The sudden availability, via TVEI funding, of modern computer facilities also encouraged the growth of both applied technology and information technology in the curriculum. Increasingly over time TVEI supported development work in some of the more traditional academic subjects, leading to courses in, for example, modular science, applied and work-related modern languages and integrated humanities.

Because many of these areas were new, there were no pre-existing syllabuses and no established and agreed bodies of knowledge to guide practice. Accordingly, the teachers charged with developing the new courses had almost unprecedented freedom to determine curriculum content. At the same time the rhetoric of TVEI, which emphasized the acquisition of personal and practical skills and the relevance of learning to adult life, encouraged teachers to devise programmes that were activity-based and which did not focus solely upon the acquisition of academic knowledge. Whilst the need to work towards nationally recognized qualifications might have imposed some major limitations upon their freedom in this respect, in practice the growing competition between traditional, university-based examining boards and the vocational awarding bodies, coupled with the potential loss of candidates because of the increasing numbers of TVEI students, meant that such bodies were eager to validate new courses, many of which relied largely or wholly on internal assessment by teachers of students' practical skills as well as of students' knowledge.

In addition to the kinds of changes to assessed courses described above, those teachers who participated in TVEI schemes frequently became involved in managing other, non-assessed activities for TVEI students. Particularly common in many TVEI pilot programmes were periods of work experience or work placement, residential experiences and a variety of out-of-school events designed to widen awareness and to develop students' personal and social skills. In addition, many were responsible for organizing blocks of time within school, created by suspending the timetable for a day or two or by allocating a regular half-day slot each week, during which students took part in a variety of practical and cross-curricular activities ranging from industry days through Young Enterprise or mini-company schemes to technology awareness events. All of these usually involved teachers working with colleagues to plan and run sessions that were quite outside their normal teaching experience.

Thus, in terms of curriculum content, the work of those teachers involved in TVEI pilot schemes undoubtedly changed considerably. Since there was no central blueprint for these changes, many teachers were actively involved in reviewing what their students might usefully learn and in developing an appropriate curriculum for them in accordance with their own educational and pedagogical beliefs. This flexibility meant that courses and learning experiences did not have to be wholly tied to traditional (and often alienating) bodies of academic knowledge but could relate more closely to students' individual needs, experiences and interests. Moreover, the reduced emphasis upon knowledge acquisition in favour of the development of a broader range of skills meant that teachers' work was less dominated by a pressing need to 'cover the content', thus allowing scope for more time-consuming experiential learning. This flexibility also allowed space and time for teachers to modify both the pace and focus of learning in accordance with student responses and to accommodate new topics as opportunities arose.

This active involvement in shaping curriculum content, coupled with the readiness of examining bodies to validate new courses that were both teacher-devised and teacher-assessed, contributed considerably to a feeling of increasing teacher freedom and empowerment that soon became part of the rhetoric of TVEI. At the same time the resulting acquisition of new skills, the sense of being part of an important national curriculum development project, in some cases actual career advancement and promotions, and finally the public celebration of teachers' innovative efforts at the annual TVEI reviews in LEAs, through local and national TVEI conferences and in a whole series of TVEI publications, all combined to develop a very strong feeling of professional confidence amongst those teachers involved in the TVEI pilot schemes:

> The experience of TVEI gives me confidence in what I'm pushing. I value the people that I know in TVEI – they reinforce my beliefs.
>
> (Teacher interview, 1991)

> It allowed us to grow . . . people stepped out of their normal role, it expanded our capabilities.
>
> (Teacher interview, 1997)

Inevitably, the view of TVEI presented here offers a somewhat rosy and simplistic picture of teachers steadily asserting their curriculum autonomy and imposing their own versions of TVEI policy-in-practice. Clearly, the reality was much more varied: some schools undoubtedly accepted TVEI funding but did little to change their existing practices; TVEI pilots involved only some teachers in some schools, and so were sometimes very divisive; the extension of TVEI to all teachers was vastly diluted by the greatly reduced funding levels and by the priority then being given to National Curriculum development. Indeed, it is quite possible to view the more positive conception of TVEI as a new 'myth', created by proponents of the initiative who had a vested interest in employing a rhetoric of success and innovation to justify the effort and expenditure that had been invested. Despite these caveats, evaluative evidence of a general trend towards teacher development, empowerment and curricular autonomy in the early years of TVEI is reflected in the literature (see, for example, McCabe 1986; Gleeson 1987a; Lines and Stoney 1989; Hopkins 1990) and can provide a useful exemplar of a collaborative culture and of very active teacher agency, which contrasts sharply with subsequent developments in the early years of the National Curriculum.

Impact of National Curriculum

The initial framework for the National Curriculum was very different from that offered by the TVEI pilot scheme. Whereas participation in the latter was voluntary and well funded, with relatively open-ended curricular objectives, the National Curriculum was compulsory for all teachers, offered little or no additional funding and was notable for the degree of detailed curricular prescription that it embodied. Teachers were required to teach nine compulsory subjects (ten in secondary schools), each with prescribed attainment targets and detailed programmes of study laid down throughout the period of compulsory schooling. There was also to be a standardized system of student assessment at ages 7, 11, 14 and 16. All schools were to be monitored for compliance with National Curriculum requirements, initially by LEA advisers and subsequently by inspectors from the new national Office for Standards in Education. Assessment results and, subsequently, inspection reports were to be made public in order to facilitate parental choice of school, a potentially crucial factor when funding was related to student intake.

Although the original working groups selected by the Secretary of State to draw up the detailed curricular specifications for each subject did involve a number of educationalists, they did not include any practising teachers. Moreover, some of the working groups' more progressive recommendations were frequently overturned unilaterally by the Secretary of State in favour of much more traditional knowledge-based approaches. This trend towards an imposed 'curriculum of the dead' (Ball 1994) became even more apparent with subsequent revisions to the National Curriculum, where consultation with members of the 'educational establishment' was increasingly abandoned in favour of central diktat. The accompanying discourses constantly implied that teachers had failed to safeguard educational standards and cast them in the role not of professionals, making decisions about the curriculum, but of technicians, following orders devised elsewhere and in need of closer direction. Apparently the notion of teachers' curriculum autonomy was finally to be abandoned in favour of overt central control.

In many ways these developments indicate a change in government thinking about the curriculum. In terms of curriculum content, there was a rapid shift away from a vocational and skills-based focus towards a renewed and strengthened emphasis upon academic subject knowledge, characterized by detailed central prescription and enforcement of what was to be taught in schools. At the same time, however, it was clear that the focus of government action had now widened to include not only curriculum content but also curriculum standards, and this was reflected in the new arrangements for standardized national testing and inspection. Curriculum methods, however, remained for the time being a matter of professional discretion, outside the scope of government intervention.

When the National Curriculum was first introduced, secondary teachers' initial reactions were inevitably mixed. In terms of content, there were some who, unimpressed by the cross-curricular and vocational developments of TVEI, welcomed the reassertion of the importance of traditional subjects. However, the degree of curricular prescription affronted many, who expressed anger and resentment at this perceived usurpation of their rights:

> National Curriculum change has systematically undervalued the professional voice.
>
> (Teacher interview, 1992)

> Government interference in history has undermined professionalism. I'm no longer allowed to teach what I've been taught, I have to teach what's been set for me.
>
> (Teacher interview, 1994)

To make matters worse, what was being prescribed was often at odds with teachers' own beliefs about good practice:

> I feel very angry about what they've done to English . . . we'd honed it to perfection, it was wonderful and then they just threw it all in the air, changed it for no particular reason.
>
> (Teacher interview, 1994)

> I've been forced to do things that I don't consider to be the right way of going about it.
>
> (Teacher interview, 1995)

In particular, the heavy content load limited teachers' flexibility to take important decisions within the classroom:

> Teachers are finding things forced upon them so they can't use their professional judgement any more . . . you can't expand on a subject if the kids are responding or move on if they're not.
>
> (Teacher interview, 1995)

> What's happening now is that it's tending to be the curriculum that's driving what is taught as opposed to the individual needs of pupils.
>
> (Special school teacher, 1995)

This was seen by some teachers to be depressing student motivation:

> A lot of the National Curriculum is not relevant to them and a lot of what we're expected to teach, they find dull and boring.
>
> (History teacher interview, 1995)

The same teacher also found that her own motivation was also diminished:

> to be quite honest, I hate teaching history now, who doesn't? I can't . . . engender any enthusiasm for certain aspects.

Cross-curricular initiatives and whole-school approaches to curriculum planning developed through TVEI were gradually abandoned because of lack of time and because of the subject-specific organization and staggered introduction of the National Curriculum, as shown in these comments from teacher interviews in 1992:

> We talked about links with other departments . . . but we just haven't had the time to liaise – and the National Curriculum Working Parties never liaise!

> We tried to identify overlaps, but as more of the National Curriculum is coming on stream, departments are handing things back to us . . . the National Curriculum pushes people back into departments.

Some adopted a stance of resigned compliance towards the imposed changes:

> We might moan about it quietly but we will do it and then whenever they change their tune, we'll have to dance to that one as well.
>
> (Teacher interview, 1994)

Others attempted to be much more proactive in maintaining a sense of professional control:

> . . . we had to try breaking through the jargon . . . getting it down to the bare bone, the minimum that we had to do that would meet the requirements, that would then allow us to get on with our job of teaching.
>
> (Teacher interview, 1994)

However, a number of contextual factors conspired to make such proactivity more difficult. One was certainly the speed and extent of imposed change, which was further exacerbated by the constant revisions to National Curriculum requirements. This led some teachers to delay expending too much effort on curriculum planning until the situation became more stable, as illustrated by the following comments from teacher interviews in 1994:

> I think . . . is it worth investing all this time getting it just right because it might change in a year or two?

At the moment things are a little bit on hold [while we] wait and see what's going to happen to the subject.

Another important factor was the lack of time for meaningful curriculum planning, as teachers' work became increasingly intensified by the plethora of new demands being made upon them:

More and more time is taken up with record-keeping and assessment and less and less time with actual teaching.

(Teacher interview, 1992)

The changes keep changing and changing and changing. No time to organize the extra work the changes involve. Everything is hurried, incomplete, chaotic.

(Teacher interview, 1993)

Most significantly, there was a considerable amount of evidence that, in schools where TVEI had generated a genuinely collaborative culture, this was under severe threat from the subject-specific emphasis of the National Curriculum and the general intensification of working life:

because of the pressures of your subject area, you find you don't really get a chance to talk to other colleagues outside, say, the maths area and I think everyone's the worse for that.

(Teacher interview, 1994)

Despite the scale of the changes, formal provision for staff development was very limited, and mostly targeted at heads of department who were supposed to 'cascade' their learning to their colleagues. It was also highly functional and subject-specific, leading some to complain of an almost total lack of support in generic areas such as pedagogy, special needs or student development. Departmental meetings also became very focused, dominated by the need to draw up schemes of work within limited time-scales – often an example of 'contrived collegiality' (Hargreaves 1992) to meet instrumental ends rather than an open-ended collaborative enterprise. As a result of the constant changes, the limited support available, the continuing public criticisms of schools and the increasing pressures of work, many teachers suffered a very real loss of professional confidence:

I began to doubt my confidence for the first time in years this last year . . .
For the first time ever I was questioning my own ability or ability to cope.

(Teacher interview, 1994)

Despite the pessimistic picture painted so far, there were inevitably some exceptions in terms of teachers who were able to find and exploit the 'spaces for manoeuvre' (Bowe *et al.* 1992) within the National Curriculum:

. . . despite the fact that they're telling you what you've got to do, they can't make you do it in a certain way. You still make the ultimate decision . . . at the front-line level, that this is how I'm going to do it.

(Teacher interview, 1995)

Growing familiarity with National Curriculum requirements also increased teachers' confidence in deviating from them:

I think we now feel more comfortable with the content, slightly more comfortable with the assessment and therefore . . . not as straitjacketed, that we must do it like this, by the book.

(Teacher interview, 1995)

This trend was strengthened by subsequent reductions in the formal requirements placed upon schools as evidence emerged of significant curriculum overload (see Dearing 1993). Indeed, some teachers even believed that involvement with colleagues in planning National Curriculum provision had actually increased their curricular understanding, their skills and their confidence. For example, a decision not to buy a maths textbook when the new requirements were introduced had resulted in greater professional interchange in one department:

I actually think there's more imagination in teaching now . . . maths teachers talk more about maths than they ever did before.

(Teacher interview, 1995)

Similarly, a series of meetings in a technology department had resulted in broader awareness and enhanced performance:

We have a good understanding of what other people are doing . . . I do feel that their professionalism has improved because . . . they do have an aim and they do have good guidance in terms of what they have to deliver.

(Teacher interview, 1995)

Such examples, however, remained the exception rather than the rule. Furthermore, teachers' ability to adopt a proactive approach appeared to be coming under growing pressure from a number of additional factors not directly related to National Curriculum requirements. As well as further increases in the intensification of work and teacher insularity mentioned above, these included a severe lack of resources in many schools; a more managerial approach to the organization of teachers and of schools; stringent accountability requirements, including exposure to an invasive model of external inspection; and the regular publication of league tables of schools' assessment and examinations results. These will be discussed in more detail in subsequent chapters.

Discussion

Both TVEI and the National Curriculum can be seen as clear attempts by the state to reassert central control of the school curriculum. Both were accompanied initially by claims that teachers had 'failed': in the case of TVEI that they had failed to meet the needs of industry, and with the National Curriculum that they had failed to maintain appropriate standards. However, the two initiatives were quite different in terms of the structural framework which they presented. Whilst TVEI was based upon a very broad set of aims, was relatively well resourced and invited innovation by teachers, the early versions of the National Curriculum incorporated detailed prescription of curriculum content, assessment and evaluation, was underfunded and represented a retreat to the traditions of the past.

Although these fundamental structural differences clearly suggest quite diverse consequences for teachers' work, in practice they represent a context within which teachers have to operate rather than an inevitable *fait accompli*. Whilst a loose framework may offer more scope for curriculum autonomy, this will not be realized unless teachers actively assert their control in this area. As shown above, some teachers involved in TVEI pilot schemes were initially very hesitant about this, wanting reassurance that they were 'doing the right thing'. Similarly, a tightly prescribed curricular framework remains dependent upon the actions of teachers to transform it into practice. Thus even with the National Curriculum, some teachers were able to maintain a sense of control and to exploit the situation to enhance professional dialogue with their colleagues. Thus, the degree to which teachers will be proactive in imposing their own individual and collective professional judgements upon external curriculum requirements is variable and not solely attributable to the nature of those requirements.

Another factor that is highly relevant to the nature of teachers' work is the degree of 'classification' and 'framing' of the educational knowledge included in the school curriculum. According to Bernstein (1971: 49–50): 'Classification . . . refers to the degree of boundary maintenance between contents . . . frame refers to the degree of control teacher and pupil possess over the selection, organization and pacing of the knowledge transmitted and received in the pedagogical relationship.' Strong classification, he argued, vests authority in elite subject groups in universities and limits the power of teachers over what is taught, whilst strong framing reduces the freedom of action of both teachers and learners within the educational process. Accordingly, changes in the strength of classification and framing are associated with a disturbance in existing patterns of authority, leading to 'changes in the structure and distribution of power and in principles of control' (1971: 63). In so far as TVEI encouraged both cross-curricular approaches and the development of teacher and student initiative in the teaching and learning process, it can be argued that it represented a signifi-cant weakening of both classification and framing. Equally it could be claimed that these two aspects were strengthened by the reassertion of the importance of subject divisions within the National Curriculum and by the pressures to prepare students for standardized national assessment of exten-sive bodies of subject knowledge. Whilst, as we have seen, teachers' conse-quent empowerment or disempowerment is not a foregone conclusion, these changes do either strengthen or reduce constraints upon teacher autonomy and make it harder or easier for them to assert control over their work.

In terms of the content of students' learning, the emphasis in TVEI upon the development of skills and personal qualities, on teamwork, on the applied use of advanced technologies and upon individual empowerment would seem to have more in common with the rhetoric of the 'new work order' than does the National Curriculum, with its focus on the acquisition of bodies of academic knowledge, on competitive individualism and on con-formist behaviour. This may reflect the extent to which the 'new work order' employs the social-democratic language of empowerment and choice to mask and to gain acceptance of potentially alienating changes in the organiz-ation of work (Helsby *et al.* 1998). Equally, it could indicate a change in government priorities away from concerns about education as vocational preparation and towards education as social control, with schools as sites of cultural reproduction, legitimizing existing social differences and hierarchies (Ball 1994).

Whatever the motivation behind earlier versions of the National Curricu-lum, its content is now subject to revision. Already much of the original Key Stage 4 curriculum has been discarded and under recent government pro-posals primary school teachers will be granted a two-year suspension of the requirement to follow detailed programmes of study in six subject areas: instead they will be expected to concentrate upon basic literacy and numer-acy skills. A completely revised National Curriculum will be introduced in the year 2000 which will almost certainly involve yet more changes to teachers' work. However, the extent to which they will be involved in agree-ing curriculum content, or the freedom that they will be given to interpret it in accordance with their own professional beliefs or the needs of their students, remains to be seen. In the meantime successive governments have shown an increased interest in other aspects of teachers' work, and the next chapter will focus upon the vexed question of pedagogy.

Note

1 The most significant of these data-sets are those relating to the long-running Lan-caster TVEI Evaluation Programme, funded by a consortium of English and Welsh

LEAs and by government departments, and the 30-month study of 'The Professional Culture of Teachers and the Secondary School Curriculum', funded by the British Economic and Social Research Council (Grant no. RO00234738). The data were gathered through extensive semi-structured one-to-one interviews with secondary school teachers, managers and LEA advisers and also through a number of surveys of secondary school teachers conducted at different times over the last 15 years.

five

CHANGING HOW
TEACHERS TEACH

It is, in many ways, a foolish endeavour to try to separate curriculum content and assessment from curriculum method and organization, since these four aspects of the school curriculum are so much intertwined. For example, the need to convey a large body of fixed knowledge in a range of separately assessed academic subjects tends to encourage organizational fragmentation and didactic pedagogies, whereas the development of students' personal, practical and core skills usually demands the active practice of such skills by the student with ongoing feedback and coaching from the teacher. At the same time such experiential and activity-based learning can be time-consuming and its realization may demand longer blocks of timetabled time, whereas the coverage of extensive bodies of knowledge may be better accommodated within short and regular 'drip-feed' organizational forms. Similarly, standardized pen-and-paper testing which measures factual recall often points towards an emphasis upon content coverage and repetitive drilling rather than inviting open-ended and exploratory learning. Conversely, gains in a range of personal and practical skills tend to require the observation of individual performance over time, with a consequently heavy reliance upon internal teacher assessment.

Notwithstanding the interrelatedness of these four aspects of curriculum practice, recent government policies appear to have treated them separately. Thus TVEI, whilst indicating a broad and general direction for change, did not specify the precise nature of either curriculum content or assessment. Instead it placed great rhetorical emphasis upon encouraging innovative and student-centred approaches to teaching and learning, which were frequently associated with new organizational developments such as block timetabling and modular courses. Indeed, the official review of the first year of TVEI pilots argued that:

A major unifying influence is the progressive adoption of student centred approaches across the whole of a student's learning experience, thereby bridging subject areas. Thus many people involved in the projects have seen the introduction of new courses as an opportunity to effect a change in emphasis towards more active learning and towards helping students learn to learn.

(MSC 1984: 12)

By contrast, the National Curriculum provided tight specification of both curriculum content and assessment, but had little to say about either curriculum organization (beyond indicating the amount of curriculum time to be devoted to each subject) or, more significantly, about pedagogy. An official publication on the National Curriculum produced in 1989 by the DES asserted positively that the 'organisation of teaching and learning' should remain 'a professional matter for the headteacher and his or her staff' (DES 1989: para. 4.3). This remarkable change of emphasis indicates the volatility of policy-making in this area, which continued to fluctuate after the introduction of the National Curriculum. Alexander (1991) argued that neglect by the government of teaching methods was a mistake in terms of gaining control over the curriculum, and subsequently a number of rhetorical interventions were made by both ministers and civil servants, suggesting a desire to expose classroom pedagogies to scrutiny and intervention.

This renewed interest in teaching methods was particularly pronounced in relation to the primary sector which, following the recommendations of the Plowden Report (Central Advisory Council for Education 1967), had developed a strong tradition of child-centred, as opposed to knowledge-centred, pedagogy. In 1985, three years before the introduction of the National Curriculum, two government papers (DES 1985; HMI 1985) had already begun to redefine the role of the professional primary teacher away from that of a generalist and relatively autonomous classroom practitioner and towards that of a more managed and managing team player exhibiting particular skills and qualities. According to Lawn (1996: 69), these documents portrayed a future in which '[t]he craft skills of teaching have been codified' and '[t]eaching has been redefined as a supervisory task'. However, it was not until 1991, following strong attacks on teachers by right-wing think tanks, that the government became more proactive and the then Education Secretary, Kenneth Clark, launched a sustained critique of progressive education and child-centred methods which were blamed on the 'trendy theories' of supposed educational 'experts'. A discussion was invited of primary school teaching methods and a report commissioned and produced within two months (Alexander *et al.* 1992). According to Ball (1994: 44) this report marked both the beginning and the conclusion of any debate: 'Progressive child-centred methods and the Plowden Report were subjected to a public deconstruction, progressive teachers were disciplined and the groundwork was laid for a thoroughgoing reintroduction of traditional teaching methods'.

Woods *et al.* (1997) have shown how this influential document served to construct a new version of the 'good teacher' which emphasized subject expertise and specific pedagogic and managerial competencies. Calls for more 'whole-class' and knowledge-based teaching, coupled with the normalizing effects of inspections of classroom practice by headteachers or by Ofsted inspectors (Merson 1990) and the impact of a heavily content-laden and subject-based National Curriculum, began to have an effect upon the classroom approaches of many teachers. However, responses were far from uniform and whilst some teachers were pushed towards greater didacticism, others were able to adapt, maintain or even enrich progressive and child-centred approaches (Acker 1997; Osborn 1997; Woods and Jeffrey 1997).

The situation in secondary schools was somewhat different, since in that context subject expertise and subject identity had always tended to be at the forefront both of organization and of practice. Indeed, up until the 1970s it had been possible to enter secondary teaching purely on the basis of possession of a degree in a particular school subject and with no other introduction to educational thinking or pedagogy. Certainly this apparent disregard for the importance of teaching methodologies had since been overtaken by a number of factors, including the development of postgraduate teacher education courses based on educational disciplines and with a strong 'methods' component; the work of the Schools Council and others in focusing upon the 'processes' of teaching and in developing the notion of the 'reflective practitioner'; and the pragmatic need to deal with increasing disaffection with school and to motivate students used to accessing more immediately entertaining information through the widening availability of mass communications technology. Nonetheless it is probably true to say that pedagogy in secondary schools never attained the importance and centrality that it did in primary schools and there was, if anything, a general convergence of certain more traditional classroom management styles (Helsby and Knight 1998).

The evidence suggests, however, that both TVEI and the National Curriculum *did* have an effect upon the pedagogies of many secondary school teachers, despite the fact that the latter initiative did not overtly or directly seek to influence teaching and learning styles. Clearly it is very difficult to generalize about classroom practice since direct observation by outsiders is extremely limited and students rarely offer a public account of their classroom experiences. Whilst Her Majesty's Chief Inspector of Schools feels confident in asserting that '[t]here is still a long way to go before pedagogic standards are as high as they should be' (Woodhead 1995: 9) and that 'there may be some 15,000 incompetent teachers currently working in our schools'

(1995: 15), these statements are extrapolated from data gathered during Ofsted inspections. Whilst the cumulative evidence from these inspections offers the most complete picture of classroom practice currently available, the basis of that evidence is questionable. The infrequency and short duration of inspections mean that they can be little more than snapshots of teaching and learning activity, whilst the criteria for 'good practice' are contentious and inspectors have frequently been criticized for the inconsistency of their judgements. Moreover, teachers themselves may seek to influence the outcomes of an inspection by a display of unrepresentative behaviour: for example, Merson (1990) claims that a reluctance to take risks may lead to an unduly conservative sample of practice being observed and reported on by the inspectors, whilst anecdotal evidence suggests that both teachers and students may conspire to present an untypical performance that matches the presumed requirements of inspectors.

The main source of evidence for changes in pedagogy, therefore, comes from teachers themselves. Whilst it may be difficult for them to make objective assessments of their own practice or of the degree to which it is traditional or innovative, 'knowledge-based' or 'student-centred', nonetheless they are in a position to recognize changes in that practice and in the way that their students respond to these. In this sense major curriculum initiatives such as TVEI and the National Curriculum, which change the context of teachers' work, offer a useful focus for exploring perceived changes in teaching methods. In the case of TVEI, the inherent interest in teaching and learning styles means that there are also some research data to support teachers' own perceptions, although such research is equally beset by the above-mentioned difficulties in accumulating reliable evidence of classroom practices.

Teaching and learning styles in TVEI

Teachers in the early TVEI pilot schemes were confronted with a significant challenge. Not only were they expected to alter the content of what they taught to make it more relevant to adult and working life, they were also invited to develop new approaches to their teaching. Indeed, Gleeson (1987b: 2) saw these as the two key aims of the initiative: 'In essence the project may be viewed as an attempt at major innovation to stimulate curriculum development and to introduce new approaches to teaching and learning through a limited life project'.

Changes in pedagogy were not directly specified but were clearly implied in the original aims of TVEI which called for innovation so that:

(iv) [students] become accustomed to using their skills and knowledge to solve the real-world problems that they will meet at work;

(v) more emphasis is placed on developing initiative, motivation and enterprise as well as problem-solving skills and other aspects of personal development.

(MSC 1984: 24)

The assumption here was that existing educational practices did not develop these attributes, or at least not to a sufficient extent, and that change was therefore necessary. Whilst some of the TVEI objectives might be partially met by allowing students to be involved in work placements or residential experiences, to visit a variety of community and work locations and to have contact with the quaintly designated category of 'adults other than teachers', nonetheless the majority of curriculum time for TVEI students was spent working with teachers in school. Thus classrooms became the prime location for experimentation and innovation, with consequent pressures upon teachers to ignore or modify the twin bases of their traditional claims to professional expertise, namely their subject knowledge and their pedagogical skills.

Whilst there was no practical guidance from the centre as to *how* teachers should go about adapting their teaching styles to achieve these aims, the rhetoric surrounding the innovation rapidly became loud and prolific. Slogans such as 'active learning', 'experiential learning' and 'learning to learn' abounded alongside calls for teaching to become more student-centred and for 'ownership' of the learning process to be shared. Several teachers interviewed in 1987 in the first year of a fourth-round TVEI pilot scheme showed considerable anxiety about both the meaning of such concepts and about the way in which they might be realized in practice:

I felt very uncertain to begin with . . . there was no guidance, you were just told to get on with problem-solving and experiential learning and you had to find your own way.

It was claimed that this was particularly true for teachers in minority subject areas with one-man or one-woman departments who sometimes felt that they were simply 'left alone to get on with it'. A degree of moral support was reported from the school TVEI co-ordinator or from the local curriculum development group, but this was described by one teacher as 'the blind leading the blind'.

Despite the uncertainties, the calls to teachers involved in TVEI pilot schemes to develop new teaching and learning strategies were accompanied by smaller class sizes, by new equipment and by additional resources, all of which encouraged and facilitated innovation. Even in the first year of implementation, some of the teachers in this sample were able to describe the changes that they were making within their TVEI classes:

The new syllabus gives us the opportunity for a new approach, it's about giving the children scope for *doing* things.

I've tried to use more problem-solving and I've tried to relate it to the outside world . . . it makes you more aware of your teaching capacity, you need to be more imaginative.

Even though I was already teaching a practical subject . . . [TVEI] was completely different from mainstream teaching, it wasn't chalk and talk, and pupils were working at their own speed.

Although this particular teacher had gradually come to accept the new approaches, the transition had not been altogether comfortable:

It was alarming at first, there was not much to show for what we had done. Also, there was no way of knowing whether you're doing it right.

This last point was echoed by several other teachers in the same sample, one of whom complained of a lack of feedback on the pedagogic changes that she was trying to make:

Is anyone taking any notice of what I'm doing?

This uncertainty over the 'correctness' of the new methodologies being developed echoes comments by Davidson and Parsons (1990) on the dangers of teachers adopting a shared vocabulary without necessarily attaining shared meanings. Whilst some believed that TVEI called for a radical change in pedagogy, others claimed that the teaching styles involved were not fundamentally different from those developed within vocational preparation programmes or for the new GCSE courses.[1] Moreover, a number of the teachers interviewed in 1987 pointed to factors which constrained the development of problem-solving approaches or experiential learning:

Problem-solving is hard to do with low-ability kids, they are so used to being told what to do. You have to take it very slowly to get them into it . . . but then you get so far behind with the syllabus that you have to stop and push them through it.

Setting up experiential learning takes a lot of time and people are not experienced in doing it. They are worried that they'll miss bits out, so they haver between the two styles . . . nobody is quite confident enough to commit totally to this, which is a big problem.

The somewhat mixed picture portrayed above is fairly typical of teacher responses from the other 15 LEAs in the Lancaster TVEI Evaluation Consortium. In most pilot schemes, the teachers involved were provided with the incentives and resources to support potentially significant changes and improvements in their classroom practices. These included smaller class sizes, which encouraged closer and more personal staff–student relationships (Sikes and Taylor 1987); unprecedented access to the new information and other technologies that could support alternative forms of learning; and the creation of longer blocks of time in the timetable, which facilitated experiential learning both within and outside the classroom. In addition to this, the weakening of 'classification' and 'framing' and the introduction of new areas of study which lacked the authority of academic tradition (Evans and Davies 1987), coupled with the growing emphasis upon the internal assessment of skills and application of knowledge, served to increase teachers' scope for experimentation. At the same time the plethora of formal and informal staff development activities, the sharing of 'good practice' and the psychological support of being part of a national curriculum development project all served to encourage risk-taking and innovation.

What is more difficult to ascertain, however, is the extent to which this widespread support for new teaching and learning strategies effected genuine and significant changes in practice. Despite the fact that TVEI was constantly evaluated at local, regional and national levels, the evidence gathered remains inconclusive and sometimes contradictory. There are a number of reasons for this: for example, the difficulties and sensitivities of observing and judging teachers' classroom practice, the heavy reliance upon retrospective and second-hand accounts by teachers and students and the sheer diversity of the developments make it difficult to draw any firm, generalized conclusions. There is a degree of agreement that the initiative did prompt some changes in pedagogy. A 1986 survey of TVEI teachers from 153 schools in 57 LEAs found that nearly half believed that they had changed their teaching methods 'very much' or 'a lot', whilst a parallel survey of 3331 fifth-year students showed that two-thirds of them believed that their TVEI lessons were different from other classes, especially with regard to the teaching approaches adopted (Hinckley 1987). Similarly, a survey of 7000 fourth-year students conducted in 1984–85 through the Lancaster TVEI Evaluation Programme showed significant differences in response between TVEI students and an opportunistic sample of non-TVEI students from the same schools: the former were more likely to agree that they 'always' or 'often' worked with other students or used equipment in their lessons, and were less likely to report regularly working on their own (Helsby and Bagguley 1990).

Evaluative studies involving classroom observation are less quantifiable but they too tend to indicate changes in methodology (see, for example, Davidson and Parsons 1990; Merson 1990) although the work of one of the national evaluation teams (Barnes *et al.* 1987a; 1987b) cast some doubts on the extent of these changes. They identified three ideal types of teaching style, namely 'controlled', 'framed' and 'negotiated', which they summarized as follows:

In the controlled style of teaching, the content and skills are tightly controlled by the teacher, and students are expected to adopt them through standard exercises and with minimal understanding of the principles which justify them. In the framed style, the students are offered an induction into the knowledge, processes and criteria which constitute the teacher's frame of reference, in order eventually to operate the frame for themselves. In the negotiated style, a teacher continually discusses both goals and methods with students, acknowledging their priorities with the intention of strengthening their responsibility for learning.

(Barnes *et al.* 1987b: 2–3)

In practice, the team found few genuine examples of the negotiated style, despite the fact that its emphasis upon involving students in discussing and taking responsibility for their own learning appeared to be closely related to TVEI aims.

Clearly a move towards a more negotiated style of teaching is not easy: it requires new skills and behaviours in both teachers and students which may be at odds with their previous experiences, with their preferred mode of operation and with the general ethos of the school. It also implies a certain loss of authority and control by the teacher and may be very time-consuming to develop and monitor. Whilst the evidence from evaluations does not confirm a wholesale move towards such practices, it nonetheless indicates the beginnings of change in the teaching and learning strategies adopted by some of the teachers involved in TVEI pilot schemes. Clearly the degree of change is likely to have varied from teacher to teacher and from school to school. Looking back at the early years of TVEI, some teachers were confident in reporting significant development, as shown in these extracts from interviews conducted in 1997:

The learner became much more significant . . . there was more emphasis on their ability to do things, as opposed to them learning facts, and an increase in relevance, with things set in an external context.

There was more pupil involvement, teachers moved from more didactic styles to more interactive, more hands-on.

Others, however, were more circumspect:

You get the feeling that it's changing, but you'd need to get into classrooms to see if it were happening.

(Teacher interview, 1993)

It's patchy. I think people are more conscious of students learning by doing, learning from experience and getting them involved – but I don't know how far people are adopting new styles . . . TVEI has raised people's awareness.

(Teacher interview, 1992)

There's a much greater awareness of the need for greater diversity of teaching and learning . . . also an awareness of outcomes being wider than just the results of assessment and exam-passing ability.

(Teacher interview, 1992)

If the suggestions of changed practice amongst some teachers and the last two comments about raised awareness are correct, then we can only speculate as to how far new teaching and learning styles might have developed over time if TVEI had been extended to all teachers with the same levels of funding and of support as during the pilot schemes. However, the resources offered for TVEI extension were extremely limited. Even more significantly, the announcement of the extension coincided with the release of details of the proposed compulsory National Curriculum based upon traditional subjects and standardized, knowledge-based assessment. This reassertion of strong 'classification' and 'framing' rapidly diminished any incentive for teachers not yet involved in TVEI to move towards more 'student-centred' or 'negotiated' teaching. For many of those who had been involved, the evidence suggested that their TVEI experiences had made them more confident in dealing with the changes and even in continuing to engage in more innovative practices (Helsby and McCulloch 1996). However, as time went by the changing policy context made it increasingly difficult to sustain some of the more progressive approaches:

There was a push into child-centred learning – not apparently what we should be doing nowadays! . . . It was definitely very strong in TVEI. Now they want us to go back to teachers as the fount of all knowledge.

(Teacher interview, 1997)

Some excellent developments had taken place regarding teaching and learning styles, record of achievement etc. The demands of National Curriculum are stifling these developments, so much content – chalk and talk at Key Stage 4.

(Comment from teacher survey, 1993)

I still use the methods I developed in TVEI, moving around and groupwork. But overall, I don't know. Perhaps when TVEI was in full swing we tried to extend it, but it was wiped out when the National Curriculum was considered.

(Teacher interview, 1993)

Whilst the impact of TVEI continued to be felt in some quarters, there were now strong forces pulling in a different direction.

Teaching and learning styles in the National Curriculum

As already indicated, National Curriculum regulations did not specify any particular teaching approach: this was left entirely to the professional judgement of teachers. Indeed, a senior official at the Teacher Training Agency, interviewed in 1996 as part of the 'Professional Culture of Teachers' research, argued that the National Curriculum actually made it easier for teachers to develop their own teaching and learning styles:

> The coming of the 1988 Education Act provided a curriculum structure that was better than one could get out of textbooks, and for the good teachers it freed them up to develop their pedagogy in relation to a curriculum framework which was given them.

A small proportion of the teachers interviewed between 1994 and 1996 as part of the same piece of research appeared to agree with this assessment:

> I think I understand what the curriculum wants and therefore I feel able to make a positive contribution to what's taught, knowing that, yes, what we've suggested as being taught will actually fulfil the criteria.
>
> (Technology/food teacher)

> . . . in terms of improving the quality of it . . . if people know what they're doing, that's a good starting point.
>
> (History and geography teacher)

> I actually think there's more imagination in teaching now because we specifically don't have a set textbook, so we can sit around our table at lunchtime and say, 'Well, I'm teaching Pythagoras and I thought I'd do it by investigation – does anybody have a good idea of a book we could use?' So I actually think that maths teachers talk more about maths now than they ever did before.
>
> (Mathematics teacher)

This positive view of the potential pedagogic benefits of the National Curriculum was also echoed by another mathematics teacher:

> . . . you could argue that, as long as I know what I've got to teach definitely, that could give me the freedom to teach it how I think.

However, the same teacher went on to explain how current pressures were thwarting this potential freedom:

> But I don't really feel that that's what's happening in practice. I think pressures of time, lack of time are becoming more noticeable all the time so . . . I've tended to stick with what they know and what they can cope with, rather than having the time to set up something innovative and different.

Certainly the initial round of 178 teacher interviews in 1994 and early 1995 elicited more negative than positive comments about the effects of the National Curriculum and related changes, and it was not until the follow-up interviews a year later that many teachers began to appear more confident of their ability to accommodate its constraints. One of the key concerns was the emphasis upon content knowledge rather than skills:

> The National Curriculum has made us more concerned with students demonstrating knowledge rather than skills.
>
> (Headteacher interview, 1997)

This was seen by many as having a direct impact upon teaching and learning styles, with a claimed reversion to more didactic methods in order to cover the new and extensive content:

> National Curriculum is resulting in a return to rote learning and a move away from exploration and 'real learning'. It is impossible to believe that those responsible for the changes know anything at all about children from ordinary homes or the kinds of schools which they attend.
>
> (Comment from teacher survey, 1992)

> It's difficult to develop a variety of teaching and learning styles and get through the content of the National Curriculum.
>
> (Comment from teacher survey, 1992)

> When the National Curriculum first came in, some of the more experiential ways of learning that might have taken a bit longer disappeared almost overnight, as people were struggling to get to grips with the National Curriculum. It all went back to being very content-led.
>
> (Teacher interview, 1997)

Some felt that their freedom to teach was being restricted by content overload:

> Sometimes the over-prescription in certain areas can be very obstructive to teachers. It can get in the way of honest, down-to-earth teaching.
>
> (Teacher interview, 1994)

> We used to produce curriculum models which were child-proof. Now we seem to be producing ones which are teacher-proof.
>
> (Teacher interview, 1994)

> I find though that with the schemes of work from the National Curriculum, it is extremely prescriptive. We've got very little freedom and teacher initiative and inventiveness.
>
> (Teacher interview, 1995)

For some, this was not helped by the increasing political emphasis upon the outcomes, rather than upon the processes, of education:

I learned how to do quadratic equations when I was 13. I didn't know what I was doing, I didn't know why I was doing it. I didn't understand it . . . There's a danger we're going back to that now because of the pressures on outcome and if all I wanted was good examination results, I could do it that way.

(Teacher interview, 1995)

Flexible learning was a big plus here, we did a lot . . . but we received a firm smack on the head when the whole agenda changed. TVEI was looking at the development of the whole child, and no one said anything about outcomes or grade Cs. As it filtered through, it put the skids under that. Then there were the 'Three Wise Men' . . . the whole focus shifted to outcomes, rather than processes.

(Headteacher interview, 1997)

The introduction of published 'league tables' of assessment results on a school-by-school basis increased pressures upon teachers to direct their efforts towards maximizing the achievement of examination success, and in particular the number of GCSE passes at grade C or above:

National Curriculum assessment means that you are teaching more to the test or exam, there's a loss of flexibility. The investigative approach in science is laid down in a particular way in the National Curriculum . . . it's become so rigid and formalized.

(Teacher interview, 1993)

It's so critical to get grades at a certain level – that seems to be the agenda nationally, locally and in schools.

(Teacher interview, 1997)

Because schools are now driven by results, you teach to get the results, so they can't answer the interesting questions . . . teachers feel they have to finish this today, they need to cover the curriculum.

(Deputy headteacher interview, 1997)

This, coupled with the 'discourses of derision' directed at progressive methodologies, was seen by some as encouraging teachers to 'play safe' in terms of pedagogy and to revert to traditional approaches, as shown by these comments from LEA advisers interviewed in 1997:

. . . experimenting with teaching and learning styles now has more risks, i.e. worse exam results.

It's been weakened because of the political climate. Teachers now ask 'Do I still believe that they can achieve X through facilitation?' There's been a lot of political talk about modern methodology, and so the less confident have shied away from it.

Teachers themselves reported that the pressures to accommodate new and changing requirements actually detracted from their classroom teaching:

I feel under great pressure to deal with all the initiatives and form-filling involved in so many of the changes in education. Worst of all, I feel that much of my energy is being diverted from my classroom teaching which is, in the end, the most satisfying and fulfilling part of my work.
(Comment from teacher survey, 1992)

Multiple curriculum changes have put so much pressure on teachers, they're not as prepared as they should be for lessons, not as up to date.
(Teacher interview, 1994)

We do need to equip them more for life, and not have so much Shakespeare and Dickens, the balance is all wrong . . . In English, we used to talk about anything and everything, but there's no time to do that any more, because of all the things you have to do and tick off.
(Teacher interview, 1997)

In many schools, a lack of resources resulting from reductions in educational spending were further inhibiting the scope for developing and improving pedagogy:

. . . you've got increased class size . . . we're teaching a slightly heavier timetable and, you know, that has an adverse effect I think on the quality of your teaching.
(Teacher interview, 1996)

. . . depending on what text books we've got in school and what resources the library has, that will make us decide what we teach for the extended piece of work . . . I've found recently that the library doesn't stock half the material that we require.
(Teacher interview, 1995)

. . . half the lessons are going on outside specialist rooms, often in a dining room . . . try teaching there just before lunch or just after lunch and you've the clatter in the background, so we're very restricted . . . I have the top set this year, that's 35 pupils. Now there are only tables for 32 pupils.
(Teacher interview, 1996)

However, set against this fairly negative picture there were also examples of teachers taking a more positive and constructive view of the effects of the National Curriculum, even in the early years of implementation. On the one hand, some expressed a determination to retain valued aspects of teaching practice despite the constraints:

There is a big pressure, you have to watch it doesn't force you to become didactic to cover the topics. We have to fight to keep fieldwork. We haven't done it this year, to make sure we hit the targets. The practical work is also under threat, we need to preserve those.

(Teacher interview, 1993)

On the other hand, these two teachers, interviewed in the same year, were confident that the National Curriculum, far from inhibiting development, actually facilitated it:

The National Curriculum will make us all change, with more group-work, where we don't feed information to them but set them a task. Problem-solving is coming into a lot of curriculum areas.

. . . we have to look at what we offer. Things are more open now, more flexible, we have to talk to each other more, perhaps because there are more pressures.

More common, however, was the belief that things were easier once teachers had become used to the new requirements and were no longer intimidated by them:

. . . we're more aware of what the restrictions are and we can work round them. As you become more used to a system you think, 'Oh yes, I could do that and I could get away with it'.

(Teacher interview, 1995)

As I have got on with it and got to grips with it, it has started to turn.

(Teacher interview, 1994)

There's enough scope to change things or improve things and still fit in with the criteria that are expected.

(Teacher interview, 1995)

The situation was further eased by the 1993 Dearing Report and the consequent revisions to the National Curriculum which came into force in 1995. These included a reduction in required content, a vast simplification of attainment targets, a reduction in assessment and reporting requirements and a freeing of 20 per cent of total curriculum time for schools to use as they saw fit. Many teachers welcomed these changes:

. . . we're on the road to recovery with the Dearing curriculum.

(Teacher interview, 1995)

As a result of growing levels of professional confidence, some teachers were again turning their attention to teaching and learning styles:

We seem to have got an overview of it . . . we now feel that we can start looking at what I call styles of learning. We can go back and do more of the role play, the project work . . . independent learning in the library.

(Teacher interview, 1995)

The fact that SATs have gone off the horizon means we can actually start to look at what we teach and how we teach it without having to teach for the exam. Because that's what we would have done, we would have done a lot more testing, we would have done a lot more content, a lot more revision . . . If SATs were there we would sit in with the textbooks without doing some of what I call the fun things, which went when National Curriculum first came in.

(Teacher interview, 1995)

Others were able to make clear distinctions between their freedom to make decisions about *what* they taught (which for most had clearly been curtailed by the National Curriculum) and their ability to exercise professional judgement in relation to *how* they taught (which, for these teachers at least, remained intact):

. . . my day-to-day operation in the classroom is still very much to do with processes, to do with working relationships, to do with how to relate to youngsters to get the best out of them . . . what I am doing in terms of content isn't irrelevant but it isn't the priority.

(Teacher interview, 1995)

. . . you still have to teach the lessons every day, it's still your job that you were trained for, and despite the fact that they're telling you what you've got to do, they can't make you do it in a certain way. You still make the ultimate decision . . . at the front-line level, that this is how I'm going to do it.

(Teacher interview, 1995)

I have to use my judgement and my knowledge of those students to – well, I can teach it this way to that class but next year, perhaps, the class are not as good or are better, so I teach it a different way . . . I have to use my skill and knowledge to adapt to different situations.

(Teacher interview, 1994)

Discussion

TVEI and the National Curriculum offer interesting and very different examples of the changing context in which teachers must develop and exercise their pedagogic skills. In very broad terms the evidence suggests that TVEI pilot schemes offered encouragement, resources and support for developing innovative and progressive approaches to teaching and learning.

Conversely, whilst the National Curriculum regulations treated classroom practice as unproblematic and largely ignored it, factors associated with the initiative tended to push many teachers back towards 'safer' and more traditional approaches. Of particular significance in this respect were the large amounts of prescribed subject knowledge that students were expected to acquire, the standardized testing of factual recall and the publication of league tables of assessment results, a marked intensification of working life, a lack of adequate resources and the consequently widespread sense of professional demoralization.

At one level, it is tempting to suggest that, as a result of these differences, there was a distinct trend towards more varied pedagogies amongst teachers actively involved in TVEI pilot schemes and a contrary tendency for teachers to revert to more didactic styles during the early years of National Curriculum implementation. However, whilst this assertion may contain an element of truth, it is too simplistic and fails to take account of the variety of responses by individual teachers in individual classrooms. Whilst TVEI-style support can indeed encourage progressive and varied approaches, it does not guarantee them. Equally, the factors accompanying the introduction of the National Curriculum need not necessarily lead to didacticism. Ultimately, it is up to individual teachers to assert control over their own classroom practice, although the circumstances within which this is done may help or hinder pedagogical flexibility.

Meanwhile the framework within which teachers must work continues to change. As indicated above, there is evidence of a renewed interest from the centre in teaching and learning styles: indeed, Anthea Millett, Chief Executive of the influential Teacher Training Agency, has labelled pedagogy 'the last corner of the secret garden', and argued that it should now be opened up to public scrutiny in the interests of teacher effectiveness and school improvement (Millett 1996). At the same time Her Majesty's Chief Inspector of Schools, Chris Woodhead, whilst acknowledging that it is 'only teachers in classrooms who can really make the difference' (Woodhead 1995: 14), has gone on to assert that '[d]eliberate and explicit efforts to improve teacher performance need to continue' (1995: 17). Central definition of teacher competencies and prescriptions of 'good practice' appear to loom large in current initiatives alongside a rhetoric of teacher professionalism. By contrast, however, the recent launch of 25 'Education Action Zones' in deprived areas of England has been accompanied by the suspension of National Curriculum requirements and other central regulations alongside calls for innovation and experimentation. The involvement of employers and the relatively generous central funding are in many ways reminiscent of TVEI. *Plus ça change . . .*

However, whatever structural changes there may be in the future, teachers' pedagogical decisions are ultimately heavily dependent upon both their own professional beliefs and their levels of professional confidence. Both of these factors may be profoundly influenced by the culture in which they work. As indicated in Chapter 2, culture not only comprises the set of beliefs, values and norms of behaviour shared by a particular group but also refers to the patterns of relationship and forms of association between group members – the 'content' and 'form' of culture (Hargreaves 1992). In making these distinctions, Hargreaves argued that the form of culture was the more significant. The next chapter will therefore look at recent changes in the forms of teacher culture and their impact upon teachers' work.

Note

1 The General Certificate of Secondary Education replaced both the General Certificate of Education O level and the Certificate of Secondary Education as the main 16+ qualification in 1988. The avowed intention of the early courses was that they should contribute to a broad, balanced and relevant curriculum, and there was a strong emphasis upon internally assessed coursework.

six

CHANGING PATTERNS
OF ASSOCIATION

A good deal of the literature on school improvement, particularly that in North America, has criticized traditional norms of teacher isolationism and has repeatedly extolled the virtues of 'collaboration', of 'collegiality' and of strong 'communities' of teachers. At the same time the prophets of the 'new work order' have loudly proclaimed the merits of teamwork and co-operative endeavour in order to motivate staff and maximize their contributions to company goals. Whilst these various notions of working together have a seductively warm ring, they are beset both by a widespread lack of clarity in their definition and by a failure to recognize the diversity of practices, purposes and effects of such arrangements (Little 1990; Hargreaves 1994; Lima 1998; Westheimer 1998). Such differences are highly relevant since the balance between individualized and collective working practices, and the way in which they both operate, have potential implications for worker autonomy.

Lieberman (1993: vii) has identified a 'central tension' between 'teachers as individual "artisans" who are members of a professional community'. On the one hand, the organizational privacy of individual classrooms and the need to respond creatively to the changing needs of their students and to make choices between alternative courses of action *in situ* all combine to ensure the continuance of teachers' relative autonomy. On the other hand, however, the thrust of recent policy initiatives has been 'to break the bounds of privacy in teaching' (Little and McLaughlin 1993: 1) and to encourage various forms of teacher collaboration which have since come to be seen as 'pivotal to current orthodoxies of change' (Hargreaves 1994: 186). Hargreaves goes on to argue that:

> Collaboration and collegiality . . . form significant planks of policies to restructure schools from without and to improve them from within . . .

their successful development is viewed as essential to the effective delivery of reforms that are mandated at national or local levels.

(1994: 187)

Despite the recent growth in the formal structures that encourage interactions between teachers and despite the potentially supportive effects of collaboration, Huberman's (1993: 12) assessment of the current situation in schools suggests that many teachers may be experiencing the worst of both worlds:

> it may well be that in the current organization of schooling, functional interdependencies among staff are not strong enough to weather the multitude of small crises and conflicts but are not weak enough to allow each actor to get on with [their] work without having to accommodate constantly to the demands of others.

Moreover, the purposes of collaboration, and the preferred role of teachers within it, may vary substantially according to context. For example, whilst recent restructuring in the USA has been largely supportive of teachers' professional judgements and allocated them an active role in planning improvements, post-1987 reforms in the UK have been marked by strong critique and the virtual exclusion of teachers from policy discussions (Woods *et al.* 1997). In such circumstances, calls for teacher collaboration may be viewed as an administrative strategy: indeed, Gewirtz *et al.* (1995: 95) claim that the marketization of schools in England and changes in school management have been underpinned by

> a variety of new management theories in which collaboration is used for the instrumental purpose of manufacturing consent for a set of predetermined goals.

Whatever the truth of this claim, it is clear that collaboration may be promoted for very different purposes. However, whilst some educational reformers may make an instrumental link between stronger forms of teacher collaboration and the achievement of prescribed ends and some school managers may attempt to impose forms of 'contrived collegiality' (Hargreaves and Dawe 1990), both of which suggest an effective disempowerment of teachers, others have highlighted the potentially more empowering aspects of teacher collaboration. Whatever its intended purposes, working with colleagues in a regular and meaningful way may increase professional confidence – for example, by providing moral support in situations of uncertainty, by broadening horizons to embrace new ideas and new approaches and by encouraging experimentation and innovation in a supportive environment (Helsby 1998). The outcome of collaborative activity is never a foregone conclusion.

As well as being unpredictable, the exact nature of 'collaboration' is also hard to pin down. Despite the keen interest of policy-makers and the wealth of research activity in this area, there is no general agreement as to how the concept should be defined, beyond the basic fact that it involves interactions between teachers. These interactions may occur within or across institutions, subject boundaries, status levels or friendship groups. They may be formal or informal, personal or professional, and may take a wide variety of forms. Little (1990) has identified four ideal-types of teacher collaboration: storytelling and scanning for ideas and resources; giving and receiving aid and assistance; sharing ideas and materials; and joint work. There are differences between the categories in terms of their implications for teachers' classroom autonomy and independence. Broadly speaking, Little claims that the first three types of collaboration leave teachers free to pursue their own pedagogic objectives and are more basic forms of collegiality. Joint work, however, is the most likely form of collaboration to impinge upon classroom practices and is, as a result, both more consequential and less common. Evidence from the national evaluation of 'Joint Support Activities' (JSA), a centrally-funded inter-LEA collaborative project aimed at developing new forms of teacher support for TVEI extension, reached similar conclusions (Helsby and McHugh 1990). In this case five ideal-typical forms of collaboration were identified and, of these, 'integrative' collaboration, which involved some loss of autonomy in order to pursue common aims, was seen as the richest and most rewarding form. It was also, however, the most difficult to achieve in practice.

Whilst these categorizations may have some validity, they are indicative rather than descriptive of reality. Indeed, much of the work in this area is overly normative (Lima 1998) and does not do justice to the complexity of teacher interactions. For example, even 'integrative' collaboration or 'joint work' may take multiple forms, ranging from a vibrant and professionally empowering activity to examples of 'contrived collegiality' which engender compliance and low-level task completion. Which form it takes is dependent upon a variety of contextual factors, not least of which are the nature of the joint task and the attitudes and motivation of the individuals involved. As Hargreaves (1994: 189) has argued, there is no 'true' form of collaboration and collegiality, just particular forms 'that have different consequences and serve different purposes'. Collaborative working between teachers may also occur at different levels, ranging from the inter-LEA focus of JSA projects, through the whole-school context emphasized by school effectiveness researchers and policy-makers (Rosenholtz 1989) to the smaller and often more spontaneous 'professional communities' of teachers (Talbert and McLaughlin 1994). It may also have a particular life cycle: Fink's (1998) study of collaboration in an innovative school in Ontario found that an unusually strong culture of collegiality in the early 1970s had been replaced by a culture of division and contention in the early 1980s. Accordingly, it is important to look at particular examples of collaboration in practice – and indeed at examples of teachers working in isolation – in order to assess their meaning and impact in particular situations and at particular times.

Over the last 15 years in England, a number of factors have tended to change some of the patterns of association between teachers. TVEI, for example, overtly promoted and facilitated new links between teachers from different curricular areas and from different institutions whilst the subject-specific basis of the National Curriculum was said to be reinforcing the boundaries between traditional departments and increasing the 'Balkanization' of school cultures (Hargreaves 1992; Reay 1998). At the same time evidence of more frequent school-based meetings and joint planning sessions in the 1990s may be contrasted with claims of a growing fragmentation of the teaching force (Lawn 1995) and widening divisions within schools between classroom teachers and senior managers (Evetts 1994b; Webb and Vulliamy 1996; Power *et al.* 1997). Whilst data gathered from secondary school teachers over this period tend to reflect these broad trends, they also point towards variations in practice and exceptions to the general rule. The rest of this chapter will explore the effects on teachers of changes in two particular forms of association and the way in which these have impacted upon both their work and their sense of professionalism. These changes will be reported under the headings of 'networking', which implies contacts between teachers from different institutions, and 'working together', which may occur either across or within schools. Since collaboration and collegiality are ill-defined and complex processes that operate at many levels, an examination of these two aspects of collaborative activity cannot do justice to the 'hybrid' nature of teachers' professional and interpersonal relations (Lima 1998). However, the changes in these two areas are of interest since they are indicative of the potentially profound impact of educational reforms on teachers' cultures and on their working lives.

Networking

The basic structure of TVEI pilot schemes inevitably produced new forms of collaboration, of which networking between teachers from different institutions was probably the most common. Each LEA scheme was developed across several institutions: in the first-round pilots starting in 1983, numbers ranged from three (two schools and a college of further education) to 17 (MSC 1984). In all cases links were established between the institutions which ranged from various forms of resource-sharing to tight consortial arrangements (Beattie 1986). A central TVEI co-ordinator was appointed to manage the programme on a day-to-day basis and each participating institution also appointed its own TVEI co-ordinator. The availability of resources for supply cover and the project's emphasis upon 'co-ordination' meant that there were frequent meetings of institutional co-ordinators. At the same time LEA-wide curriculum development groups were set up which brought together teachers from different institutions on a regular basis.

Given the impetus towards innovation and the uncertainty of how to proceed, it is perhaps not surprising that many school TVEI co-ordinators found the regular meetings helpful in terms of gathering information, sharing ideas and gaining support:

> Initially the meetings were a crutch, the four of us were in the same boat. [The LEA co-ordinator] was only a page ahead of us, but at least he had the book. It was very useful to get to know the other schools, see how they run, get their perceptions of TVEI.
>
> (TVEI co-ordinator interview, 1987)

> The TVEI co-ordinators' meetings were very, very useful, you're put in touch with what others are doing . . . We used to live in little isolated blocks, but now you can just pick up the phone and ask, 'Have you met this problem? What did you do?'
>
> (TVEI co-ordinator interview, 1991)

It was also seen by some as contributing to their own professional development:

> It was useful for my personal development, a broadening of my knowledge and experience, both practically and educationally . . . it gave me a different perspective on educational change.
>
> (TVEI co-ordinator interview, 1987)

Those involved in cross-LEA groups looking at particular aspects of TVEI practice were also appreciative of the motivational benefits of meeting regularly with colleagues from other institutions:

> One of the pluses has been the meetings of the assessors. It helps to develop common aims and consistency of provision, it gives an impetus.
>
> (Teacher interview, 1989)

As might be expected, such meetings did not meet with universal acclaim: some found them boring or unhelpful and others disliked being out of school so regularly and missing classes. Much depended on the personality and approach of the LEA co-ordinator and members of the central LEA team. In one LEA there were complaints that the early meetings were too formal and consisted mostly of information-giving, which could be done more efficiently in written form: as a result of heeding this advice, the meetings subsequently became more useful to participants. Conversely, there was some evidence that, as experience was gained and many of the aims of the group fulfilled, the move in focus from development to consolidation could sometimes lead to a loss of motivation and commitment to the meetings (Bridgwood 1996). Nonetheless the balance of teacher opinion over the life-time of TVEI pilots in the Lancaster TVEI Evaluation Programme was firmly in favour of networking between institutions. Two teachers interviewed in one LEA in a review of TVEI in 1993 were quite clear about these benefits but also doubtful about the prospects for their continuation:

> Bringing together co-ordinators and showing them what could be done was very useful . . . but will it survive? People feel they would like to continue but it depends on the degree of competitiveness.

> What will happen after TVEI in the dog-eat-dog world? We get a lot from it – shared views, awareness of what takes place in other schools, links with special schools.

The introduction of LMS, which became operational in almost all areas of England and Wales by April 1993, involved the devolution of consider-able amounts of resources from LEAs to individual schools, which were encouraged to compete against each other by the system of pupil-related funding. Both this and the general thrust towards marketization were clearly at odds with the earlier emphasis upon inter-institutional partnership:

> The collaboration created by TVEI between schools has been eroded by LMS – instead of co-operative consortia developing initiatives we have separate institutions guarding their 'market edge'.
> (Comment from teacher survey, 1993)

> TVEI was a valuable forum for people to get together, though that's not so much the case now, with delegated budgets and opting out.
> (Teacher interview, 1993)

School managers were particularly aware of the new political situation, although not necessarily in favour of it, as shown by these comments from interviews in 1997 with a headteacher and deputy headteacher:

> Collaboration between schools is now minimal . . . it's part of the new agenda: if we do something interesting, there's a strategy of playing the cards close to your chest in the new competitive climate. The national agenda of competition has put the skids under the sharing of good prac-tice.

> Schools tend to work in isolation these days, because of the competition they're less likely to share things than they did eight or ten years ago, when there was more sharing through the TVEI consortia. It's a loss – why should we have to compete with other schools?

Partly as a result of this growing competition, but more particularly because of the increased work pressures within schools and reductions in the overall levels of funding, teachers were much less likely to be involved in links with other institutions or even to go out of school on visits or for in-service training:

> School–college links are now less strong – people are pre-occupied with their own institution, so there's less time to look outwards.
>
> (Teacher interview, 1993)

> I found it very beneficial in terms of staff development getting out and talking to others about what you're doing, and that happens very much less now. We have more INSET in-house or we train each other. The approach to going out of school is much less liberal and more targeted, we now ask who's going out, when and what for. This is very different from TVEI when you were told to get out and bring it back. You're back in your box again now, because of the shrinking budget.
>
> (Teacher interview, 1997)

The publication of league tables of assessment results and the constant pressures upon schools to be accountable and to improve their relative performance also had a strongly negative effect upon networking:

> We've got a new GCSE syllabus again and I feel the need to go out and share with other schools, but that sort of collaboration doesn't happen to the same extent now. It's not just the funding but also the issue of having teachers in front of classes, with the increased accountability, the emphasis on results and school improvement.
>
> (Teacher interview, 1997)

A series of interviews conducted in 1997 pointed towards the significance of this loss of contact with colleagues from different institutions, with teachers frequently expressing concern about its effects. It left many feeling isolated and alone:

> We rely more on supporting each other within the establishment now. During the bad times of the National Curriculum you felt you were battling on your own.

> You can get terribly isolated in school because of the workload.

The situation was exacerbated by the weakening of the LEA advisory service as a result of the transfer of funding from LEAs to schools through LMS and the consequent diminution of their role both in organizing cross-institutional meetings and in organizing INSET courses for teachers:

> The networking has gone down a lot since the advisers disappeared . . .

now it's up to the individual to get training in-house. That's bad because it's too insular, you never get the exchange of ideas.

The collaborative working and networking haven't survived and I desperately miss that. With the collapse of LEA support, you're becoming very isolated, you're not finding out what others are doing, you're not sharing . . . the TVEI co-ordinators' network was very strong here, and it's only informal contact now.

Where networking did continue, it was very infrequent and often limited to senior or middle managers. A survey of over 2000 teachers, conducted in three LEAs in 1992–93 as part of the Lancaster TVEI Evaluation Programme, showed that fewer than 42 per cent of classroom teachers felt that they had any opportunity to meet colleagues from other schools, compared to over 80 per cent of senior managers. Moreover, according to one headteacher, the meetings that did take place were also of a quite different nature from those conducted formerly:

It's more a question of watch your backs and don't share anything now. The networking hasn't gone totally, because the heads still meet, but it's not about curriculum matters or about moving forward.

For some of the classroom teachers involved (usually heads of department) the meetings that were called now were not necessarily seen as useful and were often of a low priority compared to what was happening within their own institution:

Some networking still happens in a disparate way – for example, an adviser calls a meeting on a specific topic. I wouldn't choose to network all that much: it depends who you feel comfortable working with, and there are enough people in-house.

The LEA adviser arranges meetings but I don't go to them that often now. Last night, for example, it clashed with a heads of department meeting in school, and that's more important. A lot of junior school teachers go there now. I've got less out of it over the years, and there's so much to do here.

By contrast, however, one head of geography who was interviewed a year before, in 1996, described the crucial importance of her continuing contact with an LEA geography group:

I've known these people since, oh, since I was in the geography department 17 years ago and I get on with them very, very, very well. They're like my brothers and sisters virtually. And that I find a great source of comfort because I can find out from them what's going on locally and if I'm in tune with them I feel so much relief, it's incredible, it really, really is.

This contact with the outside group offered both a source of fresh ideas and moral support for her own educational beliefs:

> . . . there are some of my colleagues' wishes here in school that I do not want to follow and I want to stick with the core of the [LEA] area, you see, because then it makes consolidarity for our work, and sharing of books and of materials makes life so much easier that way, it really does . . . sometimes I'll change my scheme of work because I've heard of a good idea from a colleague.

Working together

As well as supporting cross-institutional networking, TVEI also encouraged and funded stronger forms of collaboration where groups of teachers worked together on joint projects to develop new courses, learning modules, teaching materials, student counselling systems, records of achievement, planned residential experiences, industry days and other diverse forms of curriculum development. This happened at a variety of levels: across LEAs in JSA and other wider projects, across institutions in local TVEI schemes and also within individual institutions involved in TVEI programmes. It is difficult to draw hard and fast distinctions between 'networking' and 'working together', as the two often occurred at the same time. Equally, it is impossible to generalize about the degree to which the forms of collaboration in the early years of TVEI were 'joint' or 'integrative'. However, what the evidence does suggest is that TVEI, particularly in the pilot phases, stimulated new forms of working together which, in many cases, have been weakened or changed by subsequent developments.

Within schools, one of the most obvious changes prompted by TVEI pilot schemes was the growth in collaboration between teachers from different subject departments. This happened both as a result of the identification of cross-curricular teams responsible for non-subject-related initiatives, such as recording achievement or flexible learning, and because of the development of new, integrated courses in areas such as technology, business studies or humanities. The typical TVEI model of technology, for example, brought together former teachers of woodwork, metalwork, cookery, needlecraft, technical drawing and art to develop design-oriented provision which drew on all areas of expertise. Evidence from the evaluation of JSA projects suggested that such cross-curricular working broadened horizons and encouraged participants to think beyond their individual subject areas and in terms of the whole curriculum (Helsby and McHugh 1990). Unfamiliar exchanges of information and joint planning sessions also enabled teachers to compare different approaches and learn from, and support, each other:

It encouraged colleagues in school to work together, to link in with a whole-school approach. TVEI made us question how we did things and then offered support.

(Teacher interview, 1992)

Instead of teaching in discrete subjects we built a team to teach problem-solving, product development [computer-aided design and manufacturing], setting up a business – we wrote the course ourselves and produced our own resources. It was a major step in team-building amongst staff, people stepped out of their normal roles, it expanded our capabilities.

(Teacher interview, 1997)

Participation in developing new courses could enhance motivation and stimulate people to rethink existing practices:

It has been a real bonus for staff morale being involved in a working group.

(Teacher interview, 1993)

A lot more people were out on curriculum development, a lot more people were thinking about their subject and the direction in which it could go.

(School TVEI co-ordinator interview, 1987)

This, coupled with the feeling of support from being a member of a team and part of a wider movement, encouraged experimentation and risk-taking and, in some cases, began to break down the barriers between subjects:

Everyone had to plan a day – that's been good staff development, you plan, develop materials, organize other staff. It makes you work as a team, you're not isolated in your classroom.

(Teacher interview, 1993)

It's probably true to say that TVEI encouraged staff to be innovative and to introduce new things. There was a feeling of being part of something beyond your own subject, because of the shared meetings and because of TVEI philosophy.

(Teacher interview, 1989)

There was also some evidence that the weakening of 'classification' and 'framing' (Bernstein 1971) was having significant effects upon teachers' professional confidence. This was certainly the conclusion of two headteachers, interviewed in 1997:

[TVEI] opened classroom doors, more people worked together in teams, it increased staff confidence.

The lasting legacy of TVEI in this school is a group of staff who are confident and who know that the sky's the limit when they work together.

Clearly not all teachers had the opportunity to be involved in such cross-curricular collaboration both because of the highly selective nature of TVEI pilots and because of changed priorities in many schools at the time of TVEI extension. For those who had been involved, however, one of the most immediate effects of the introduction of the National Curriculum was a reassertion of the boundaries between subject departments:

> TVEI promoted cross-curricular developments but the National Curriculum pushed the other way.
>
> > (Teacher interview, 1992)

> The cross-curricular nature of the curriculum has gone and that's sad . . . now everyone's gone back in their little boxes . . . we've gone back to the hierarchy of subjects.
>
> > (Teacher interview, 1997)

When the National Curriculum was first introduced into secondary schools, some teachers tried to counteract the effects of what they saw as an excessive amount of prescribed content by looking for overlaps between the various specified learning objectives with a view to rationalizing their 'delivery' and avoiding duplication of effort between the various subject departments. However, this proved an extremely difficult and often impossible task. The problems were exacerbated by the lack of co-ordination at national level between the different subject working parties, by the staggered introduction of regulations for particular subject areas and by the heavy workloads for individual departments in their first year of National Curriculum teaching:

> We tried to identify overlaps, but as more of the National Curriculum is coming on stream, departments are handing things back to us . . . it ought to be done nationally . . . the National Curriculum pushes people back into departments.
>
> > (Teacher interview, 1992)

Despite the belated introduction of cross-curricular 'themes' and 'dimensions', a combination of curriculum overload, the non-statutory aspect of these elements and the heavy demands made upon teachers to align their subject-based teaching with National Curriculum requirements meant that there was little investment in their development:

> Cross-curricular themes have very low priority – schools have to put in enormous effort just to get the main courses up and running, and this has top priority. Cross-curricular things tend to take more organization than things that happen in one department.
>
> > (Teacher interview, 1993)

Attempts to work across departments ran up against both pressures of work and systems of accreditation:

> We started to look at what we all do, comparing, because of the National Curriculum, but it's been put into abeyance because of workloads.
>
> (Teacher interview, 1993)

> It's hard to break the autonomy of individual subject departments because of the subject-specific accreditation.
>
> (Teacher interview, 1993)

Even within departments, the extent to which teachers worked together was variable. In theory, the need to develop new schemes of work to meet National Curriculum requirements should have led to more collaborative effort, and indeed there was much evidence of frequent departmental meetings both within the normal working week and during school-based training days. However, many teachers believed that the time given was inadequate for the work involved, and in some cases schemes of work were developed unilaterally by the departmental head:

> . . . the two heads of department took various parts of the scheme and they wrote them. So, in effect, the amount of consultation was zero . . . that seems to be the preferred way of doing it here . . . it's always been perceived that heads of department in the school here, their job is to prepare a scheme of work, in a sense to tell people what they should be teaching.
>
> (Senior teacher interview, 1995)

Some also felt that meaningful collaboration within departments was inhibited by increases in competition between individuals and by shortage of time, as indicated in these extracts from teacher interviews conducted in 1997:

> Not everyone likes working in teams together, especially if you're looking at who gets what grades. The pressures to get results are up and to nail people who are not getting the grades.

> . . . teamwork is very time-consuming, it's easier to work on your own. We've no time to talk to each other, let alone develop teaching materials.

Many commented on the effects of the general intensification of working life that had become apparent in the wake of the 1988 Education Reform Act:

> There doesn't seem to be a profession any more. We just seem to be so browbeaten, scurrying around, snatching those odd moments to say hello to our colleagues, then we're back into class.
>
> (Teacher interview, 1996)

This aspect of teachers' work will be dealt with in more detail in the next chapter.

However, notwithstanding all of the difficulties reported by teachers in sustaining meaningful forms of co-operative activity, there were examples of teachers continuing to work together or even developing new kinds of professionally empowering collaboration. In some cases this arose naturally from long-standing relationships within a department:

> In the history department there are three professionals at work in the school. We trust each other to get on with it. We work together as a team, swapping ideas and discussing things, collaborating . . . I feel very confident in history about collaborating.
>
> (Teacher interview, 1994)

In other cases, the need to change practice to accommodate National Curriculum requirements provided an impetus for joint working. For example, in schools with little previous involvement in TVEI, the early versions of National Curriculum technology created some uncertainties because of the need for an integrated approach between the different craft areas. In one school this led to a joint review of existing strengths and possible approaches:

> Initially, we wondered how we would do the National Curriculum. This brought us closer together – in some schools it drove teachers further apart! We asked ourselves what we could do together and how we could make it work.
>
> (Teacher interview, 1996)

Provision of timetabled time for the group to meet, open recognition of professional differences and a decision not to appoint a head of technology all combined to assist the processes of constructive planning and of team-building:

> We were willing to develop ideas and courses for young people . . . we knew that the only way forward was to come together as a group, we knew our strengths and weaknesses and we've broken down the barriers.

Similarly, a maths department had deliberately exploited the advent of the National Curriculum to review their teaching and jointly plan ways in which it could be improved whilst meeting the new requirements:

> . . . at every faculty meeting, each person has a time when they have to give an example of something that they'd taught that has gone well, so that other people can get ideas of how to teach it . . . some people come up with some very good ideas for things that we could look at for improving results in the future, and so, yes, I mean we're all learning all the time.
>
> (Teacher interview, 1995)

These last examples echo other research findings on the potential import-ance of subject departments as sites of professional learning (Siskin 1994; Talbert and McLaughlin 1994). However, access to wider perspectives also remains important: as Bullough and Gitlin (1994) point out, confining learn-ing to local sites can inhibit critical thinking by discouraging scrutiny of institutionally accepted roles and relationships.

Collaboration and change

Collaborative associations between teachers may provide a useful form of support at times of curriculum change and uncertainty. On the one hand, shared thinking and access to alternative ideas and sources of expertise can widen and improve the range of possible solutions to the problems of responding to imposed changes, whilst the solidarity that comes from being part of a wider group tends to enhance confidence and encourage experi-mentation. At the same time, exposure to different perspectives and partici-pation in development work within a supportive context can challenge taken-for-granted ways of seeing and doing things and thereby broaden pro-fessional knowledge and enhance professional skills. For these reasons col-laboration is a potentially empowering experience and is often advocated as a means of improving the quality of schooling, especially at times of edu-cational reform.

As indicated above, however, collaboration may take many different forms, some of which are far from empowering. Indeed, an excessive empha-sis upon joint working within closely specified parameters may discipline group members into compliance with imposed demands or encourage the development of uncritical 'groupthink' (Fullan 1993). Equally it can be 'comfortable and complacent', confirming rather than changing existing practice, 'contrived' to meet administrative purposes, or simply 'superficial', making few demands on those involved and lacking purpose or direction (Hargreaves 1995: 155). Since the more positive and empowering forms of collaboration are based upon relationships of trust and involve some loss of individual autonomy, they cannot be mandated.

Both TVEI and the National Curriculum promoted or demanded curricu-lum change and both affected the patterns of association within and between schools, often increasing teacher interactions in different ways. Whilst TVEI, at least in the pilot stage, offered resources and release from teaching duties to enable staff to meet and work together in a fairly open-ended way both within school and across institutions, the National Curriculum offered few additional resources and set a relatively tight agenda for development. More-over, other factors emerging at the same time tended to increase competition between schools and discourage cross-institutional working. Certainly many of the teachers interviewed through the Lancaster TVEI Evaluation Programme believed that there had been a decrease in collaborative links between teachers from different schools and a corresponding increase in insularity and individual feelings of isolation.

Data gathered both during and after the Professional Cultures of Teachers project in 1994–96 tended to confirm this trend, despite the clear increase in in-school meetings. However, they also pointed to examples where teachers had been able to exploit the impetus for change and to manipulate the prevailing institutional circumstances in order to create more meaningful and professionally empowering forms of collaboration. For some teachers this occurred in the early days of National Curriculum implementation, whilst for others it developed as they became more familiar with, and less inhibited by, national requirements. Either way, however, it is clear that such collaboration is always time consuming and that time is an increasingly rare commodity in schools. The next chapter will explore in more detail the ways in which the pace of teachers' work has been rapidly accelerating in response to various aspects of current educational reforms.

seven

CHANGING PACE OF WORK

As indicated in Chapter 1, a number of factors associated with the 'new work order' are already beginning to be translated into employment practice and in many cases have tended to increase the day-to-day pressures and workloads of ordinary employees. For example, the relentless quest for continuous quality improvement means that many workers are constantly expected to develop new ways of working and to acquire new skills, whilst at the same time improving their performance and producing 'more for less'. The devolution of responsibility to smaller work units has not only created additional tasks but also increased demands for accountability, with a consequent growth in form-filling and record-keeping by employees, whilst the new emphasis upon teamwork has frequently meant more time spent in meetings and in joint planning and review sessions. Finally, the creation of a more flexible labour market and the growth in unemployment have significantly increased the pressures upon those in employment to work harder and to comply with heightened expectations of performance.

It seems clear that the work of teachers has also been affected by many of these developments. Certainly the ubiquitous mantra of 'raising standards' has meant that most teachers have had to cope with significant changes in their working lives as a result of a general restructuring of education systems, and have come under increasing pressures to produce better 'results', often with diminishing resources and without additional funding. The introduction of LMS in England, and associated activities such as school development planning and marketing, have greatly extended the range of tasks carried out within schools, whilst new, accountability-oriented requirements like data-gathering, record-keeping, teacher appraisal and school inspection have all created additional pressures and burdens. Finally, the reduction in in-service teacher support and the growth in competition both between schools and between individuals in schools have left some teachers feeling isolated and unable to cope (Helsby 1997).

Whilst teachers' working lives have tended to become more 'intensified' (Apple 1986; Hargreaves 1994) it is difficult to be precise about the extent of this process. A survey conducted by the International Labour Office in over 40 countries in 1991 found that most teachers were experiencing stress and time pressures and that their overall workloads had increased, particularly in terms of new administrative duties and the time needed to deal with unruly students (ILO 1991). In their studies of the work of teachers in the UK, Campbell and Neill (1994a; 1994b) attempted to categorize some of these increases. Thus, for example, they claimed that a term-time working week of 50 hours in primary schools and over 54 hours in secondary schools had become the norm, compared to the 46.75 hours recorded in secondary schools by Hilsum and Strong in 1976 (Hilsum and Strong 1978). Only about 40 hours of this working week were spent in school, with the rest of the time spent working off school premises in the evenings and at weekends. Campbell and Neill also found that the patterning of teachers' work had been restructured, with only between 45 per cent (primary) and 41 per cent (secondary) of that time spent in contact with pupils. A substantial minority of teachers' time (10 per cent in primary schools and 14 per cent in secondary schools) was spent on low-level activities and/or non-teaching-related administration. In addition, involvement in meetings, inter-school liaison and school-based and other forms of training days accounted for over four hours of the average working week for primary teachers and over four and a half hours for secondary teachers (Campbell and Neill 1994a: 204–5; 1994b: 157–9).

Statistics alone, however, can only paint a partial picture, since they tell us little about what these changes mean to teachers themselves and in what ways they impact upon their working lives. Certainly this is not the first time that teachers' workloads have increased and, depending upon the situation, a widening of responsibilities could be associated either with exploitative practices and deskilling or with professional development and advancement. As Lawn (1987b: 50) points out:

> The definition and practice of teachers' work changes according to local demand, national priorities, the historical period and, not least, the teacher's own view made in response to these factors.

Lawn goes on to describe the major changes made to the management of schooling in England during the Second World War when, despite greatly increased duties and extended working hours, some teachers were inspired by their sense of partnership in a new national public service. Lawn's quotations from the diary of May, a wartime elementary teacher, are in some ways reminiscent of the complaints of today's teachers:

Daily struggle to accomplish many extra tasks which are not productive of any educational good has resulted in my frequently losing sight of the true aims of teaching . . .

However, the increased pressure and workload were, for this particular teacher, balanced by a sense of mission and a belief in the importance of her work:

At the same time I am conscious that there is a greater need than ever for positive ideas and constructive thought and action and I am feverishly trying to twist the happenings of today into some form which will bespeak good.

(1987b: 53)

Sadly, the political situation in England in the 1980s and 1990s has been quite different from that of the 1940s, with traditional notions of 'partnership' roughly cast aside and teachers excluded from decision-making processes and subjected instead to public attack and criticism. Accordingly, the framework within which teachers were expected to work harder was more suggestive of deprofessionalization and technical compliance than of professional growth and creativity. Gewirtz (1997) argued that the nature and texture of intensification within a climate of increased surveillance and competitiveness were having significant emotional consequences for teachers as well as affecting their social relations and their pedagogy. As a result of this they were experiencing a loss of autonomy along with increased activity and stress. Similarly, Ball (1994: 49) identified 'an increase in technical elements of teachers' work and a reduction in the professional . . . [t]he spaces for professional autonomy and judgement are [further] reduced'.

Clearly not all teachers experienced a sense of deprofessionalization because of the changes in the number and nature of work tasks. Some school managers, for example, have developed a heightened sense of professionalism along with their new management skills (Ball 1994; Grace 1995), and some teachers have seen the changes as an opportunity for curriculum review and have exploited both this and their broadened responsibilities to achieve personal growth. Campbell and Neill (1994a) identified an enhanced professionalism amongst primary school teachers, whilst Hargreaves and Goodson (1996) found evidence of teacher 'reprofessionalization' in certain aspects of their work alongside a process of 'deprofessionalization'. However, the mounting evidence that many teachers are experiencing a chronic work overload with reduced time to reflect, to plan carefully and to talk to colleagues (Hargreaves 1994) suggests that any sense of increased professionalism occurs *in spite of* recent changes or even that it is, as some have claimed, a misrecognition of a process of intensification which persuades teachers to collude in their own exploitation. As Hargreaves points out, however, the same circumstances impact differently upon different teachers and their responses are not uniform. Whilst some react with increased commitment and longer working hours, others may adopt survival strategies which involve placing a limit upon the hours worked and the tasks undertaken.

Another factor that must be taken into consideration is that teaching has always involved a potentially heavy and stressful workload. Connell (1985) argues that the lack of any clear object to the labour process of teaching, and the diversity of teachers' work tasks, mean that the definition of teachers' work can expand indefinitely. There will always be more that a teacher can do, and the only limits are those set by teachers themselves as they seek their own personal resolutions of the conflicting demands of the job. However, as Connell also points out, the competing ideologies surrounding education and education reform give priority to the needs of everybody but the teacher and imply a call for sacrifice in the interests of children, the community, society or the economy.

Evidence from secondary school teachers interviewed in the course of the Lancaster TVEI Evaluation Programme and through other projects such as the Professional Cultures of Teachers study suggests that the vast majority believe that workloads have increased in recent years. Some of the older teachers contrasted experiences during their early years of teaching with the current situation, as shown by these comments from interviews in 1995, 1996 and 1997:

> . . . when I first started teaching I could cope. I would hate to cope now with a young family and teach. I would find it very, very difficult.

> I feel sorry for people coming into the profession at the moment because they've never known what it's like to just have that little bit of breathing space to think about the job more, instead of 'What am I doing tomorrow? What's on tomorrow?' It's very much hand to mouth, you know, you're just trying to stay one step ahead of the game.

> Before there were times when you could relax and socialize, now it's work, work, work.

Similarly, a young teacher in her first post, interviewed in 1995, compared her own experiences with the tales that she had heard of teachers in earlier times:

> . . . sitting in the staffroom, . . . playing dominoes and knitting. If I went into that staffroom today, right, if I had a free period – because, you know, you rarely get a free period, it's usually on cover – but if I went into the staffroom and started knitting, that would be it, my name would be mud in the school.

Indeed, the same teacher described the difficulties that she had encountered in developing relationships with her colleagues:

> . . . you haven't got time to socialize, you haven't got time to really know people. It's taken me two and a half years to make friends in this school. So I think that's hard as well, especially if you're new to the profession.

A number of factors were identified as contributing to this perceived increase in workload. The vast majority of these related to recent educational 'reforms', introduced with the avowed purpose of improving education. Indeed, teachers interviewed in 1995 and 1996 highlighted only one cause of increased work pressure that had arisen spontaneously, and that was the changing nature of the school's clientele:

> . . . the children [have become] more demanding in the last few years, and with them doing their own work, individual work, they need more attention, individual attention.

> . . . problems are now being encountered which are filtering through from society into the schools, staff being verbally and physically abused, drug addiction [among] the pupils and the consequences of that.

Lack of motivation, lack of respect for authority and shorter attention spans were all creating new challenges for teachers:

> We've got to give them a diet of things that they can relate to . . . it's a difficult situation, we've got to be pretty amazing in front of a group of children now to capture their imagination . . . whether we can compete with the presentations that TV can give us and film can give us is another matter.

For some teachers, this was creating significant problems, and the time needed to enforce discipline was seen as detracting from teaching. This technology teacher, interviewed in 1996, found working in the new context demotivating:

> I don't know, if I went through this again, whether I'd go into education . . . I don't know whether I'd want a lot of the hassle that you get now, . . . it's really pupil behaviour, I think, that's taken a lot of the pleasure out of the work. You've got to spend so much time dealing with the discipline which cuts into the major part of your role which is actually teaching.

A geography teacher, interviewed in the same year, found that similar difficulties were arising because of the decision to integrate children with special educational needs into mainstream classes:

. . . we've more difficult children coming into the school. A lot of [special educational needs] children, which is absolutely ludicrous because they aren't getting the proper treatment and then my high-fliers aren't getting the proper treatment. So there's frustration in the classroom between teacher and pupil at the same time. And that frustration builds up of course into an aggravation that can lead to discipline problems fundamentally.

These problems were exacerbated for many teachers by resource cuts which meant that they were having to teach larger classes:

. . . more and more parents want their children in this school . . . so the classes are bigger and we're having less timetabled free time because more classes have to be catered for. Because our headmaster is on his own budget, we can't employ more staff so what staff are in he just has to squeeze more and more. And this is our loss of freedom.

(Teacher interview, 1996)

In another school which ran a 40-period week, a teacher interviewed in 1994 said that each of his colleagues was having to teach one more lesson than in the previous year (teacher interview, 1994). A history teacher described how he now taught more than half of the children in the school and therefore had to mark over 350 books per week, whilst a maths teacher interviewed in 1996 complained of the lack of adequate teaching materials and the extra time needed to share and plan the use of existing resources:

. . . a lot of materials are in demand at the same time for the four maths classes. So it's a lot of fiddling around and you've got to have planned much more in advance so you can share the materials . . . you're constantly juggling your resources around and you haven't sufficient . . . it's not impossible, it just gives you a few more grey hairs.

(Teacher interview, 1996)

Several teachers mentioned the expanded duties of form teachers ('you're expected to be a social worker as well') and some felt resentment at the multiplicity of their roles and at the fact that so much of their time was now taken up with activities that they felt contributed nothing to their teaching:

. . . you're an agony aunt, sorting problems, chasing letters, collecting money, checking dress, passing on or collecting information. Some of it is quite nice, but you've not got the time to do it. I'd like it clearly defined what we have to do.

(Teacher interview, 1994)

When I started in this game many years ago, I was a *teacher* and enjoyed it! Now I am a chief examiner, setting practical exam sessions within impossible guidelines, a moderator, a marker, a record-keeper and filing clerk, a careers adviser, a tutor, a 'meetings' attender and occasionally a teacher. PS Soon to be an appraiser.

(Comment from teacher survey, 1993)

On top of the difficulties caused by unmotivated students, indiscipline, large classes, expanded duties and inadequate resources, another source of pressure and irritation highlighted by many teachers was the dramatic increase in recording and reporting requirements:

... the difference that I've found with the National Curriculum is there's far more paperwork. Particularly the assessments, which take hours and hours and it's got to be done, obviously not in teaching time ... I suppose it's part of my work as a teacher but it just seems to have increased over the last few years. One bit of paper by itself doesn't really make all that much difference but when you sort of start adding it all together, it really does.

(Teacher interview, 1995)

... the amount of time you spend doing pointless records that are never looked at and never sent for is time you could be preparing really good lessons and marking ... the amount of paperwork is like snow, it just comes down like snow.

(Teacher interview, 1994)

A teacher interviewed in 1996 contrasted this situation with that of other professionals:

... those people are actually timetabled to do their paperwork. They don't take it home, they have a day a week where they do their paperwork and that's part of their actual job role.

Many also emphasized how excessive paperwork detracted from what they felt were the more important and more valuable aspects of their work:

The amount of paperwork worries me greatly because that tends to take me away from the human relationship side.

(Teacher interview, 1994)

The bureaucracy and the admin side of it is crushing. I have to do an hour's admin every night before I actually do my own job, which is marking and preparing. And of course long-term preparation just gets shoved to the holidays or the weekends.

(Teacher interview, 1996)

Ofsted inspections were not only seen by teachers as threatening and largely unhelpful (see Chapter 8) but also as exceptionally time-consuming, as indicated by these comments from teacher interviews in 1995 and 1997:

Oh, the build-up to it was actually horrendous and I think a lot of it was a waste of time because it wasn't worth it.

We've just gone through an Ofsted and I decided this summer that I really should be a spinster, with no family ties whatsoever, and then I could get on with my job. Yes, it's got to that stage now.

The Ofsted inspection in April was totally consuming, and your teaching suffers because of it.

On top of all of this, teachers had had to cope with major changes in their classroom work because of the introduction of the National Curriculum and subsequent revisions to its requirements. Teachers interviewed in 1995 were experiencing a lot of pressure because of the need to meet with colleagues, to plan new schemes of work and to teach unfamiliar material:

. . . now with the National Curriculum there's an awful lot more marking and meetings . . . people are working much longer, or I am . . . I do now have to spend far more of my own time preparing and getting things up to date and making sure that everything's . . . where it should be.

. . . it's preparing new syllabuses, that's the time-consuming thing, and being ready to teach a group of students something that you've not taught them before.

Very many commented on the frustration and the additional workload created by frequent revisions to National Curriculum orders and the cumulative effects of constant change:

. . . it's the fact that you're just starting to get on your feet with one thing and you find that you've got a whole new change introduced and you've got to change everything again.

. . . everything is constrained by time, and in addition to that we've had lots of problems with endless changes with National Curriculum.

One teacher summarized the feelings of many when she tried to explain the reasons for teachers' unhappiness:

I don't think it's about prescription, I think it's about the chaos which has been imposed upon schools in terms of reorganization, reorganizing the curriculum, you know? Perhaps scrapping old schemes of work and having to do new schemes of work, and everything coming at the same time, teaching days changing, you know, probably from a slow steady pace to a more frenetic pace.

The problems created in schools in the years following the 1988 Education Reform Act were so great that Ron Dearing, a leading industrialist, was asked to undertake a review of the National Curriculum and of the framework for assessing students' progress. His final report of December 1993 recommended that National Curriculum requirements should be slimmed down and that assessment arrangements modified following a more detailed review by the Schools Curriculum and Assessment Authority (SCAA). Significantly, he also recognized the damaging effects caused by the constant changes in requirements and recommended that there should be a five-year moratorium on curriculum change. Whilst this was welcomed in principle by teachers, few really believed that stability would be achieved, as shown by these comments from 1995:

> I know we've been told we've got five years, but I think the feeling is that we are into almost like a continual cycle of change, that even if they're changed in fairly minor ways, they will be changed.

> I don't think the pressure will be any less because I know, looking ahead, that we've got new GCSEs to introduce in September 1996, and that will be two years that we have to ensure that those pupils are getting the right diet. That we've been changed again and so there will be major changes, plus the lead up to that exam in Years 7–9. So no, I don't think the pressure's going to be any less. I don't think this idea that it was going to bring us five years of stability is true at all, I think it's still going to be five years of change.

Indeed, another teacher interviewed in 1996 believed that, far from getting better, the situation for teachers would actually deteriorate:

> I see it getting worse in the near future . . . and I can see a mass exodus of staff, good teaching staff, because they just can't take any more.

Certainly the increase in pressure and workloads was having a significant impact upon many of the teachers interviewed. There were repeated references to the way in which work demands were increasingly impinging upon people's personal and social lives:

> When you're up till all hours preparing documents for inspection and marking, your social life goes out the window.
>
> (Teacher interview, 1995)

> . . . it really cuts into your free time on an evening, and you've got to do work on Sunday. I never plan to do anything on a Sunday because I know I'm going to have to work, so that I've only got one day off a week. And I think for people with families it must be hell, I think it must really affect their family lives.
>
> (Teacher interview, 1995)

Several married teachers did indeed refer to the stresses and strains that arose within families as a result of the extended working hours:

In my own case it's the actual number of hours that I'm having to put in within the school environment even before I go home and then having to put more hours in again, with a young family it's creating an enormous amount of stress because somebody else has to pick up the pieces.

(Teacher interview, 1996)

I'm so ratty with my own kids . . . I seem to be able to be understanding with the kids [at school] and have lots of patience with them, and as soon as I get home and my kids step out of line, bang, I blow up at them. It's awful really and I'm sure it's the stress of holding down the cork on the bottle.

(Teacher interview, 1995)

The following two teachers, interviewed in 1996, foresaw potential problems, regardless of marital status:

Being single, you have to be careful that you don't fall into the trap of devoting all your life to school.

It would be very interesting to find out what the divorce rate within teaching is . . . the actual reason quoted behind those divorces would be the workload that people are taking home now compared to what it was five years ago. It's enormous, both in terms of paperwork and, I think, the actual stress that's being placed upon individuals.

Some teachers tried hard to keep their work lives separate from their personal lives. Indeed, one teacher described how she always came into school early to prepare lessons or mark books and would work through lunch and after school if necessary in order to keep her evenings and weekends free. Whilst she saw the problems encountered by other teachers as signs of poor organization, her view was exceptional. Some argued that the separation of home and working lives was impossible, not only because of increased workloads, but also because of the nature of the job:

I resent the impact that it has on my social life and my life outside school, so you can't turn off because it's interaction with people and you think 'Oh, is it me? Why is this going wrong, why is this kid doing this?' That daily challenge to your personality really affects you.

(Teacher interview, 1995)

. . . it's had a tremendous effect on my personal life, being a teacher . . . it seems that you can never actually get away from the job.

(Teacher interview, 1996)

As well as the effect of increased workloads upon people's home lives, there was widespread evidence of a significant impact upon the quality of teachers' work within schools and, consequently, upon job satisfaction.

The following comments from a teacher survey in 1992–93 are fairly typical:

> Too many changes too quickly. Impossible to feel satisfied with any task well accomplished.

> Too much going on at once and totally impossible to cope with change because of lack of time and all the other pressures.

> I simply do not have the time to do my job effectively.

> The changes keep changing and changing and changing. No time to organise the extra work involved. Everything is hurried, incomplete, chaotic.

Indeed, more than three out of five of the 2010 teachers in that survey believed that they were having difficulty keeping up with current professional demands. The following two comments, from teacher interviews in 1995 and 1996, suggest that the multiplicity of roles and the varied demands being placed upon teachers make it impossible to perform any of them effectively:

> I don't actually have the time to put into planning or thinking about my teaching as I used to. I'm doing a lot more teaching sort of on the hoof, which bothers me because I know it isn't as good . . . as I'm capable of doing. But it's the amount of time I have in the day really and the other roles which pull you in different directions, because it's the other deadlines really.

> I feel that you're trying to keep so many balls in the air at once that you're doing a lot of jobs to perhaps a lesser standard than you could have done in the past. I feel that sometimes there's a degree of mediocrity in what I'm doing as there's so much on my plate, and I think that that's true for a head of department, a classroom teacher.

There was some evidence of teachers continuing to struggle against the odds to fulfil their many tasks, even when work was threatening to take over their lives or when their efforts were counter-productive. The following comments from interviews with teachers in 1996 point towards a possibly misplaced sense of conscientiousness:

> I do find it hard work. But there again, you see, there's always this old argument, there's nobody telling you to do it a lot of the time. [You do it] to get through the volume of work and, yes, because at the bottom line I like a job well done and I wouldn't be content myself if I felt I'd just dropped something and chosen not to do it, you know, I take my responsibilities quite seriously, I suppose too seriously. But I do think that you can end up really . . . living to work rather than the other way round.

... it looks back to this idea of professionalism almost in a negative way which is that you assume a professional stance and say 'Well I am going to do my job to the best of my ability, therefore to do that I have to stay until six o'clock because I'm not going to cover it otherwise.' And to a certain extent you lull yourself into a false sense of security, which is that 'I'm meeting the demands of the job by staying for that length of time'. But you're not meeting your own needs and, in the long term, you're not meeting the needs of your job because you're putting yourself under stress. You're underperforming ... creating stress at home, inability to cope with the pupils in the way that you should be doing because things that before would not have got on top of you are starting to get on top of you.

It was further suggested that teachers were reluctant to seek help when they did encounter difficulties and instead tried to struggle on alone:

The majority of teachers that I know try to cope with it. This is where the problem arises and I don't think they ask for help early enough. We tend to think that if we can't cope, we are inadequate, therefore, you know, we've got to sort ourselves out.

(Teacher interview, 1995)

Many teachers reported a significant loss of professional confidence as a result of the changes:

After teaching for 20 plus years, I have never felt so totally exhausted, nor so pessimistic about my ability and competence to cope with what is now expected of me.

(Comment from teacher survey, 1993)

... we're finding that it's not getting easier ... we're struggling as if we're still at college, post-college days and that, after 17 years of teaching, I think is appalling.

(Teacher interview, 1996)

In some cases teachers were responding to these pressures by switching off from any sense of professionalism and retreating to a more limited conception of their role:

... you know, don't you, what morale's like in schools, particularly? That's something to do with increased sort of chaos, I think, in increased paperwork ... it is crazy and I think ... more and more people are feeling less professional in the sense that they say 'Oh, why should I bother?'

(Teacher interview, 1995)

In many cases, however, teachers were said to be experiencing severe stress, illness and burnout, as suggested in these interview extracts from 1996:

> A lot of members of staff, as far as I'm told, are on tablets for blood pressure and stress.

> . . . we're increasingly aware that stress is a big problem in teaching. I mean we've seen it here, we've a colleague who's no longer in school, people are looking for early retirement. People are taking time off, if you like, through illness, but it's illness that's brought on by the sheer weight of the work that they've got to do. Different people cope with it in different ways but yes, I think it's increasing.

This last comment reminds us that not all teachers experience stress as a result of multiple changes and increased workloads. A younger teacher interviewed in 1995 suggested that she was less stressed than others because she had entered teaching when rapid change was already a fact of life:

> It surprised me when I worked out why the changes were stressing me less than they were stressing my colleagues, because I've never known it stand still for any length of time, so I'm used to it changing every time somebody feels like it.

However, this was certainly not true of all younger teachers, some of whom were struggling to develop their own teaching in a context where in-service support was extremely limited or non-existent (see Chapter 10) and where advice from more experienced colleagues was lacking because they were themselves under too much pressure. Stress-related illness had affected several of our interviewees, including a very experienced head of a geography department who was interviewed in 1996:

> I've been off long-term with illness, for 13 weeks, so I'm only just back in school. And it was burnout. I was literally working all the time. Trying to keep my social life going as well, and I'm afraid the candle snuffed in the middle eventually.

Working in a small but popular school with an inadequate staffing budget, this teacher described how her workload had steadily increased to the point where she was so tired at weekends that she was struggling to find the time to do routine things like gardening, walking or tidying the house ('I find that now I'm even on a timetable to do these things as well'). She was convinced that many of her colleagues were in a similar state:

> . . . there are other members of the teaching profession and I'm just the tip of the iceberg, there's going to be a dreadful crash with all the pressures that are put on us at the moment.

At school, she found there was no longer any time for social interchange ('We don't have the ability to relax any more. We're on edge all the time') and she had started to avoid going to the staffroom because:

> I find the staff are so low that they either sit there like zombies, who are ill, or they just don't have time to say anything.

Another teacher with 11 years' experience who was interviewed in 1996 was also showing severe signs of stress. This stress was caused partly by the burden of trying to reconcile an excessively heavy workload with the demands of a young family and partly by his inability to carry out his duties to his own satisfaction:

> I would say on average I'm here now at around six o'clock every night . . . then I'm having to sort out the family and starting again with tons of paperwork. And I'm still, in my own opinion, failing within the job I'm doing.

This teacher was a member of the senior management team (SMT) in a small school as well as a classroom teacher and had recently taken on additional roles because of a forthcoming Ofsted inspection. Like others, he was finding that the multiplicity of work roles, and the pressures of performing them well without any proper time allowance, were having a very negative effect upon him:

> If you go from five [areas of responsibility] to seven and you're being measured then against seven areas of responsibility but you've not been given allocated time or an allocated structure to work against, immediately you've got pressure. You've got pressure that you're placing on yourself where you see yourself as underachieving, as not meeting the needs of either management or the pupils. And then on top of that you've got an external body coming in who are not really aware of the context within which they are assessing, and saying you haven't followed the curriculum . . . I know what I should be doing but I can't do it because I've not got the time, so what I do is I do them because we have to and do them badly and find myself very, very frustrated with that.

A strong sense of professional duty was driving him to protect his classroom teaching from the pressures, but these were surfacing in other contexts:

> I'm an actor. I will walk into that place and I will be what's required of me in terms of those pupils . . . the stresses and the strains . . . I take home and I find that the actual stress shows itself at home, not at school.

This raised a particularly keen conflict of values which was then creating further pressure:

. . . you're married to the job and they're picking up the pieces at home. I find that very difficult, because my own philosophy is that this is a job and that my own family and my children are far more important but that I'm being pushed more and more – and it's usually me that's doing the pushing – into a corner, where to meet the requirements that are being asked of me in the job, the job is actually the thing that is directing my life, and not the things that I actually value. And that in itself creates stress.

Once again, this teacher was convinced that his own case was far from unique and that the recent changes and increased workloads had had a devastating effect upon the teaching profession:

. . . the changes, I think, have created a lot of difficulties and a lot of stress upon people in terms of their professionalism. I think there are a hell of a lot of teachers walking round the place now who are in a state of shell shock . . . The rate and pace of change that's being inflicted upon them without the time to take stock and evaluate, in conjunction with external accountability being placed upon them being based upon those changes, and I think the whole combination has created an enormous amount of stress within the teaching profession, and I don't think it's isolated to just the basic teacher. I think whatever level you peel off, be it headteacher, deputy head, senior management, departmental head, basic teacher, the actual level of stress and expectation placed upon teachers has gone right through the ceiling.

Conclusion

The balance of the evidence presented above suggests that most teachers have been adversely affected by recent educational reforms and that work overload and stress-related illness are widespread. When workloads were mentioned, none of our interviewees felt that they had lightened, whilst the vast majority believed that they had increased greatly or excessively over the last few years. It could, of course, be argued that people who aspire to professional status are unlikely to agree that their work is easy or undemanding. Equally, however, they may be reluctant to admit to any problems in coping with the work, and so the fact that over three out of five survey respondents agreed that they were having difficulty in keeping up with current professional demands may be significant.

Much of the research evidence on recent educational reforms shows that teachers react in very different ways to changed and changing requirements such as those imposed by the National Curriculum. Whilst some are incapacitated by them and suffer withdrawal, stress or burnout, others are able to impose their own interpretations upon the requirements and creatively exploit them to their own educational and professional ends. A number of contextual factors appear to have an influence upon teachers' responses and may either enable or inhibit them from finding 'spaces for manoeuvre' within the imposed framework. Amongst the most significant of these are teachers' professional confidence, the availability of both space and time for reflection and a strong culture of collegiality (Helsby 1996b). Since much of the evidence points towards greatly extended workloads and the increasing pace of teachers' working lives, it becomes harder to sustain collegial relations and to find time for reflection. At the same time the need constantly to make rushed decisions, to cut corners and to accept lower levels of performance all tend to have a negative effect upon professional confidence. Accordingly, many teachers may feel deskilled by the intensification of their work and become demotivated or disengaged.

However, and as reiterated constantly throughout this book, there are always exceptions to the rules and teachers who appear to thrive on the changes, despite the increased workload. Moreover, the picture is never constant and the effects of intensification are likely to change over time. For example, whilst the extent of curriculum change was an important factor in creating pressure in the early years of National Curriculum implementation, teachers have gradually become more used to both dealing with its structure and managing change. In addition to this, there has also been a reduction in some of the curriculum and assessment requirements, and so this source of pressure has been greatly reduced for many teachers, whilst new pressures have arisen elsewhere. One of the most significant of these pressures is the increase in the demands for formal accountability, and this is the subject of the next chapter.

eight

CHANGES IN ACCOUNTABILITY

A recurring feature of recent educational reforms has been the growth of formal accountability mechanisms. This has been particularly striking in England, because of the contrast with the earlier traditions of teacher autonomy, and is a significant factor in claims of deprofessionalization. The changes are multiple: teacher appraisal, new recording and reporting requirements, national testing, the publication of league tables of school performance with regard to attendance levels and examination results, increased rights to information for parents and for school governors, and the imposition of a new, national system of inspection which judges both schools and teachers. Such developments are portrayed as important to educational effectiveness and improvement, and also to meeting government responsibilities whilst opening schools to the forces of marketization and providing information for 'consumers'. However, they have major implications for the nature and content of teachers' work and stand in marked contrast to the 'professional autonomy' model of accountability (Adelman and Alexander 1982) that held sway up to the mid-1970s and that left control of educational evaluation in the hands of educational professionals.

Schön (1983) identified a number of causes for the general crisis of confidence in professionals that developed in the 1970s. These included the growing perception that professionals had failed to find adequate solutions for the problems of society; a number of notorious incidents or 'scandals' where professionals were seen to have misused their autonomy; and an increasing tendency to question specialist knowledge and claims to expertise, especially as a result of public debunking of the professions. All of these factors can be applied to the English education system: claims of 'failure' arose as the economic crisis of the 1960s and early 1970s was increasingly blamed upon schools; the so-called 'William Tyndale affair' appeared to confirm these shortcomings (Auld 1976); and the questioning of teachers' professional expertise was encouraged by Prime Minister Callaghan's Ruskin College speech and the subsequent 'Great Debate' on education. Dale (1989: 133) described the consequent changes as a shift from 'licensed autonomy' to 'regulated autonomy': 'Control over the education system is to become tighter, largely through the codification and monitoring of processes and practices previously left to teachers' professional judgement, taken on trust or hallowed by tradition'.

Subsequent efforts to make teachers more accountable and to bureaucratize the control of education took various forms, ranging from the establishment and strengthening of the Assessment of Performance Unit, attempts by the DES to develop a core curriculum which emphasized standardization, output and testing, a growing emphasis upon the monitoring of teachers' classroom performance, the publication of inspection reports, the extension of the powers of governing bodies and the introduction of teacher appraisal in schools. TVEI introduced the concept of categorical funding, whereby bids for inclusion in a funded project had to conform to certain pre-specified criteria and success in gaining resources meant acceptance of contractual accountability for meeting those criteria. In this case, however, the looseness of the criteria and the lack of experience amongst MSC officials in monitoring educational outcomes as opposed to budgetary auditing meant that, certainly in the initial stages, stringent accountability remained more theoretical than real.

The burgeoning accountability movement was given more substance by the Education Reform Act of 1988. According to Kogan (1989: 141), this Act 'impose[d] a national core curriculum which flatly contradicts the assumption underlying the professional accountability model' and ensured that 'the public contractual model of accountability, too, [was] drastically changed' by the weakening of the LEA. Finally, the new provisions for LMS dramatically strengthened the powers of headteachers and governors at the expense of classroom teachers. Initially, compliance with National Curriculum requirements was to be monitored by LEA advisers, but the 1992 Education (Schools) Act established a national system of school and teacher inspection which relied upon four-yearly investigations by privatized teams of inspectors, trained and commissioned by, and answerable to, the new Office for Standards in Education.

Thus, the bureaucratic structures of teacher accountability were established, despite the dangers that that accountability might be applicable to a less extensive area of activity than the broader notion of 'professional responsibility' and might encourage ritualistic compliance with specified procedures, rather than a commitment to a set of principles of good practice (Hoyle and John 1995). Even at this level, however, bureaucratic accountability was not without its cost, particularly in terms of a tendency towards 'hyper-accountability' (Hoyle 1995), where an excessive amount of teachers' time is spent on activities related to accountability which detract from the time available for teaching. Moreover, the substitution of bureaucratic accountability for professional autonomy risks producing an adverse effect upon teachers' morale and motivation, suggesting that good teachers might be less willing to invest fully in improving their practice, despite the fact that such accountability has been introduced in the name of raising educational standards. The number of 'failing teachers' likely to be identified by such measures and removed from the classroom remains a subject of contention, although there is as yet little evidence of any widespread move to expel them.

In practice, the effects of this increased accountability upon teachers' work were indeed profound. Firstly, the feeling of 'not being trusted' caused an enormous amount of resentment amongst teachers, especially since this lack of trust was seen as largely unjustified:

> ... most teachers are far happier with the idea that they can make decisions about what is taught and they don't abuse that. And they resent a lot the fact that somebody is telling them, not subject content but the framework ... I think on the whole they do take their jobs seriously, they are responsible people and they would value greater freedom. They would value the trust. I think it's this resentment of not being trusted that really does the damage.
>
> (Teacher interview, 1996)

> ... one of the things that always got complained about is this idea that teachers are inherently untrustworthy. This idea that, left to ourselves, we'd all be sat there with the kids throwing paper aeroplanes at each other across the classroom while we sat and, I don't know, read a book or something.
>
> (Teacher interview, 1995)

Comparisons were made with other professions, leading to a view that teachers were being unfairly penalized by the government:

> ... the Labour and Conservative parties have both highlighted bad teachers as something that they're going to pick up on if they win the next election, but where's bad doctors or bad architects or bad solicitors, you know, why is it always bad teachers?
>
> (Teacher interview, 1995)

The constant 'discourses of derision' about teachers and the highly negative tone of public pronouncements by politicians or by leaders of educational quangos caused deep bitterness amongst teachers. This was seen as undermining professionalism and as contributing significantly to teachers' low morale, as indicated by these comments from interviews in 1996:

> . . . you have people like Nick Tate [Chief Executive of the SCAA], a few weeks ago, and the recent Ofsted report. They seem to be concentrating on the negative qualities rather than saying 'This is going well but we need to pay attention to this', and therefore I feel that professionalism is being questioned all the time. I've never known teachers' morale so low in 28 years' teaching.

> I'm very unhappy with the inspection service generally, mainly because of Mr Woodhead and his endless pronouncements about 15,000 bad teachers and all this . . . I mean that is completely undermining morale, I'm certain of it.

Teachers were happy to accept the notion of accountability and were even ready to acknowledge that a small number of teachers might indeed be 'failing'. However, there were strong feelings that the extent of any 'failure' was grossly exaggerated, and great exception was taken to the fact that it was senior people close to central government who were doing this. Many felt that the public image of teachers had been badly damaged by these constant attacks and by the corresponding sensationalization by the media of any isolated cases of poor performance:

> I'm not disagreeing with teachers being accountable, certainly to the general public and the powers that be, but I feel that there's such a bad lead coming from the government and Ofsted and people in the SCAA, there's so much rubbish that is actually written and said about education that, you know, as in anything else, the more people say it, the more the general public will believe it.
>
> (Teacher interview, 1996)

> And of course the media has done a lot of damage, with the odd, rare bad teacher, the odd, rare bad pupil or school. But it's been hyped up and it becomes a blanket cover.
>
> (Teacher interview, 1996)

There was also a sense of deep injustice that the increases in accountability were being imposed at a time when teachers were effectively being asked to do more for less. Whereas in North America calls for fundamental change were accompanied by additional resources and appeals to teacher professionalism (at least in the 'second wave' of reforms), in England they came in a context of diminishing resources, inadequate opportunities for staff development and constant criticisms of teachers, all of which were seen as highly demotivating:

> Teachers' morale is low because they are more accountable than ever to more internal and external bodies and yet training, remuneration, time allocation and esteem in no way match the constant, heavy and ill-conceived demands for change.
>
> (Comment from teacher survey, 1992)

One of the consequences of the increased accountability was a heightened emphasis upon external testing of student achievement. Thus the teacher-assessed coursework element of GCSE qualifications for 16-year-olds was removed or greatly reduced, new forms of national testing were proposed or introduced at the end of the other three key stages, and teachers were asked to keep detailed records both of the basis and of the results of any internal assessments. This sudden and overt lack of trust in teachers' professional judgements was deeply resented, along with the increased workload in terms of recording and reporting:

> One cannot teach for testing, and our professional judgement is so doubted that record-keeping to justify known levels of achievement is deforesting the planet!
>
> (Comment from teacher survey, 1992)

> You're much more accountable now, much more accountable in lots of different ways, you know, through to the way you discipline pupils, even. You know that on the academic side of it as well, it's assessments, reports, you know, justifying yourself, what you've done, why you've given that child an A or a B or whatever. Where before you could just say 'Well, that's my judgement of them', but now you've got to have evidence. You've got to back it up with evidence . . . where I think at one time people just accepted.
>
> (Teacher interview, 1996)

A former senior HMI, interviewed in 1996 as part of the Professional Culture of Teachers project, also highlighted the damaging effects of this lack of trust in teachers' judgements and lamented the fact that diagnostic assessment, that could lead to improvement, was being abandoned in favour of accountability-oriented assessment:

> . . . if they're not trusted to carry out assessment, then . . . their professionalism is really knocked for six, because their whole judgement is then questioned . . . Yet on the other hand most thinking teachers and many people in education know for a fact that the assessment that brings about improvement is teacher assessment . . . but we don't have that kind of assessment because nobody will trust the teachers to do it.

Some concessions were made when, after a successful teacher boycott of Year 9 SAT tests, the government accepted the recommendations of the

1993 Dearing Report that the National Curriculum should be reviewed with the aim of reducing the statutory content, giving more weight to teacher assessment and lessening the administrative demands upon teachers. Dearing himself proposed that progress be made by 'reducing prescription so as to give more scope for professional judgement' (1993: para. 3.8), although this was to be 'matched by accountability to parents and society, including that from simple tests in the core subjects' (1993: para. 3.40). Thus, whilst some subject areas were exempted from SATs, more weight was placed upon the tests in core subjects, which therefore became 'high-stakes' forms of assessment. Teachers whose subjects had been exempted showed considerable relief:

> If I had [SATs] there'd be massive problems in this department, there really, really would be, because of the pressures from time and from outside forces. And also not knowing what the outside forces want.
>
> (Teacher interview, 1996)

Another teacher, interviewed in 1995, was clear that the operation of National Curriculum assessment before the Dearing Report ran counter to the notion of professional judgement and indeed deskilled the teacher:

> . . . it was a matter of the child either got a tick in this box, that meant that they'd got attainment target 2 at level 3A, or they didn't get a tick in that box. There was not judgement there by the teacher, it was a strict test, an audit on the child, and all the teacher was doing was what you might want to call a secretarial task in observing whether or not the child had done that. And it was purely observation, it was not a facilitation there whatsoever.

He was, however, much more optimistic about the revised arrangements:

> Dearing is trying, I think he's genuinely trying to put some professionalism back into teaching . . . Now that you're working to the programmes of study and you don't have to report levels, mid-key stages, the teacher will decide themselves what level they want to look at . . . making a judgement themselves what this child best fits into. And so therefore the value of the teacher as compared to ticking boxes is much greater.

Despite this optimism, considerable concern remained about the pressures created by such assessments on both teachers and students, as evidenced by these comments from teacher interviews in 1996 and 1995:

> In this country they're SATed at 7, 11, 14, they sit a public examination at 16, if they want to go on to higher education, they sit a secondary public external examination at 18. At what point would a representative of the government who had been involved in the SATs say that they

are going to increase educational standards? In my opinion, it is that they are going to increase enormously stress on the pupils.

Now we are getting an added pressure with Key Stage 3 testing, with harassment of getting the added pressure of Key Stage 2 testing, this is just something totally new for them. People felt under pressure to get good results which has increased now by the publishing of league tables.

League tables were generally disliked by teachers, even when they cast their own school in a favourable light. It was suggested that they had an adverse effect upon important areas of the curriculum that did not feature in the tables:

> . . . you'll be told for instance that there should be personal and social education in the curriculum, but I know of some teachers now who are thinking 'well, that actually doesn't appear in the league tables'. If they do more science or they do more maths, that actually appears in the league tables, and I think a lot of things that are over and above the basic curriculum are now being looked at as, you know, 'Do we include this?'
>
> (Teacher interview, 1995)

They were also seen as running counter to traditional values and as damaging to collegial approaches:

> I do not agree with these league tables at all. I do not agree with the publishing of school results, because that just sets up competition . . . when we should be supporting and encouraging each other and helping each other along. It's dividing the profession right down the middle.
>
> (Teacher interview, 1996)

Assessment and league tables were not, however, the only forms of accountability affecting teachers, and many complained of the multiplicity of forms and lines of accountability that had emerged in the wake of the 1988 Education Reform Act:

> . . . people's performance can be a lot more easily evaluated, either internally or by Ofsted.
>
> (Teacher interview, 1996)

> As a professional teacher and head of department, it's my accountability to others for the National Curriculum. I'm accountable to my head to make sure that I'm delivering it, I'm accountable to parents to make sure that I'm delivering and to give them assessments at the relevant points and to prepare pupils for the exams, and I'm accountable, in some respects, to the people in my department in that, as head of department, it's my responsibility that we're on track and that we're

doing the right things, and to guide them in the right direction, because I'm partly paid for my experience.

(Teacher interview, 1995)

There was a considerable degree of cynicism about claims that the multiple initiatives to increase teachers' accountability were about raising standards: rather they were seen as a means of reasserting central control over the profession:

I feel that the government has gone out and cast its net into every other education system that exists and bitten here and picked what it felt was going to be politically adept for them in terms of accountability. Not what was going to be best for the pupils. Not what was going to be best for raising standards in the country, but what was going to be politically adept and what would create a stranglehold over the teaching profession in terms of accountability.

(Teacher interview, 1996)

Many resented the fact that the accountability applied only to teachers, and not to the government or to any of the bodies that it had created to oversee the work of teachers, as shown by these comments from 1996:

. . . particularly in terms of the fact that you've got those externally created bodies, by the government, of accountability in the forms of SATs and Ofsted, the way in which what we teach, how we teach it and to whom is being centrally dictated, and we are being called upon to be centrally accountable too . . . we've got an awful lot of quangos that have been created [but] are not held to the same degree of accountability that the schools are, and I think that creates frustration.

They're looking all the time at accountability from schools, from teachers, from governors, from headteachers, but they're actually not putting in accountability within the changes that they've created themselves . . . you've got to evaluate, plan, project and evaluate, and it doesn't seem to be happening centrally . . . I think they are changing things to increase central control.

Whilst some form of accountability in teaching was seen as important ('I do think you need standards in any profession, and you need to be answerable to whoever', was the comment of one interviewee in 1995), there was a strong belief that teachers already took their responsibilities seriously and that the new pressures were quite unnecessary:

. . . in a lot of teachers' cases, where they are highly critical of their own performance anyway . . . pressure that's being placed on them was unnecessary.

(Teacher interview, 1996)

Not only was the pressure viewed as unnecessary, it was also seen as excessive:

> SATs, the publication of results, a tight inspectorate and the market are all working on us, the pressures are getting inexorably worse.
>
> (Teacher interview, 1997)

> In the last few years the pressures have increased, almost beyond endurance . . . with this supposed accountability, everything has to be reported, documented and laid out in acceptable form. The paperwork gets in the way of teaching.
>
> (Teacher interview, 1995)

Comments from a teacher survey in 1992–93 highlighted the extensive amount of paperwork that now had to be completed:

> More and more classroom teaching time is spent filling in paperwork, providing information which is often duplicated on even more forms. Surely there should be a limit.

> The National Curriculum is obsessed with assessment, record-keeping and accountability. It is prescriptive without being supportive.

> More and more is being recorded and assessed about less and less contact time.

Most felt that, far from helping to raise standards, this actually detracted from classroom teaching:

> I find the requirements of National Curriculum assessment a pain in the neck. I love teaching but absolutely hate unnecessary paper exercises! Most of my colleagues also feel the same way. Let teachers teach, for God's sake!

> There has been a proliferation of paperwork which makes no real contribution whatsoever to good teaching.

> More and more of my time is taken up with record-keeping and assessment and less and less time with actual teaching. I feel hemmed in by criteria laid down by the National Curriculum. It's like teaching in a box.

A maths teacher interviewed in 1995 echoed the views of Hoyle and John (1995) on the limits of accountability in terms of improving education and the importance of professional responsibility:

> . . . if you're going to maintain your standards, it has to be you that does it. If you're going to do your best for the kids, it's got to be you that ensures you do that.

She went on to describe how the earlier versions of the National Curriculum had impinged upon that sense of professional responsibility and how the element of compunction had been extremely counter-productive in terms of motivation:

> . . . what I objected to previously was having that sort of professionalism cut away because it was all decided for you, it was all carrot and stick, it wasn't self-motivation. It wasn't you doing it because you knew it was right, because you're well versed in your subject and in your profession. It was you doing it because there was somebody stood behind you with a big stick making you do it, and I personally found that to be very demotivating.

Given the perceived impossibility of perpetually inspecting teachers' classroom practices, she felt that the loss of a sense of professional responsibility could have serious consequences for teachers' commitment and, therefore, for the quality of education:

> . . . the only person who can monitor you is you. And without an aspect of professionalism then I suppose . . . it could just revolve around being an easy life.

This idea of the limits of external surveillance was echoed by a technology teacher also interviewed in 1995:

> . . . you've got the guidelines. You know what you're supposed to be doing and people would assume that you're doing it. Because somebody doesn't come and actually check on what I'm doing.

Of all the new accountability measures put in place in recent years, however, it is the imposition of a particular form of teacher surveillance, namely the four-yearly Ofsted inspections of schools, that appears to have generated the greatest degree of disquiet, fear and anguish amongst teachers. One very experienced geography teacher and head of department who was interviewed in 1995 vividly described his own sense of anxiety over the recent changes:

> I feel that perhaps now there always seems to be somebody, somewhere over my shoulder, looking over my shoulder. It's a long time now but thinking back prior to National Curriculum, you did your own thing . . . with the best of intentions, you wanted the pupils to move forward academically, geographical knowledge and so on, but now you've got a ladder to climb. And it's almost like gladiators climbing the wall, and you feel there's somebody behind you and if you don't make the right steps then they'll be on you.

Although there were no immediate plans for an Ofsted inspection of his school, he concluded that this was the source of his apprehension:

It's not the school. It's not the headteacher . . . I suppose the Ofsted inspector is the one that, you know, you're wondering all the time, are you up to the standard that they're setting. Not really sure of what that standard is. So that's the concern, that's the worry. About whether I'm teaching the subject right, whether the subject's being delivered right in the school.

The geography department in this school included three other highly experienced teachers, two of whom were also members of the SMT. Examination results were good, and the head of department was very confident about the abilities and performance of his staff. In spite of the evidence of good practice, however, the prospect of being judged by an outsider and compared to other schools filled him with uncertainty and alarm:

I think the department as a whole is doing all they can do . . . I know every one of my three people in the department is teaching well. I don't know how I know they're teaching well, but I know that there's order in the classroom. I know that the scheme of work is being covered. We have regular assessments and I know that the marks they're coming up with, that the kids are coming up with, are appropriate to the whole range of marks we're getting in the school and within the sets that those teachers are teaching. But that's our assessment of our own teaching. It's the external view of it. Perhaps it's because I don't know what's going on in other schools and how they're doing it.

There was a strong fear that Ofsted inspectors would apply a different standard, which was exacerbated by the uncertainty of what that standard might be:

So we are comfortable in our position, but when the outsider comes up and looks, then you're always worried that they will, because of their different standards, that they will think that you're not . . . So it's this uncertainty of what they are expecting to see in the lesson. How they would judge what you are doing . . . I'm sure they must have some hard and fast criteria for saying what 'satisfactory' is, but I don't know what it is.

This uncertainty was exacerbating an existing sense of personal insecurity about teaching ability:

I suppose I'm always doubting my ability as a teacher, I've been teaching twenty-odd years now and yet I still have doubts, am I doing things right? And I suspect that if I had an inspector inspecting me, I'd probably come out as 'satisfactory', this sort of wide but safe middle ground. Because I don't think I'm particularly dynamic, but then again I don't think I'm particularly duff. So I have this vague idea that I'm an all right teacher, a middle-of-the-road teacher.

It was not the thought of having his teaching observed that caused this teacher so much anxiety, but rather the way in which the Ofsted system of inspection had been set up and the messages which it conveyed. Certainly he would in principle have welcomed classroom observation by another teacher as a formative aid since

> . . . that teacher can feed back in a non-threatening way their views of it, whereas I think there always is this idea of the *threat* of the Ofsted inspector.

Similarly, he had no qualms about observation by an LEA adviser since the feedback, like that of HMI in earlier times, would have been primarily constructive and supportive. The prospect of an Ofsted inspection, with its emphasis upon punishment and blame, filled him with profound concern and anxiety:

> . . . it might be fear. It's fear of people having a different view of the job I'm doing than my view of the job I'm doing, and I think I'm doing a decent job and I think my department's doing a decent job. And the old adviser, you could talk to him on a man-to-man basis, and I know that the old adviser wouldn't have ripped me to pieces. He wouldn't have complained about what I'm doing because I knew I was doing it well. But I've got the fear that the inspectors are coming in with a different set of rules and different standards, and I've got this doubt that maybe I'm not 'satisfactory' as I thought I was. So . . . the carpet is slipping under the feet a bit and I don't know whether it's going to go flying away and I'll end up flat on my back.

Whilst this particular case has been quoted at length, many of the comments made have been echoed by other teachers. Certainly the prospect of a forthcoming Ofsted inspection was frightening many teachers, who were consequently devoting large amounts of energy to preparing for it:

> . . . schemes of work can be dictated by the schemes of assessment and by homework policies, discipline policies, all these things are becoming, even in the last 18 months, much more written down, partly because of fear. And I mean fear of inspection next October. I think there is fear, yes. So we have to be seen to have all the right bits of paper.
>
> (Teacher interview, 1996)

At the same time the fear and stress created by Ofsted was seen as highly damaging both to teacher morale and to levels of professional confidence, with consequently negative effects upon teaching:

> I see Ofsted as an unnecessary evil, because they have created so much harm and damage . . . This is an intimidating approach and, from reports

of my other colleagues in — [LEA] there can be tears on a regular basis when they're around, which is no good because you've got a demoralized workforce to begin with, and if it's further eroded, then it's not going to give confidence and it comes back on to the children eventually.

(Teacher interview, 1996)

The workload associated with an Ofsted inspection, both in terms of preparing for it and drawing up the necessary action plan afterwards, was extremely high, as indicated by these comments from teacher interviews in 1995:

Prior to inspection . . . 12 months before we were intensively looking at what we were doing. Are we covering all the strands, you know, do we meet all the things that would be looked for in quality teaching? . . . there's been a lot of staff effort devoted to writing an action plan as a result of the inspection which we had in September.

. . . we had our Ofsted in here last March, so we've obviously spent a long, long time trying to get our schemes of work as we would want them, and it's not easy.

A technology teacher interviewed at the same time was anxious for his department to have a good report and foresaw that a considerable amount of his time would need to be devoted to preparing for the inspection:

I know I've got to satisfy certain criteria. I know the major part of my task over the next 12 months is to have a lot of pieces of paper which have got to tie together in practice.

Other teachers were finding that the additional tasks meant that they were overstretched and underperforming and/or that their teaching was suffering as a result:

Well, there are areas that I'm doing because we have to do it because Ofsted's coming, but I know I'm doing them badly because I've not got the time to do them properly.

(Teacher interview, 1996)

The Ofsted inspection in April was totally time-consuming and your teaching suffers because of it.

(Teacher interview, 1997)

For those who had already been through the experience of inspection, there were repeated reports of teacher stress and illness caused by its pressures and uncertainties, which again were not seen as making any positive contribution to enhanced teaching:

Staff were off school after the Ofsted inspection who've never been off before. The pressure was not so much when Ofsted were in school, but from putting everything together and wondering what the result would be after all that work. Afterwards, people were off ill.

(Teacher interview, 1995)

. . . it was almost taken as routine that everyone gets wound up when the inspection's on and before that. I mean we started a year before really with meetings about preparing for inspection and so on, and that just builds up the whole thing, and people were very stressed, some more than others. And I think it's a great shame that we're constantly driven by that, not by necessarily how we can improve things and how we can make things better, because that is out of our hands really. There are certain things that we can do to make things better which we can no longer do or are just not feasible given all the constraints.

(Teacher interview, 1996)

Certainly the feedback received after the inspection was not seen as particularly helpful. Some claimed that it failed to tell them anything that they didn't already know, whilst others criticized it for its lack of content or for its failure to match criticism with advice on improvement:

I found that the amount of feedback from the inspection service was a complete and utter joke. A chap sat in the back of my room for practically two days, he had nothing to say to me, you know, nothing really happened. He spoke to [my head of department] afterwards, everything was quite happy. We ended up with a report that's about three lines long, and where does that leave us?

(Teacher interview, 1996)

. . . they tell you what's right, they tell you what's wrong but they don't give you any advice as to how you might be able to do various things . . . the build-up to it was actually horrendous and I think a lot of it was a waste of time because it wasn't worth it.

(Teacher interview, 1995)

Even the very occasional reports of positive reactions to inspection were hedged by doubts about its developmental value and particularly about the value for money that it represented:

And the message that's come from lots of schools that have been [through an Ofsted inspection] . . . is yes, it wasn't such a bad experience after all and in many cases the teachers have felt quite lifted by it because they weren't doing as badly as they feared they were. So that was encouraging but, beyond that, the amount of developmental value it had was very, very limited. And you know the view is, well, if you give us the £25,000 or whatever it costs, we can do a lot more with that.

(Senior teacher interview, 1995)

The same senior teacher argued that any potential developmental value had been obliterated by Ofsted's more recent emphasis upon 'rooting out bad teachers'. Another teacher, interviewed in 1996, believed that being made to jump through the hoops of an Ofsted inspection actually diminished teachers' sense of professionalism and their ability to use their own professional judgement:

> You see when you're filling in a piece of paper, which you don't want to fill in because you don't really think it helps anything at all, and it takes a lot of time and it takes away a person's ability to make decisions for themselves. I feel, on the one hand, teachers are very much encouraged to go out and teach on their own to a class, make decisions, think on their feet, and then the next minute it's, 'you have to conform to all these new rules and regulations and pieces of paper', and I think there's a bit of a paradox there.

Similarly, it was suggested that the emphasis upon documentation and procedures could well lead to deprofessionalization if teachers were not directly involved in the decision-making processes:

> I think there's a danger with a lot of the documentation, the procedures, that we . . . could actually reduce people to the level of the mechanic. The difference, I think, at the moment is that we actually involve people in working out what those procedures are going to be and what the policies are going to be. If we ever stop doing that, then I think we do reduce people to the status of mechanic.
>
> (Teacher interview, 1995)

Finally, disquiet and doubts about the beneficial or developmental effects of Ofsted inspections came not only from teachers but also from politicians from both the main parties, as shown by these interview comments from 1996:

> Ofsted have not got it right . . . it's the damage that's being done to motivated teachers, to good teachers who feel threatened by a process which they feel doesn't, in some cases, address [their] very real problems.
>
> (Senior Conservative MP and educationalist)

> . . . the Ofsted people are trained in this ridiculous training to tick boxes and to keep blank, impassive faces.
>
> (Former Labour MP and educationalist)

Conclusions

The evidence confirms that the accountability measures introduced into education in recent years are indeed having a very significant impact upon teachers' work. On the one hand, the many additional tasks created by the need constantly to record, document and report to both internal and external audiences are certainly contributing to the intensification of teachers' working lives, a finding also noted in relation to primary schools by Woods *et al.* (1997). On the other hand, there is a considerable amount of evidence that the insistence upon formal accountability, coupled with the constant critique of teachers as being untrustworthy and 'failing', is creating a notably adverse effect upon the morale, motivation and confidence of many teachers.

Perhaps the most damaging forms of accountability for teachers are the publication of league tables of schools' assessment results and the Ofsted system of inspection. It is ironic that both of these measures have been introduced in the name of improving educational provision. Thus it has been claimed that, in line with the beliefs of the 'new work order', the competition promoted by league tables will spur teachers and schools on to greater effort and therefore to greater achievement. Similarly, the motto of Ofsted is 'Improvement through Inspection', despite the fact that the main emphasis appears to be upon making judgements of individual teachers and schools and 'rooting out' those who are deemed to be failing – a somewhat negative view of 'improvement'.

Clearly a system of regular school inspection could, in principle, provide a useful prompt to internal review and be a helpful source of external feedback. Moreover, as Woods *et al.* (1997: 120) remind us: 'Inspections can hold different meanings for different teachers, and can have variable and contradictory effects'. Indeed, they cite the case of a primary headteacher who found that, despite the disruption and increased workload, a positive Ofsted report had increased her confidence and enhanced her professionalism. However, this may be an exceptional case: certainly no such positive outcomes were reported by any of the teachers interviewed in any of the Lancaster studies. Instead, the process was seen by the vast majority as inordinately time-consuming, threatening and unhelpful, with many teachers reporting varying degrees of stress and illness as a result of the experience.

The introduction of league tables is also having a marked effect upon schools, most particularly in terms of narrowing the focus of teachers' work. As shown in Chapter 5, many teachers are becoming increasingly concerned with covering the prescribed content and 'teaching to the test'. Accordingly, they are tending to use more traditional and didactic approaches in the classroom. At the same time the increased competition and the pressures to achieve particular examination grades are inhibiting collegiality and reducing contacts between schools. Within some schools efforts are increasingly directed towards those parts of the curriculum, and to those aspects of individual subjects, that are formally assessed and reported on, often to the detriment of wider learning and broader areas of experience. Similarly, students whose predicted examination grades are near the borderline of the critical grade C pass may be given more attention than others in an effort to boost the school's reported results. For those committed to a broad view of education and to equal opportunities for all students, it is difficult to view this narrowing of focus as an improvement.

Finally, the questions of professional confidence and of professional responsibility are relevant since, for many teachers, the recent increases in accountability measures appear to be having a negative effect upon both of them. This issue touches upon the fundamental nature of teachers' work and the extent to which, on the one hand, it can be codified, routinized, prescribed and measured or, on the other hand, it demands the open-ended exercise of judgement upon non-routine problems. In the former case, the imposition of bureaucratized accountability procedures may be appropriate, whilst in the latter it is not, since there needs to be a strong element of discretion and trust. Developments in recent years could be seen as an attempt to impose a view of teaching as a routinized and measurable activity: it remains to be seen in the long term how far teachers will accept this view and therefore lower their professional sights.

nine

CHANGES IN SCHOOL ORGANIZATION AND MANAGEMENT

The way in which schools are organized and managed is an important factor not only in establishing the framework and context within which teachers work but also in defining the scope or limits of their professional autonomy. Along with the recent changes in curriculum, in workloads and in formal accountability mechanisms, there have also been significant alterations to the internal organization of schools that have had profound consequences for those working within them. The transformations that have been effected have not occurred spontaneously, but rather have been driven by a combination of policy initiatives, legislation and training programmes that have originated at the centre and that appear to be largely in accord with the business management emphasis both of the 'new managerialism' and of the 'new work order'. These 'reforms' have tended to reinforce the developing ideological trend towards a commodification of education, an industrial model of organization and management and a repositioning of both teachers and managers within the newly created 'business units' (Beresford 1995).

In many ways the turning point – or at least the symbolic justification – for these changes was the industrial unrest of the mid-1980s and, in particular, the bitter and protracted teachers' strike of 1985. Indeed, Lawn (1996: 89–90) has described this as 'without a doubt a watershed in the political and work relations of education' in which 'direct intervention and control of teaching has replaced the old idea of consensus in policy making and management'. In contrast to the expansionary post-war years, when the need to recruit more teachers had enhanced not only their career prospects but also their status and autonomy, the subsequent economic and demographic downturn restricted opportunities for mobility and promotion and moved the balance of control back towards the employers. As teachers' salaries declined in real terms, a series of unsatisfactory pay offers and dissatisfaction with salary and career structures provoked industrial action by teachers in the form of a 'withdrawal of goodwill' and a series of one-day and three-day strikes in different geographical areas. The withdrawal of goodwill meant a cessation of voluntary involvement in non-teaching activities connected with school administration, organization and management as well as a refusal to provide routine teaching cover for absent colleagues or to supervise school lunches. It is noteworthy that, in many cases, these actions caused some divisions and bitterness between teachers and school managers, as the latter were put under pressure to undertake these duties themselves in order to keep their schools open.

Whilst the guerrilla tactics adopted by the teachers were successful in causing a considerable degree of disruption to the service, a lack of unity amongst the different teacher unions finally led to the acceptance of a deal that was not particularly generous and, importantly, that included an agreement to enter into discussions on linking pay with terms and conditions of service. Before the agreement could be fully implemented, however, the new Education Secretary, Kenneth Baker, adopted a more autocratic line and announced his intention of taking powers to dictate unilaterally both salary levels and conditions of service. The subsequent Teachers' Pay and Conditions Act of 1987 abolished teachers' negotiating rights and imposed a new contract specifying minimum working hours and duties. This contract extended the working year by five days, which were to be allocated to school-based training. At the same time a new pay structure was introduced based upon a single grade for classroom teachers with a number of incentive allowances to be allocated by school managers for additional responsibilities.

According to Walsh (1987: 148), the new employment situation increased managerial control of teachers' work and posed a significant threat to their independence: 'The changed labour market conditions that confront teachers have allowed the employers to assert a form of bureaucratic contractual control that fits ill with the notion of professional autonomy'. This contractual control has led to a broadening of the specification of teachers' work beyond traditional pedagogical responsibilities to embrace additional administrative and, in some cases, managerial duties (Busher and Saran 1990). These new tasks include various forms of record-keeping and the provision of diverse kinds of information as well as participation in staff meetings, assemblies and parents' evenings. There is also an explicit duty to manage other staff and to co-operate and participate in school management and administration as required by headteachers. All of these new responsibilities come in addition to normal teaching loads and, as seen in Chapter 7, have contributed to an intensification of working life and, for some teachers, to a decline in professional confidence.

Whilst the changes point towards a potential disempowerment of class-room teachers, a number of other measures were introduced which appeared to increase the authority of school managers. For example, the 1986 Education Act opened the way for the appraisal of teachers' performance through classroom observation by headteachers or other senior managers, whilst both this Act and the 1988 Education Reform Act greatly increased the powers of school governors, who were given employer rights over the appointment, promotion, disciplining and dismissal of staff in their schools. In particular, the institution of LMS through the 1988 Act and subsequent legislation (and the further option of gaining even greater independence through becoming grant-maintained) moved most or all of the budget and local decision-making powers away from the LEA and to the school. Formally these new powers were vested in the governing body, although in many cases it was the head-teacher who retained the greatest influence in this arena.

The introduction of LMS presented headteachers with a range of new tasks, from budget management through strategic planning to negotiating with school governors, many of which diverted them from traditional concerns with curriculum and educational leadership (Evetts 1994b). At the same time an increasing proportion of in-service teacher education was devoted to particular forms of management training which, along with a plethora of popular educational management guides, promoted a technical-rational and systems-based approach to school management which was dominated by commercial, as opposed to educational or social, considerations (Gewirtz *et al.* 1995). Traditionally masculine values such as efficiency, objectivity and instrumentality are consistently encouraged in the 'new educational management order', where the preferred role of the headteacher is that of hierarchical leader, charged with developing a strong corporate culture and applying business solutions to educational problems whilst ensuring the compliance of school staff. The centrally advocated processes of school development planning tend to encourage systems-based approaches and, despite the appearance of collegiality and teacher involvement, to reinforce the decision-making authority of the headteacher (Grundy and Bonser 1997). School development planning also generates texts which provide codified accounts of teachers' work practices, thereby facilitating surveillance and potentially devaluing and deskilling the people involved (Giddens 1991). Finally, it forces both teachers and managers to link educational planning directly with financial and resource management in a context of diminishing budgets.

Overall, as shown in Chapter 3, there is a considerable amount of evidence that recent educational reforms have reinforced the authority and leadership role of headteachers at the expense of classroom teachers, leading to a centralization of power in schools. The increasing gap between managers and managed is exacerbated by potential value conflicts. Ball (1994: 58) identifies the development of a division of values and purpose, of professional culture if you like, between managers, oriented to the budget, the market, entrepreneurial activities and the drive for efficiency, and teachers, oriented to the National Curriculum, teaching and learning, student needs and the drive for effectiveness.

School managers are not, however, necessarily wedded to the new market values nor are they omnipotent. Indeed, previous research has suggested that, whilst headteachers have seen some of their powers increased, others have been eroded (Fergusson 1994). Certainly funding levels are set externally and school managers are held accountable for achieving educational targets which are increasingly determined centrally. These factors have led to suggestions that LMS has resulted in a devolution not of power, but rather of responsibility for managing an underfunded education system and of blame for the financial cutbacks (Angus 1994; Hartley 1994).

As indicated above, these changes have profound implications for the work of both school teachers and school managers and also for the working relationships between them. Evidence from an interview with a senior teacher in 1994 highlighted the gap that was developing between school managers and classroom teachers:

> I think there's also a distinction beginning to emerge within teaching that perhaps people who occupy more senior posts in teaching can actually see themselves as professionals, whereas people who are actually doing the job see themselves very much as being driven by what's required of them, you know the whole thing is specified for them.

He argued that this sense of professionalism did not have its basis in educational expertise but related instead to an involvement in new management practices:

> The role of senior teaching staff is to manage but I think, interestingly, the sort of professionalism that is coming in to the top end of the teaching profession now is that of manager more than educationalist.

Increasingly, school managers were being given experiences and training in generic management skills which were not generally available to classroom teachers, and this he saw as increasing the separation between the two groups:

> . . . a fantastic amount of investment has gone into the development of the senior team, an increasing amount, and what they're getting is management input, not specifically educational management theory and practice, so they're changing. I'm not saying they're in isolation, they can't be in isolation, but they are becoming more separate, I think, from what was the case in the past.

Even heads of department, who might traditionally have been expected to bridge any gap between senior managers and maingrade teachers, were being excluded:

> . . . at the same time the middle managers are not being given the same opportunities . . . unless the middle managers can begin to absorb some of the culture, the change, then you are going to become increasingly more isolated.

These suggested differences between teachers and senior managers in terms of training and development opportunities were confirmed by responses to a teacher survey conducted across three LEAs in 1992–93. In this survey senior managers were more than twice as likely as main-grade teachers to agree that they had received some form of support from the LEA over the previous two to three years (81.3 compared to 40.4 per cent) or that the system of professional support and development had improved over that period (50.6 compared to 23.2 per cent). At the same time over 62 per cent of teachers believed that they rarely had the opportunity for personal professional development, compared to fewer than 38 per cent of senior managers.

Whether or not it was attributable to differential access to development opportunities, many teachers certainly identified an increasing cultural gap between themselves and senior managers, as shown by these comments from interviews in 1995:

> There is a bit of a divide about professionalism with the 'new managers'. This brings in a two-tier professional system. Taking on other additional 'professional' activities is viewed by one side as the important thing. There is a divide creeping in between professional and professional.

> Senior management teams almost have 'a monopoly on wisdom' because they talk about problems and solutions. This is a cultural matter.

> There have been clashes between the management team and the rest of the staff. There is an obsession about training . . . Managers are intoxicated with their new-found power.

Many teachers pointed to the way in which managers were increasingly distanced from teaching, creating a lack of understanding and a number of tensions between the priorities of the two groups:

> There's an inevitable gap between teachers and senior managers, they do so little teaching compared to admin that they lose contact with what's happening.
>
> (Teacher interview, 1994)

There is definitely a different form of management now, and there is frustration on the 'shop floor'. The main thrust of my job is teaching, the main thrust of senior management's job is not teaching. Goals are interlaced, but in many ways disparate.

(Teacher interview, 1995)

For some, this divergence of goals was beginning to impinge upon classroom practice, as senior managers imposed new systems which reduced teachers' professional autonomy:

Senior management has a blinkered view as to the teacher's role. I would like much more freedom to develop maths as I would like, the school system imposes on me.

(Teacher interview, 1995)

Another maths teacher and head of department interviewed in the same year explained at some length how top-down imperatives to maximize school performance in the league tables of examination results was in direct conflict with his own deeply held philosophy of education:

I feel professional to a great extent, but not 100 per cent, and there's pressure for it to be less. The pressure comes from school management, especially the head, and the league table of exam results and that philosophy of approach. There's pressure on the department to change. Our first aim is for pupils to enjoy maths and for it to be accessible to them all, and also to maximize results for *all* pupils. But this emphasis on enjoyment and accessibility probably means we don't achieve as many top grades as we could with a different approach, cramming them . . . the department felt we had done well, but maths and English came out negative on an internal school value-added scheme. I can explain that away to my own satisfaction, without being complacent, but I've been asked to do something about it, to look at the implications for teaching, and that leaves me very uncomfortable.

Other teachers interviewed in 1995 also remarked upon the growing pressures from school managers to improve both their own performance and the measurable results:

We have a head who has high expectations – there is pressure to do more and more in the same time.

There's competition for places, so management are constantly on your back to get results. They're always on about attendance because attendance figures are published.

Despite teachers' perceptions, it was also clear that many school managers did not necessarily agree with what was happening. One deputy head-teacher, interviewed in 1995, claimed that because of the levels of accountability, outcomes have become more important than I would like them to be.

Two headteachers, interviewed in 1992 and 1993, described how they saw their role as protecting their staff from the worst consequences of the fast-changing reforms:

There's a danger that everything becomes a knee-jerk reaction. One of my biggest jobs is to maintain the sanity of my staff and the stability of the curriculum, to see a way through.

My job is to control as best I can the rate of change, to ensure that changes are manageable, to avoid 'innovation overload'. I can't control the shifting goalposts – I need to assess which target is the most important to hit, I need to prioritize and focus on the basis of the best information available.

However, another senior manager, interviewed in 1994, was somewhat less optimistic about his ability to manage the changes and recognized the conflict between educational and managerial values which he faced because of the pressures to ensure adequate funding for the school:

Two or three years ago I began to question what I was doing. I began to think in terms of pound signs instead of kids. I was the link person with the primary schools in the area. I made sure that I gave a positive impression to them so they would come here and earn £2000 for the school next year. The interest in the kids was secondary. In that way I very much questioned the values I am beginning to take on. I see the kids in terms of jobs for staff, of keeping the school open. It gets to the point where you think twice about excluding a child. Now that's ridiculous – that's getting away from down-to-earth teaching principles.

A senior manager of a special school, interviewed in 1996, criticized the proliferation of top-heavy management structures which he believed had been introduced in response to the perceived demands of the national inspection system:

What I think Ofsted has done, it's certainly created an enormous amount of management structure that may not necessarily be needed, there's a distinct line management approach that's appeared, there is a definite pattern occurring, not just in this school, right across the board.

He also believed that the consequent extension of management tasks had created unrealistic workloads for managers and deeply resented the prospect of his performance being judged in these new areas of activity:

. . . the actual workload at certain levels within the management structure has zoomed off the scales. And of course not only has it zoomed off the scales, but these people are going to be held externally accountable for their performance within that field.

Another deputy head, interviewed in 1995, also attributed an increase in managerial responsibilities to the effects of national inspection:

> . . . since Ofsted, according to our action plan, we're trying to get more monitoring at senior management level and we now have a senior manager sitting in once a week at department meetings actually looking at schemes of work.

At the same time a headteacher, interviewed in 1997, lamented the fact that her energies were diverted away from teaching and into site management tasks:

> I'd like to appoint a non-teaching manager to deal with things like buildings, and I'd prefer to work on curriculum issues, but I was advised not to.

However, the greatest number of complaints from senior managers focused on the inadequacy of the budgets that they were expected to manage:

> Now heads are just concerned about balancing the books, I don't see how schools can carry things forward on a tiny amount of money.
>
> (Headteacher interview, 1997)

> We're always doing things on the cheap, and when things go wrong it's us that carry the can, not the government, despite the underfunding.
>
> (Senior teacher interview, 1997)

Another senior manager who was in principle very much in favour of LMS, which he saw as 'opening up a whole new area of professionalism for teachers', was nonetheless unhappy with the levels of funding:

> . . . in my more cynical moments I feel that the whole exercise really is about reducing costs.
>
> (Senior teacher interview, 1995)

The low levels of funding created pressures not only for teachers but also for managers, who were working increasingly harder and taking on more tasks:

> One of the features of the senior management team is that, on average, we leave at half past six at night. The head is frequently here until nine o'clock at night and I mean that's again a significant change in the working pattern . . . I'm a senior teacher and the person I replaced last year was a deputy head. A few years ago this school had a head, two deputies

and three senior teachers. We now have in our senior management team the head, a deputy, two senior teachers and the head of sixth form.

(Senior teacher interview, 1994)

Time needs money and at the moment there are too few people wearing too many hats. When I became head, my deputy post was not filled . . . I extended the senior management team, but they all have massive commitments . . . I'd like to give people a single brief.

(Headteacher interview, 1997)

A special school manager interviewed in 1996 described the pressures of having to take responsibility for inadequate funding. His school was going through a difficult period of transition and he contrasted the current situation with what would have happened before LMS, when the LEA might have helped by providing additional levels of supply cover:

Now, because of local management of schools, that is not the case. The case is, you've got your allocated budget and you deal with it as a managerial issue . . . you've people coming to you saying this needs doing, that needs doing, and you've got to be honest and say 'Yes, it does need doing', but in the back of your mind you know there isn't money to do it. And I find that highly stressful.

One response to low budget levels was to seek additional resources from external bodies or to bid for inclusion in any of the current funded initiatives for schools. For some of those who had been successful in that respect, there was a degree of enthusiasm for the new enterprise culture:

We've learnt that it pays to be an innovative establishment. By a process of continuous improvement and development, we've been able to move forward quite rapidly and we've become a technology school and a technology college. This came from the enthusiasm and willingness of staff to embrace change and to innovate.

(Senior teacher interview, 1997)

This positive attitude was, however, exceptional. Much more frequent were the complaints of having to spend inordinate amounts of time writing bids and chasing funding and trying to fill gaps on an *ad hoc* basis. There were also complaints about the need to meet changing, external criteria:

How do you plan around all the initiatives? For example, the [Single Regeneration Budget] gives you half a teacher, but that goes after three years. They need to fund us properly. Last week I was talking to someone about lottery bids for the arts! Just give us the money and don't make us jump through all of these hoops, with changing criteria for all of the bids.

(Headteacher interview, 1997)

. . . it's very time-consuming to get the money and to show that you meet *their* criteria.

(Senior teacher interview, 1997)

Comments from other managers echoed this view that schools were expected to subordinate their own aims to the agendas of outside bodies, such as Training and Enterprise Councils (TECs), in order to secure relatively small amounts of funding.

More control is exerted by the TEC as to how the money is spent. They're looking for targets to be met, and the targets are the TEC's, not the school's, and there's little negotiation here.

(Senior teacher interview, 1997)

The TECs are not a gravy train. They have an agenda, they're a top-down not a bottom-up group, they only give out money if it fits their priorities.

(Headteacher interview, 1997)

There were also bitter complaints both about the fact that funding had to be won rather than being freely allocated and about the levels and costs of accountability required, as indicated by these comments from senior managers interviewed in 1996:

You're made to feel you have to qualify for things, rather than having the money delegated and being trusted to use it.

I think there's a huge sense of frustration and irritation with the way the government works . . . what they're effectively doing is drawing money off which could come directly through educational budgets to schools into a variety of projects which then spawn a bureaucracy which then sucks resources away.

Similarly, teachers resented the amount of paperwork that accompanied many of the new projects currently operating in schools and even declined to become involved because of this:

Any new initiative that involves a new way of working often demands that we provide screeds and screeds of paper. I'm a keen teacher but don't want to write it all down. That would spoil my teaching and become an end in itself.

(Teacher interview, 1997)

Others, however, were under pressure to bid for inclusion, even when the projects ran counter to their own perceptions of educational need:

Teachers have taken up an initiative not because they believe in it but because there is money in it. LMS was attractive but, when one really analyses it, it is not.

(Teacher interview, 1995)

There was a high degree of agreement amongst both teachers and managers that the low levels of resourcing were having a number of adverse effects upon the provision of education and upon the quality of the service offered. In the first place, the lack of funding to appoint more teachers meant that class sizes had risen, that teachers were working harder and that the range of educational experiences and opportunities offered to students was being narrowed:

> We now have larger classes too, because of LMS, we can't afford to replace or have more teachers.
>
> (Teacher interview, 1994)

> We're working harder because of LMS and the financial constraints.
>
> (Teacher interview, 1994)

> We're going backwards . . . the National Curriculum and across-the-board budget cuts have tended to wipe out all that TVEI did, so that we can't offer the range of courses, employ the range of staff or offer the range of teaching and learning techniques.
>
> (Deputy headteacher interview, 1997)

Some reported that their schools were making more frequent use of inexperienced teachers in order to save costs. In this example, taken from a teacher interview in 1995, curriculum staffing needs appeared to have been subordinated to strengthening the SMT:

> . . . we were told to appoint somebody newly qualified because they were cheap and yet a few weeks later we were told that three teachers had been promoted to the rank of assistant deputy head, which I find despicable.

Others complained of a growing tendency to appoint or deploy teachers who were not subject specialists:

> I had to accept a person who had been trained in PE, who could no longer teach PE because of a back problem, into my department, who is now supposedly a geography specialist and is teaching GCSE geography . . . and you've got to be responsible for what they produce . . . when we had the inspection we were criticized . . . they said they would prefer us to have a specialist teaching in history and geography.
>
> (Teacher interview, 1995)

As well as the potentially adverse effects upon the quality of classroom teaching, the growing use of non-specialists was also placing additional pressures upon heads of department, who were finding that they had to give advice, produce teaching materials or draw up schemes of work unilaterally rather than collaboratively. The following comments are taken from 1995 interviews with a head of technology and a senior teacher:

Well it puts a lot more pressure on you because you have to prepare the materials for that person to deliver because they don't have the basic knowledge of the subject.

. . . more and more people come into departments that are non-special-ists . . . I can think of another colleague who actually teaches in four departments. So when it comes to things like departmental meetings, she has to make a decision as to which one she's going to go to . . . so it may be that more of this is done by a sort of remote control thing, the head of department writes it.

Several complained of a lack of understanding on the part of the school's senior managers of the difficulties of staffing classes with non-specialists or of dealing with large class sizes in practical areas of the curriculum:

. . . there's a complete lack of understanding on behalf of the senior management team, that they don't realize that you can't go into certain areas and expect teachers to deliver that particular subject if they haven't been trained in that area.

(Teacher interview, 1995)

. . . we don't have anyone on the senior management team who has had experience of teaching in a practical lesson, it does have a knock-on effect because they themselves obviously are not aware of what the requirements are. Their own experience, as far as teaching children is concerned, is having children behind desks, they don't have any concept of what it's like to teach in an area where children have learned to move around freely, and we do get some conflict as far as that's concerned with regard to group sizes. They would expect you to teach with a stan-dard class size of twenty odd, which is very, very difficult.

(Teacher interview, 1995)

The increased pressures and the lack of additional resourcing were also seen as having a negative effect upon teachers' motivation to innovate, and instead there were suggestions of increased parochialism and a retreat to more traditional and less demanding practice:

It seemed that, as soon as TVEI funding stopped and LMS came in, everyone was looking after their own and asking 'What's in it for me?' . . . it reinforced the old insularity.

(Teacher interview, 1997)

. . . it became more difficult to say we'd carry on the various inno-vations, we didn't have the means to generate things. Bottom-up ideas are very beneficial, but you're dependent on money to resource good ideas. People continued to work collaboratively but there was not the same drive. They were asking for small amounts of money that the school couldn't afford, for tapes, materials and things like that. Those signals pretty quickly dried up the curriculum innovation.

> (Headteacher interview, 1997)

The same headteacher was extremely annoyed at being put into what he saw as the impossible position of raising adequate funds to support any form of curriculum development:

> We are a model Thatcherite school, high-achieving and efficient, but we are not able to generate a budget for innovation.

He also complained of the lack of opportunity for in-service teacher development: not only was access limited to courses funded by the centrally determined Grants for Educational Support and Training (GEST), but the costs of releasing teachers to attend such courses was prohibitive:

> GEST monies are limited for schools compared to the size of staffing and are subsidized by schools . . . every £1 from GEST funding costs us £2 in supply cover.

Several teachers also commented on the more limited opportunities for career advancement:

> Our profession is falling apart, there is now much less of a career structure. Promotion is not worth the remuneration.
>
> (Teacher interview, 1995)

> . . . whereas at one time there was a clear career progression, that structure has now been effectively destroyed by budgetary constraints.
>
> (Senior teacher interview, 1995)

A teacher on a temporary contract, also interviewed in 1995, was less concerned about career progression than career continuation, and pointed towards the increased insecurity experienced by beginning teachers:

> There are more short-term contracts, teachers are more expendable, and they know it, you're having to look over your shoulder. I need to look at what I'm doing.

For those whose position was more secure, there were concerns about the lack of reward for good classroom teaching and the growing emphasis in promotion procedures upon managerial and other experience outside of the classroom:

> I think you should be doing the day-to-day things. People go up the ladder by not doing the day-to-day things.
>
> (Teacher interview, 1995)

Another felt that the traditional system of rewarding seniority had been overtaken by other considerations:

> . . . there is something different about the hierarchy. At one time it was more age-related, there was a certain kind of 'dug-inness'. Senior management are younger now. At one time the expectation was that, if you did a reasonable job and stayed the course, you would eventually become management.
>
> (Teacher interview, 1995)

Changes at the top, as well as an increase in a systems-based approach to school management, were highlighted by several teachers:

> Headteachers have a different attitude to headship.
>
> (Teacher interview, 1995)

> Most schools have a clear management structure where decisions have to be followed through; it was *ad hoc* before. It's all down to the monitoring procedures and the appraisal procedures. It is all at a distance and mechanistic, not personalized.
>
> (Teacher interview, 1995)

> Generally in school there have been changes in procedure, mechanisms which guide action have forced this. The whole teaching profession has become more structured.
>
> (Teacher interview, 1994)

This more structured approach was usually accompanied by a marked increase in documentation:

> There's a trend towards more of the job being defined and written down, by the government downwards.
>
> (Teacher interview, 1995)

> There's pressure in school to have [pastoral work] more structured, with something on paper . . . it's part of the trend to have procedures written down.
>
> (Teacher interview, 1995)

Some teachers had learned to accommodate the new situation and had become adept at meeting its requirements:

> We did a lot of work on monitoring and evaluation that fitted with school development planning . . . it's now so deeply embedded that I can write performance indicators standing on my head!
>
> (Teacher interview, 1997)

Others actively resisted the trends towards documentation and prescription and made great efforts to work their way around the requirements and to create spaces so that they could continue to take the initiative in important areas of their work:

> . . . we had to try breaking through the jargon . . . getting it down to the bare bone, the minimum that we had to do to meet the requirements that would then allow us to get on with our job of teaching.
>
> (Teacher interview, 1994)

> It means, I think, being creative with what's presented to you and trying to find as much freedom within that as you can possibly muster.
>
> (Teacher interview, 1995)

Another group, however, simply looked back nostalgically to the days when classroom teaching had been the main consideration. The following comments are from teacher interviews in 1995:

> At one time you just came in, did registration and taught your subject. Now it's development planning on a three-year cycle, with a policy on everything. There's a lot more admin and policy-writing . . . the demands are greater, there are more meetings.

> . . . in the late sixties and early seventies, at the beginning of my career, I was younger and you had more freedom to do what you wanted, staffing ratios were different, there were fewer non-teaching jobs, smaller class sizes, everything was more flexible, people did things outside of school voluntarily, because it was not a chore and they were not over-tired. There were no year teachers, there was not that tier. They've created a lot of jobs and a lot of bureaucracy since then, which take people out of the classroom, and class sizes have gone sky-high.

Several teachers made spontaneous references to the teachers' action of the mid-1980s and, even after ten years, this evoked strong feelings amongst interviewees. On the one hand, some believed that it had been a significant factor in the perceived loss of public sympathy for teachers and in the consequent lessening of professional status. Others, however, believed that it was the government action in imposing new terms and conditions of service that had damaged teacher motivation and morale and that it was this that had had an adverse effect upon teachers' sense of professionalism. The specification of a working year of 1265 hours' directed time was particularly contentious in this respect, with many seeing this as an insult to the amount of effort formerly invested by teachers:

> It changed for us when the question of lunch-time and after-school supervision became an issue. We were treated as less than professionals after the teachers' action, that was a great sea change. There are now many who no longer give freely of their time. Attitudes have changed

towards the employer: 'I'll do what I have to do well, but not any more than that'. Very few people are here until seven o'clock now.

(Deputy headteacher interview, 1994)

The government has affected teachers' attitudes by trying to tie them down, but since the teachers' action, teachers are not willing to do things after school. They now ask 'Is that designated time?', it's destroyed a lot of good will.

(Teacher interview, 1994)

Some claimed that the very idea of being told what to do ran counter to their sense of professionalism, although it was no longer clear how far such direction originated from the centre and how far it was dictated by the head-teacher and SMT:

There's government imposition, then the LEA input and then the head's interpretation, so we don't know how much is government-imposed and how much is school-imposed.

(Teacher interview, 1995)

They used to blame the LEAs, but it's worse since LMS, which divided us into little separate schools. The LEAs were a buffer between us and the government, now it's in the hands of the head, and they become like little emperors . . . I feel [the relationship between staff and SMT] is all one way, we send information up to them but get no feedback, we're not told when pupils are excluded or why. The legislation is filtered through the head, and we get his version.

(Teacher interview, 1995)

Other teachers also noted a lack of meaningful communication between teachers and senior managers:

We're given time to discuss things like new buildings, but it's always a foregone conclusion – what you say doesn't count.

(Teacher interview, 1994)

Some schools are hierarchical and there is a big divide.

(Teacher interview, 1995)

This was seen as highly damaging to the collaborative spirit that had pre-vailed formerly:

. . . what is disappearing, I think, is an overall commitment to the insti-tution . . . that is the aspect that is being ground away and I think that's being ground away by a hierarchical management structure.

(Teacher interview, 1995)

In particular, there was an enormous amount of resentment at being held responsible for particular outcomes when the power to manage the situation was withheld. The necessity to go through the motions of consultation only made matters worse:

> . . . we are held accountable in that respect but we are not given the power to make decisions, we are impotent as far as that's concerned. It's something that we have to push upstairs and the decision is made for us, and quite often it's the wrong decision that's made on our behalf . . . we get asked and we're criticized if we don't comment but at the end of the day we have no say in the matter whatsoever, it's as blunt as that.
>
> (Teacher interview, 1995)

There were still some, however, who continued to invest fully in their institution despite the setbacks and despite the deteriorating conditions. This teacher, interviewed in 1995, described the paradoxes of struggling to maintain a professional attitude whilst giving 'more for less':

> We have become 'willing slaves'. 'Slaves' in the sense that more and more work is thrown at us to do. This would not have happened in 'the professions'. Conditions of service have been eroded, teachers' unions have not been effective, pay is now less in real terms than it was. As a body of people we have become less professional. 'Willing' in the sense that people seem happy to take on the extra responsibilities out of the goodness of their hearts.

Conclusions

The evidence presented above comes mostly from the mid-1990s, when LMS was well established in schools and other aspects of 1980s legislation had also been translated into practice. Whilst some senior managers may have expressed a degree of enthusiasm for the developmental benefits of managing resources at local level or for the new entrepreneurial spirit in education, others were far less positive and the vast majority of teachers could only identify the more negative aspects of the changes to school organization and management. Of particular concern to many teachers was the increasing divide between themselves and school managers, whom they saw as becoming distanced from curriculum and teaching matters and increasingly preoccupied with budgets and with management systems. However, some managers were equally unhappy with this enforced change in their role, suggesting that some structural changes can have significant effects on behaviour in schools even when all of those directly involved do not wish to change. Certainly teachers and managers alike were deeply concerned by the perceived inadequacy of current educational budgets, which they saw as having a detrimental effect both upon working conditions in school and upon the quality of education that was offered.

Despite the unpromising framework, there were examples of both teachers and managers striving to work their way around the new organizational paradigm and refusing to play the roles allotted to them by the educational reforms. Thus some school managers struggled both to protect their staff from what they saw as the worst features of the changes and to maintain a commitment to educational, as opposed to managerial, values. Similarly, some teachers continued to assert their professional responsibilities for educational quality and to endeavour to do their utmost to ensure that their teaching did not suffer because of the reforms. However, it was also clear that the changes were encouraging a less proactive approach amongst many teachers and an extension of managerial control.

Divisions between school managers and classroom teachers are not inevitable, although they are certainly encouraged by recent legislative changes, which give additional authority, responsibility and rewards to the former whilst curtailing the autonomy of the latter through a more closely defined job description and greater accountability for the achievement of specific, measurable outcomes. Similarly, impersonal systems-based approaches to change or masculinist and 'hard' forms of managerialism (Trow 1994) are not automatically adopted in schools, despite the thrust of government-sponsored management training schemes and current accountability procedures. Notwithstanding the obvious constraints, both teachers and managers retain a degree of choice as to how they will behave within the new structures and how far they will accept or resist the proposed scenario. To some extent, the choices that they make depend on personal qualities, beliefs and value systems, although cultural influences are also important in determining the extent of their resistance to, or compliance with, imposed requirements. A key factor in boosting professional confidence and determining the degree of proactivity in responding to external imperatives is access to professional development opportunities, and in this respect there are marked differences between the two groups. The next chapter will explore some of the recent changes in this area, in terms of both formal course provision and opportunities for work-based experiential learning.

ten

CHANGES IN TEACHERS' PROFESSIONAL DEVELOPMENT

As argued throughout this book, the nature of teachers' work is not entirely dictated by the structures within which they operate but is also a result of the myriad decisions and choices that they make in the course of their day-to-day working lives. Teachers may, for instance, choose to regard their teaching as simply a 'nine-to-five job' requiring the routine application of standard classroom techniques which are acquired through practice. In such cases the aims of education are seen as given and their task is simply to meet the requirements. Equally, however, teachers may view teaching as an open-ended moral enterprise which demands ongoing reflection and a perpetual quest for improvement. Classroom practice is seen as a highly skilled and complex operation involving constant creativity and improvisation, and maintaining and developing its quality is a fundamental professional responsibility. Whilst these examples may represent the opposite ends of the spectrum, they do reflect the fact that teachers' attitudes to their work may be significant in determining the kinds of professional choices which they make when confronted with demands for educational reform. To some extent such attitudes may have their origins in teachers' own personality and in the formal frameworks within which they work, but they are also closely linked to, and shaped by, the kinds of professional development which they experience.

Professional development may take a number of forms, but in teaching there are three main categories. The first is the initial teacher education which aspiring teachers must normally undertake before taking up a teaching post. The second is the formal range of courses and activities that practising teachers may experience as part of their continuing professional development. The third and final category comprises a variety of work-based learning opportunities that occur spontaneously rather than through any formal provision or organization. These include, for example, the normal classroom-based processes of 'learning on the job' and the collegial learning that may take place as a result of being a member of a 'professional community'. It is possible to identify marked changes in all three categories of professional development which have occurred over the last 15 years as a result both of centrally sponsored initiatives in the systems of initial and in-service teacher education and of the changing patterns of teachers' working lives.

Initial teacher education

Government interest in courses of initial teacher education (ITE) began to grow in the early 1980s as a result of a general preoccupation with standards in schools, concerns about the competencies of newly qualified teachers highlighted by HMI and alleged weaknesses in the quality of the courses offered by university schools and departments of education (Taylor 1994). In 1984 responsibility for monitoring the curricula of ITE institutions was given to the newly established Council for the Accreditation of Teacher Education (CATE), whose members were appointed directly by the Secretary of State for Education. All courses were to be inspected, and those that failed to meet new government criteria would no longer be allowed to award teaching qualifications. According to Furlong (1992: 163), this marked a turning point as the 'quiet backwater' of ITE became 'a major site for ideological struggle between the government and other groups with an interest in education'. During that struggle it has been suggested that ITE has been subjected to an inexorable process of 'technocratic modernisation', involving 'the extended application of scientific methods', the 'introduction of business efficiency models' and 'the extension of evaluation, monitoring and testing' (Young 1998: 55). Significantly, it is now always referred to by government sources as initial teacher *training*, rather than initial teacher *education*.

Certainly central control of ITE has grown steadily as the influence of institutions of higher education has diminished. The criteria for the approval of courses that were first developed in 1984 were revised and strengthened in 1989 and the remit of CATE was widened. These criteria have increasingly encouraged a greater emphasis upon academic knowledge in a main teaching subject, with correspondingly less attention paid to pedagogy. They have also led to the virtual disappearance of the educational disciplines of sociology, psychology, philosophy and history as separate studies and to a renewed focus upon practical training, with an increased role for practising teachers. Further encouragement was given to more school-based approaches to ITE, initially through the piloting of various 'articled teacher' and 'licensed teacher' schemes and subsequently through an insistence that school-based learning should comprise two-thirds of ITE courses. In addition, groups of schools were allowed to develop their own schemes of ITE independently from institutes of higher education. Meanwhile, government Circulars 9/92 and 14/93 defined the minimum competencies to be developed through secondary and primary teacher education courses respectively.

Central control was further strengthened by the establishment in 1994 of the Teacher Training Agency (TTA), a government-appointed quango answerable to the Secretary of State but with otherwise unclear lines of accountability, despite its pervasive influence on the occupational and professional lives of teachers (Mahony and Hextall 1997). The TTA, in conjunction with Ofsted, published plans for a national framework for the assessment of ITE (Ofsted and TTA 1996). The following year they produced a consultation document (TTA 1997) which formed the basis of a new national curriculum for all ITE courses (DfEE 1997). This document specified the English and maths curriculum that was to be taught to all primary trainees and also set out the criteria for the standards of knowledge, understanding and skills that they had to demonstrate in order to be awarded qualified teacher status.

Hartley (1998) has drawn attention to the parallels in government policies between the development of the National Curriculum for schools and that for ITE courses, claiming that both reforms can be seen as relating to the 'new managerialism'. Thus each involves a prescribed and standardized curriculum, national testing, external inspection and league tables of institutional performance, as both schools and education departments are encouraged to compete by exposure to market forces. In each case, according to Hartley, there is a narrowing of what is learnt, as both students and trainee teachers go 'back to basics' and the acquisition of defined knowledge or skills takes precedence over the development of critical thinking.

Whilst ITE was not a particular focus of questioning during teacher interviews in the 1994–96 Professional Culture of Teachers study, occasional references were made to the recent changes. Some teachers welcomed the increased emphasis upon practical and school-based training:

> You can't learn how to teach sat in a lecture theatre. You can get ideas
> of things you can use when you're teaching, but only experience makes
> you better . . . gives you more ways of coping with different situations.
>
> (Teacher interview, 1996)

Others, however, felt that the emphasis upon school-based training was now excessive. It was seen as a way of reducing costs which, because of the other pressures upon schools, damaged the quality of the training experience and diminished its learning content:

You used to have to study for four years to be a teacher, now you can learn it on the job . . . Learning on the job is probably OK, but it does diminish professionalism a lot if there's no time to read and learn, for example, about the teaching of reading. How can a licensed teacher pick this up?

(Teacher interview, 1995)

I've got worries about the changes to the [Postgraduate Certificate of Education] and the way it's been dumped in schools, it's a cheap way out and it's superficial. There's some truth in the idea that higher education is too theoretical and out of touch, but it's swung too far the other way. Some students are left to their own devices a lot, and the notion of working in teams is a cop-out.

(Teacher interview, 1995)

A young teacher with two and a half years' experience, also interviewed in 1995, was very positive about her own ITE course and contrasted it with the new provision:

Yes, it was an excellent training. And it's very interesting because we've just had students in for the first time in our department, and when I compare my training with theirs I realize how lucky I was. I don't understand, I can't understand the rationale behind some of the things that they've done. For example, their major topic in the first term was looking at cross-curricular links, whereas our major topic in our first term was why do kids behave badly? Why do kids fail? Why do kids succeed? . . . the emphasis was much more about classroom management and your classroom.

Like others, she also suggested that the new, school-based training was less thorough than that provided before, basing her judgement upon reports by the students on teaching practice in her own school:

They've been in some schools for block teaching practice for three weeks and they've had no involvement with the staff, the staff have just looked at the forms and ticked it, 'yes, yes, fine', handed it in, 'all right, yes, you've passed', and that's it, no feedback, no constructive criticism. We spent hours with ours. Hours and hours going over every lesson and, 'well, you could have done this and you could have done that'.

It was also suggested that the reforms of ITE sent out messages about the status of teaching:

. . . it comes back to this idea of how people view teachers outside the classroom, you know, about how teaching, anyone can do it and you don't really need that many skills.

(Teacher interview, 1995)

Thus, not only were the teachers of the future now being trained 'on the cheap' by hard-pressed school staff and given limited access to wider perspectives and knowledge, but the work of teachers was being presented as based primarily upon practical skills rather than specialist knowledge and expertise. At the same time, the effective loss of professional control of ITE in favour of central prescription, which itself appears to be based on rationalist thinking and a reductionist view of teaching, is strongly suggestive of a process of deprofessionalization.

Formal continuing professional development

In the 1960s and 1970s the opportunities for qualified teachers to continue their personal professional development through attendance at external courses had expanded significantly, particularly through the availability of central funding to cover most of the costs of full-time secondment to higher degree courses. In the 1980s, however, this 'professional' model of development was increasingly replaced by an 'institutional' model (Young 1998) as the focus on the development of the individual teacher was replaced by a concern with meeting the perceived training needs of the individual school. As Young points out, the low levels of funding and the pressures upon schools to behave as small businesses mean that the newly devolved budgets are more likely to be used to meet immediate and short-term needs rather than being invested in the long-term professional development of particular members of staff. At the same time, that element of staff development funding that had been retained centrally was increasingly used in accordance with government perceptions of training needs. A large proportion of this budget has therefore been allocated to management training or to training for the implementation of the National Curriculum, with the former targeted at senior managers and the latter largely restricted to heads of department. Accordingly, the opportunities for professional development in more generic areas, or for ordinary classroom teachers, have been severely curtailed.

An intermediate step between the higher-education-dominated model of the 1960s and 1970s and the 'institutional' model of the late 1980s and 1990s came in the early 1980s, with the advent of TVEI pilots and the development of a number of INSET courses in pre-vocational education. On the one hand, TVEI pilot schemes brought relatively generous funding to support the release of TVEI teachers to attend courses or to be involved in other forms of professional development activity. On the other hand, the student-centred and cross-curricular nature of many of the pre-vocational education courses being developed in schools at that time called for changes in the conventional subject-based INSET courses. In 1983 the DES broke with the tradition of not influencing in-service training priorities and offered funding for teachers to attend designated courses in any one of five named priority areas, including pre-vocational education. Because of the innovative nature of the area of study, the INSET courses were also innovative and certainly less strongly framed or classified than normal subject- and knowledge-based courses, encouraging creativity and allowing a greater degree of freedom for both course attenders and course providers – see Helsby (1993) for a fuller discussion of the effects of these changes.

The growth of opportunities for professional development for some teachers during TVEI pilot schemes also encouraged new approaches to teacher support. The novelty of TVEI developments meant that there were few pre-existing courses relevant to teachers' needs and limited expertise in institutions of higher education. Accordingly, LEA teams developed their own programmes of internally run courses, workshops and meetings, and staff development was increasingly linked with involvement in curriculum development. The inauguration of the TVEI-Related In-Service Training scheme in 1986 built upon these developments but also increased the extent of government identification of INSET priorities and encouraged a rational planning approach to teacher support which balanced individual training needs against those of the institution. There was also an emphasis upon monitoring practical outcomes, suggesting a more instrumental and functional view of staff development. These processes were taken further through subsequent government initiatives, Grant-Related In-Service Training, the LEA Training Grants Scheme and Grants for Educational Support and Training, which gradually substituted central prescription for local discretion in in-service education.

Although the opportunities for professional development and support during TVEI were restricted to a limited number of staff, they were mostly appreciated by those involved:

> TVEI funds have meant that there's money for staff to go on courses. Staff at the TVEI centre are good and offer a back-up system. The TVEI courses are always good, not time-wasting – they make you work.
>
> (Teacher interview, 1992)

> It's nice to know there's a back-up there who's not an adviser, you don't need to impress them, you don't feel they're watching you . . . [TVEI staff] are more on the ground floor, they really know what they're talking about.
>
> (Teacher interview, 1993)

> The setting up of the TVEI centre was really important for us, it was an excellent resource base. People there were doing nothing but TVEI and their advice was brilliant.
>
> (Teacher interview, 1997)

However, such TVEI-related support initiatives were soon overtaken by the introduction and spread of the National Curriculum in secondary schools and eventually by the cessation of TVEI funding. Despite the fact that National Curriculum regulations created an enormous amount of change for classroom teachers, provision for teacher support was woefully inadequate. In a survey of 2010 teachers in 1992–93, 87 per cent of main-grade teachers claimed that there had been a lot of changes in their subject area over the previous two to three years, well over half (55 per cent) agreed that they had difficulty keeping up with current professional demands and only about a quarter (27 per cent) believed that they had received adequate professional development in their curriculum area. This last figure compared to 43 per cent for senior managers.

Comments from the survey suggested that the levels of support were insufficient or even that they had declined:

> More need for LEA support, guidance in my area – we feel on our own.

> At a time of greatest demand on staff because of changes there is less time and support available to cope with it.

To make matters worse, teachers felt that they had too little time to assimilate and plan for the required changes:

> Insufficient professional training and support given to accommodate the changes. Now insufficient time given to carry out the multiplicity of tasks required by the changes recently imposed.

> Too many changes in too many areas pushed through too quickly with too little support and not enough time given off timetable to come to terms with them.

For many teachers, one of the consequences of this combination of imposed change, lack of teacher support and lack of planning time was a loss of professional confidence, a finding also supported by Vulliamy and Webb (1991: 232) in relation to primary teachers: 'the amount and unfamiliar content of National Curriculum subjects is serving to deskill teachers and in some schools may be generating a collective lack of confidence rather than confidence'.

Many teachers, particularly in the early years of National Curriculum implementation, certainly found the drastic changes demoralizing. Technology teachers experienced an exceptional degree of turmoil, as evidenced by these comments from interviews in 1995:

> Technology has changed drastically over the last two to three years . . . Being only two to three weeks ahead of the children tends to undermine confidence.

. . . keeping abreast of our own subject and the changes in our subject . . . it frightens us, I think, well it frightens me anyway. Because I think we're not too sure what we're doing and I suppose we've got, particularly my age, we've got into a rut. We're happy with that rut I suppose. A change coming at our age of life, we tend to panic, so we're not sure of ourselves.

Eleven months later, the same teacher still felt insecure and lamented the lack of available support:

. . . we're starting new GCSEs and Key Stage 4s in September but yet we have no training as such or even days where they can show us examples of work or books or anything, so we're really sort of floundering around in the deep end to start with.

Another teacher interviewed in 1995 did not believe that training was always necessary but recognised that many teachers had lost confidence in their ability to take the initiative:

. . . teachers develop a sort of belief that they can't do anything without being trained. Without going on a training course, you know, and it's clearly not true . . . I think perhaps more people lose their self-belief, like you can't possibly introduce a new exam syllabus without being trained for it.

Whatever the justice of that claim, it was evident that many classroom teachers did feel a great need for in-service training and resented the fact that such opportunities were being unfairly denied them:

Total disillusionment about staff development. Any work placements, course funds etc. handed out as perks to 'favourites'. INSET provision is useless – one might as well not bother asking because one knows the answer will be negative.

(Comment from teacher survey, 1993)

The position of teachers was compared unfavourably with that of other professions, who were seen as having greater access to continuing professional development:

Like other professions, there's a period of basic professional training, but the failure comes in the lack of continuing professional development to service the growing demands made upon teachers. It's hit and miss INSET, you're very lucky to get what you need.

(Teacher interview, 1994)

I feel that [doctors] can go on more courses and conferences than we actually can. That's one thing that has actually deteriorated in the last few years. Because there just isn't the money. Because if you do go on a course you've got to get a supply in, that's expensive, plus you've got to pay for the course more often than not.

(Teacher interview, 1995)

It was suggested that, in a situation where school managers were responsible for allocating limited amounts of money to the development of their staff, main-grade teachers were often the losers. The following comments are from interviews in 1994, with a part-time maths teacher, and in 1995, with a young history teacher in her third year of teaching:

I think in all of my four years, I've only been on one one-day course, and that was on my day off . . . people at the bottom, like me, don't get very much support at all in the way of courses.

This year I asked to go on a head of departments' training course and I wasn't allowed to go on it, and I was put down to go on an A-level course, which is really important, and they forgot to send the form off, so I'm a bit frustrated this year with training.

What in-service provision there was for developing National Curriculum subjects was usually restricted to heads of department, who were expected to 'cascade' their learning to other members of their department. Not only was the extent and quality of feedback variable, but main-grade teachers were denied the opportunity of making contact with colleagues from other institutions:

. . . many of the courses I would have liked to go on, my head of department has attended. I would have like to do more to keep up to date, to find out what teachers in other schools are doing, because I don't have much contact with them, which I think I would if there were more opportunity to do some INSET.

(Teacher interview, 1995)

As already indicated, senior managers had much greater access to continuing professional development opportunities, especially in the area of management training. There were also suggestions that the quality of courses attended by senior managers was higher than that of INSET targeted at teachers:

The volume of staff on INSET has fallen off and the standard of input, where you get in big names who can fire the imagination, is now only for heads and deputies.

(Headteacher interview, 1997)

Some teachers certainly complained about the content of the limited provision that was available. In particular, they were concerned that it was focused almost exclusively on National Curriculum implementation rather than on broader topics of professional concern:

It's been difficult recently because INSET requirements have been so oriented towards the National Curriculum. I would have preferred more on teaching and learning.

(Comment from teacher survey, 1993)

There's little opportunity for continuing professional development. There was one session planned for Key Stage 4, but nothing to develop my history teaching. There are restrictions because of lack of money.

(Teacher interview, 1995)

One government initiative intended to increase in-service provision for teachers was the introduction, through the Teachers' Pay and Conditions Act of 1987, of five compulsory school-based training days each year. The way in which these days were used varied from school to school, depending on the preferences of senior managers. Sometimes they might involve contributions from an outside presenter or from school staff, and sometimes time was given to groups of staff to work together on tasks, often in departmental groups. In the 1992–93 survey already mentioned, reactions to these training days were distinctly mixed: when asked whether the way that in-service training was organized in their school worked well, only about a quarter of main-grade teachers (27 per cent) agreed, with 48 per cent positively disagreeing with the statement. By contrast, 54 per cent of managers believed that it did work well, a figure which possibly reflects their own involvement in its organization.

One comment from the head of a technology department in 1995 suggested that the time given to departments during school-based training days was frequently taken over by the instrumental need to complete specific tasks, rather than being able to engage in activities that might contribute to professional development:

. . . unfortunately what we tend to have to do is use INSET time for standardization meetings at exam time . . . that's the only time we can literally get together to standardize work across the department for GCSE. So, a good six to nine hours of work which could be used for curriculum development is used up on GCSE . . . moderation and standardization.

A history teacher, also interviewed in 1995, found the sessions frustrating but recognised the difficulties of meeting the disparate needs of staff in a single session:

The departmental ones, cor! I mean, at the beginning of term we just had two whole-day departmental meetings! No, I haven't really found any of them particularly useful . . . they are for some people, but it must be hard to have to try to fit everyone's ideas or problems into a whole-school INSET.

For some teachers, the pressures of work, the new lack of sociability in school and the inexorable processes of developing policies and documenting everything were taking their toll. The head of a geography department interviewed in 1996 found that school-based training days had become just another burden:

> And if we do have INSET days and we're together as a group and we actually see each other, instead of these odd shadows here, there and everywhere, we find that we just don't want to do any more policy- or rationale-making because we're fed up with it.

As always, there were exceptions to this generally negative picture, with some teachers able to exploit meeting time in school to develop a richer and more collaborative approach to producing schemes of work:

> . . . these little INSETs that we had at school, it focused ideas together . . . we'd throw the ideas around and then it was left to me to do the writing. In the past the job would be given to the head of geography [who] would be by themselves and it was given down to you as a sheet of paper . . . the only way that we felt that that could happen was in a collaboration like that.
>
> (Teacher interview, 1996)

Another form of support that had largely disappeared for many teachers was the availability of advice and guidance from LEA advisers. In the early years of National Curriculum implementation, the new inspectorial role of advisers distanced them from many teachers:

> Now he's not necessarily seen as the friendly adviser . . . People are more suspicious of advisers because of the inspectorial role. The relationship has changed.
>
> (Comment from teacher survey, 1992)

Subsequently, the reductions in LEA funding and services and the involvement of the remaining advisers in Ofsted inspections and other paid work meant that they were increasingly unable to visit schools in an advisory capacity:

> . . . the LEAs have disappeared. I think the LEAs wanted reforming but a lot of teachers now are going through a sort of bereavement because they don't actually now have anybody out there they can turn to.
>
> (Teacher interview, 1994)

I can't remember the last time a design technology adviser came into school, and we are talking years now . . . I have no real relationship with the adviser, I don't have any dialogue with the adviser, I don't have any, or very little, contact with other teachers in other schools, and it just seems a total void.

(Teacher interview, 1995)

A senior teacher interviewed in 1994 believed that the lack of either advisory support or training opportunities was creating a significant gap in provision:

> . . . that whole sort of layer of consultancy has disappeared, so put together with the fact that there isn't funding now to send people on the sort of courses you would like to . . . you've got an enormous great chasm that's appeared.

He went on to describe the difficulties created when staff became demoralized and demotivated by the profound changes that were being imposed upon schools:

> . . . there are other people equally that are bewildered and other people who feel they don't really want to cope with the change that's come about. And you know in the past you could actually try and develop some of those people . . . you could actually involve them in some sort of training which may bring in some enthusiasm, but again because of the financial restraints that's disappeared, so the ability to respond to people's needs is less now . . . one of the greatest disappointments of appraisal is that there is very little in the way of resource to back up what you actually uncover.

In stark contrast to this general view of instrumental and mostly school-based INSET, with limited opportunities for any kind of course attendance for the majority of teachers, some of the older interviewees reflected nostalgically on their own past experiences of professional development. For some, their former involvement in an MA course was cited as a significant influence, allowing them time and space for professional reflection:

> . . . it provided the opportunity to stand back, to see from a distance what I was doing or trying to do as a teacher . . . I found it provided a very useful insight, an opportunity to focus in on things which, when you're involved in them, you don't see.

(Teacher interview, 1994)

> I met an individual [the course director] who had a phenomenal amount of managerial experience, both in industry and outside, and who started posing the questions rather than giving the answers, making me go and find my own answers.

(Teacher interview, 1996)

Despite the extensive curriculum changes, however, involvement in such professionally empowering courses was now rare. For most classroom teachers, formal INSET provision had become much more limited in terms of both access and scope, and they were increasingly thrown back upon their own resources.

Informal continuing professional development

As already indicated, courses and other formally organized activities are not the only source of professional development, and many teachers learn spontaneously from their own experiences of classroom teaching and from informal interactions with colleagues. Indeed, in a small pre-interview survey of 147 teachers in 1994–95, conducted as part of the Professional Culture of Teachers study, a question about perceived influences upon professional development showed that personal experience was the most common, being cited by 86 respondents. This was closely followed by colleagues in their own department (77 mentions) and their own beliefs and convictions (74 mentions). ITE was the next most frequently cited influence (39 mentions), although it was more often emphasized by relatively new teachers, with less than six years' experience. Only 17 of the 147 highlighted formal INSET activities as an important influence. By contrast, the 121 teachers in a second, post-interview questionnaire were overwhelmingly positive about their experiences of INSET in the preceding 12 months: 79 per cent rated it as of professional value and only 8 per cent reckoned it to be of no value. Teachers also believed that nearly 80 per cent of the INSET in which they had recently been involved had either wholly or partly focused upon practical activities such as receiving information, completing specific tasks, acquiring specific skills and examining classroom materials (Helsby and Knight 1997).

One conclusion that might tentatively be drawn from these data is that, whilst instrumental and practically focused INSET activities might be regarded as important and valuable at times of great pressure and change, they do not necessarily serve to develop teachers professionally. At the same time, data from interviews with practising teachers again confirmed the developmental significance of informal learning. On the one hand, many emphasized the crucial importance of classroom experience, as shown by these comments from 1995:

> . . . any development I've had . . . it's just happened. It's me developing, it's me growing, it's me changing. It's not from any outside influence that I know of.

> You learn more about teaching from being in a classroom than you do at college.

... bad classes are the ones that mean that you have to sit down and really think about what you're doing and how you're going to teach it.

A history teacher interviewed in 1996 also emphasized the importance of experiential learning and problem-solving:

... a lot of it you have to work out for yourself at the end of the day. Your own strategies and your own way, it's very much a personal thing.

He was, however, equally ready to acknowledge the influence of colleagues in professional learning:

I think it must be from in school, watching, getting to know other people and seeing other people at work and how they do things ... you do learn a lot from the people around you, your colleagues.

When asked who or what had had the greatest influence on their professional development, many interviewees did indeed cite other teachers, particularly members of their own department. These comments from 1996 are typical:

Certainly other teachers that I've worked with, individuals ... who were very, very good practitioners would be people that I'd look at and think, 'yes, that's a much better way of doing it' ... and you modify your own performance and your own ideas or the way that you'd work through that.

I think ... people in my own department have influenced my development more than anything else.

Sometimes the person involved was a head of department or senior colleague who acted as a mentor to a less experienced teacher:

... she was like a mother to me when I first arrived and she taught me everything that I know now ... she taught me the tricks of the trade.
(Teacher interview, 1996)

... definitely the person who's influenced me most has been the head of department ... definitely within my first year of teaching, it was 'oh, what do I do?', 'I'm not quite sure, how do I approach this?', you know. He was the one I got the most advice off, the teacher I've worked most closely with ... he's helped me through things.
(Teacher interview, 1996)

It was, however, suggested that the increased pressures in schools and lack of time to interact with colleagues were having a serious effect upon such learning opportunities. A senior teacher, interviewed in 1996, compared his own experiences in the 1960s with that of young teachers entering the profession in the 1990s:

I would think that, if we're going back to when I first started teaching in 1968, the biggest influence upon my teaching was the example of good professionals. Now I don't mean just maths teachers. I was very fortunate that, in my first post, in a very large maths department, were some very strong teachers and I also had the breathing space to talk to colleagues in the staffroom during non-contact time, at the end of the day and so on, who were teaching in completely different areas and I was able to draw upon their experience and knowledge. I count myself lucky that there was the breathing space in the late Sixties . . . Now I don't feel that the more experienced teachers have the time or the contact with the people who are coming into the profession.

Certainly one young teacher reported feeling a distinct sense of isolation:

I'm relatively new and it's hard to fit in here, where there's a stable, rigid staff. It sometimes feels as if you're battling on your own.
                                                        (Teacher interview, 1994)

Another described how the intensified pace of working life largely prohibited meaningful interaction with colleagues:

I think the school spirit isn't there so much . . . you don't see people: you're there for five minutes, having your cup of tea at break, after you've finished sorting out the kids who haven't done their homework, and then the next minute you're back in the classroom, and everyone's off in their own direction. We only have a 35 minute dinner break, and it's a split dinner, so you might not see anyone one day, and you're back teaching again . . . [after school] they shoot off home to get on with their work.
                                                        (Teacher interview, 1995)

Clearly these kinds of pressure affected experienced teachers as well as new ones. The head of a small geography department interviewed in 1996 lamented the fact that heavy workloads were making it very difficult for her to work collaboratively with the other member of her department:

. . . to be able to bounce [ideas] off someone else would be nicer, you know. But she's a married lady, she's got a family, so she has even less time than I do.

Despite all of these difficulties, however, there were a few examples of teachers who were able to exploit the opportunity presented by imposed curriculum changes to work creatively with colleagues and to combine curriculum and staff development (see also Chapter 6). A home economics teacher described in 1995 how the need to develop an integrated technology course to meet National Curriculum requirements had prompted a group of staff to work together to the benefit of all:

. . . we were driven by the fact that National Curriculum was coming in, we were willing . . . to look at what we were doing and adapt it, modify it and change it . . . we've learnt how to relate to each other, because we didn't have to do that before, you could sit in your own little empire . . . and that's a great strength.

The head of a technology department in another school interviewed in the same year had also used the National Curriculum changes as a prompt to encourage members of his department to become engaged in curriculum development for the first time. Again, he saw the results as highly beneficial in terms of professional development:

What I've tried to do in the last 12 months is give people more responsibility for particular areas . . . So we're moving towards a situation where I feel that . . . staff are responsible for the curriculum. I've felt for a long time that it's been mainly my burden to actually push that through and I don't think they feel that they have ownership of it if it's that kind of framing . . . I think that as a department we feel relatively comfortable in each other's company now . . . I do feel that their professionalism has improved.

Thus, whilst greatly increased workloads had clearly made it more difficult for teachers either to act as mentors to younger colleagues or to engage in the kind of collaborative and reflective activities that can lead to shared professional learning, such activities were not impossible and indeed in some cases were actually prompted by the need to respond to imposed change.

Conclusions

It is apparent that there have been significant changes in recent years to all three forms of professional development, with potentially significant implications for the future of teachers' work. Both initial and in-service teacher education provision have been subjected to much greater degrees of central prescription and have become more practical, more instrumental and more school-based. Access to out-of school courses, external advice or contact with teachers from other schools has become very restricted for most classroom teachers, increasing the dangers of parochialism and insularity. At the same time, pressures of work and the general intensification of school life have generally had an adverse effect upon the opportunities for informal professional development through interactions with colleagues, as sociability has declined and the formal meetings that take place have tended to become more narrowly focused and task-oriented. For some teachers, even personal, classroom-based learning has been threatened by the use of survival strategies and 'making do'. Whilst all of these trends suggest a possible deprofessionalization of teachers, there are other examples where the introduction of curriculum changes and the involvement of groups of staff in reviewing their teaching and devising new courses have led to important kinds of professional development and consequent gains in professional confidence.

As with other areas of educational reform, the field of professional development illustrates the way in which government-inspired changes have produced a framework which threatens to reduce the significance of teachers' work by transforming it into the application of routine procedures, as teachers are charged with the execution of plans devised elsewhere and trained in the specific skills perceived to be necessary to that task. Yet again, however, individual teachers have continued to resist this centrally designated role and have endeavoured instead to impose their own more professional interpretations upon their work. This has been easier in situations characterized by strong collegiality (see also Chapter 6). The outcomes, therefore, are variable and fluid, depending as they do on the ongoing interplay of structure, culture and agency. How far, in the long term, teachers' work will be deprofessionalized or reprofessionalized remains to be seen. A crucial factor, however, will be the extent to which teachers have access to, or are able to create for themselves, opportunities for genuine and meaningful professional development.

eleven

CONCLUSIONS

The data presented above indicate the enormity of the impact of recent educational restructuring upon teachers' working lives. The somewhat negative tenor of the quotations selected is representative of the views of the majority of teachers across hundreds of interviews and several teacher surveys. Even younger teachers, brought up with the National Curriculum, were far from unequivocal in their support of it. The reforms have been so extensive and thorough that they have changed in fundamental ways the frameworks and structures within which teachers operate and, in so doing, have challenged the very nature of their work. In the discourse of educational policy-making, the notion of the autonomous and responsible professional, dedicated to his/her students and trusted to take complex decisions in their best interest, has been largely displaced by the image of an occupational group that has somehow failed and is therefore in need of regulation and 'hard' management. A succession of government policies has overtly increased central prescription and control of education whilst at the same time exposing schools to the 'discipline' of the market – or at least of the quasi-market. As traditional educational bureaucracies have been largely dismantled and as the power of teacher unions and teacher associations has steadily declined, teachers have become more isolated in this fast-changing context and have had to find their own resolutions to the problems presented to them.

The new vision of schooling which teachers are invited to share casts them in the role of efficient and cost-effective employees, vying with others to maximize the test scores of their students and striving constantly to improve their own performance in line with government requirements. Within the 'new school order', the ideal teacher is knowledgeable about those aspects of his/her subject specialism which are prescribed in the National Curriculum, is able to teach them in accordance with centrally approved modes of pedagogy and is able to produce adequate documentation that describes teaching plans and policies as well as presenting clear evidence to support assessments of student performance. At the same time this model employee will be enthusiastically committed to the school mission, as articulated by the headteacher and SMT, and will be happy to work both individually and collaboratively with colleagues to further its realization. Teaching will be only one of the tasks undertaken, as the scope of the teacher's work broadens both within and outside of the classroom, but the new teacher will gladly embrace this multi-skilled role and, inspired and guided by school managers, will endeavour not only to meet but to exceed expectations.

Clearly such visions, like the visions of the 'new work order', are idealized prescriptions rather than reflections of reality. The extent to which individual workers choose to 'buy in' to such visions and to accept their allotted role within them is, in practice, variable and unpredictable. As Gee *et al.* (1996) point out in their study of the development of self-directed work teams in an American electronics assembly plant, training in collaborative working does not inevitably result in new work identities nor does it necessarily affect traditional power structures in organizations. On the one hand, this may reflect the hollowness of any invitation to worker empowerment in a situation where real power is retained at the centre and it is only responsibility that is devolved to lower levels. On the other hand Gee *et al.* draw attention to the fact that any new discourses are in tension with older discourses which are likely to affect, and may well subvert, any attempts to achieve social change. These older discourses include both pre-existing workplace discourses and other, wider discourses related to such things as class, gender, ethnicity, parenthood or community.

Of particular relevance to teachers are the traditional professional and social-democratic discourses of education which propose a quite different conception both of educational aims and of the role of teachers in achieving those aims. Given the strength of commitment of many teachers to these traditional discourses and the general lack of any inherent incentive to embrace the new discourse, the latter has had to be supported by structural changes to the organization of schooling which push teachers towards its adoption. The resultant struggle between competing discourses has been, and indeed is still being, played out in schools and classrooms throughout England, as individual teachers continue to make sense of successive new requirements and translate them into practice. Whilst the outcomes of these attempts to transform schooling are based upon, and constructed by, the accumulation of choices made by those teachers, the situation remains fluid. However, the evidence presented in earlier chapters suggests that recent educational reforms have enjoyed a notable degree of success not only in moving the goalposts but also in revising the basic rules of the game.

Effects of the reforms upon teachers' work

Curriculum

Since the school curriculum lies at the very heart of teachers' work and, in many respects, defines that work, any changes in curriculum content, form, method or assessment can be expected to be highly significant. Whilst TVEI encouraged teacher creativity and inventiveness within very broad guidelines, the English National Curriculum, particularly in its earlier manifestations, embodied an unprecedentedly high degree of central prescription with regard to both curriculum content and curriculum assessment. As shown in Chapter 4, the compulsory nature of this initiative and the enforced accountability measures that were introduced to ensure compliance placed serious constraints upon teachers' freedom of action and ran counter to the idea of professional decision-making to meet individual and often conflicting student needs. This prescription of practice, coupled with the imposition of standardized testing to judge both student learning and, by implication, teacher performance, was strongly reminiscent of the application of scientific management techniques, rather than of the tenets of the 'new work order'. Whilst some teachers were able to find 'spaces for manoeuvre' within the new legislative framework, a tendency which increased over time, others became resigned to the notion of receiving instructions and following orders. Although many of the requirements of the original National Curriculum have since been relaxed, the principle of central determination of curriculum content is now established and the current focus upon the basic skills of literacy and numeracy in primary schools can be seen as simply another manifestation of this new situation.

Although National Curriculum legislation left decisions about pedagogy to the discretion of teachers, the amount of prescribed curriculum content and the nature of assessment procedures combined to have a significant impact upon the classroom approaches of many teachers. Whereas TVEI had encouraged and supported the development of a broader range of strategies, this was largely overtaken by growing pressures to 'cover the content' and consequently by the temptation to return to 'tried and tested' and often more didactic pedagogies. Data presented in Chapter 5 suggest that this has indeed been the case for many teachers, a trend further encouraged by the general intensification of working life, by the importance attached to league tables of assessment results and, to a lesser extent, by the notion of 'playing safe' during Ofsted inspections. Furthermore, there is now evidence of an increasing interest from the centre in codifying and prescribing teaching methods, as indicated by the development of specified and measurable competencies for initial teacher education and by the call from the Chief Executive of the Teacher Training Agency to open up the 'last corner of the secret garden' and expose pedagogy to public scrutiny and debate (Millett 1996).

In this way another area of professional discretion is threatened with displacement by central regulation, although the extent to which this might be realizable in practice remains uncertain.

New public management

The introduction into the education service of new forms of school organization and management have also had profound effects upon the nature of teachers' work. Rather than operating within a collaborative and egalitarian public service framework, teachers must now work within small, independent units which are expected to compete with each other for business. The business analogy is further strengthened by the attempted creation of a different kind of school manager, who is expected to acquire new skills and responsibilities and who is structurally empowered at the expense of ordinary classroom teachers. The demands of LMS mean that the headteacher must now be involved in financial and staff management and in negotiations with governors, all of which detract from the time available for involvement in curriculum matters and educational leadership. Meanwhile, competitiveness between subject departments and individual teachers within schools is encouraged by new systems of resource allocation and career progression, whilst the perceived inadequacies of educational funding mean that hard choices have to be made between contending priorities.

As indicated in Chapter 9, the extent to which teachers and managers embrace the imperatives and values of the new public management systems is variable. Whilst some headteachers have been described as intoxicated with their new-found powers or as enjoying an enhanced sense of professionalism based upon their new management skills, others have striven to protect their staff from the more managerialist aspects of the reforms and to preserve for themselves a meaningful involvement in educational and curriculum issues. Similarly, classroom teachers have varied in their responses to the changes, with some continuing to uphold the values of collaboration and joint enterprise and actively asserting their professionalism in the face of the more restricted role apportioned to them by the new managerialist philosophy. Others, by contrast, have accepted the inevitability of the 'new management order' and have either sought to gain individual advantage from it at the expense of colleagues or have been led to 'construct their own subjection' within it (Ball 1994: 12).

Despite the relative empowerment of school managers, they, like classroom teachers, have had to meet increasing requirements for public accountability despite declining levels of funding. Thus the work of both teachers and managers is now exposed to the scrutiny of Ofsted inspectors, whilst both groups are held accountable for success in terms of measurable student outcomes. The evidence presented in Chapter 8 suggests that, far from spurring staff to improve the quality of the education that they offer, the impact upon them of such accountability measures has been largely negative. Not only have the processes been very time-consuming, detracting from the time available for genuinely educational activities, but they have also damaged the morale of many teachers and encouraged a narrowing of focus and effort towards the achievement of key performance indicators. This represents a marked divergence from the traditionally broader conception of teachers' work as the development of young people's capacities in more open-ended and therefore unpredictable ways.

The 'new work order' of teaching

A spate of legislative changes has produced less favourable terms and conditions of service for teachers in England as their collective bargaining rights have been removed, their working hours specified, their working year lengthened, their contractual duties and responsibilities more clearly defined and their classroom practice subjected to managerial appraisal and inspection. Teacher unions and teacher associations have increasingly been excluded from policy discussions and decision-making processes, and repeated attempts made to encourage local pay bargaining and to introduce a system of performance-related pay, despite union opposition to the principle of either. The devolution both of school budgets and of *de facto* employer responsibilities to headteachers and governing bodies has encouraged a diversification in employment practices, including the increased use of school support staff and of newly qualified teachers. As suggested in Chapter 3, these measures have combined to produce an increasingly flexible and differentiated workforce (Lawn 1995), in accordance with the principles of the 'new work order'.

Another feature of the 'new work order' that is very apparent in English schools is a general intensification of working life, as teachers take on additional responsibilities and, with no commensurate rise in funding, are encouraged to do 'more for less'. In many cases the increased workloads have led to a decline in professional confidence, to anxiety and even to stress-related illness. As suggested in Chapter 7, however, responses are not uniform and there are some teachers who have thrived on their new responsibilities, despite the increased workload. Moreover, the situation is not static, and factors such as the National Curriculum, which necessitated a great deal of additional work at the time of its introduction, have become easier to manage with experience. On the other hand, new initiatives continue to surface, all of which demand a reinvestment of teachers' efforts and energies, and the promised period of stability remains elusive. In the proclaimed age of postmodernism, it seems unlikely that teachers' work will return to the more leisurely pace of former times.

The notion of continuous quality improvement that is inherent in the vision of the 'new work order' implies a constant upskilling or reskilling of the workforce. In education, the spate of recent reforms has also necessitated the acquisition of new skills by teachers although, for most of those below the level of head of department, any professional development during this period has mostly taken place within schools and has been predominantly 'do-it-yourself'. As shown in Chapter 10, there is resentment amongst some teachers about the implications for the status of teachers' work of an increasingly practical and school-based model of both initial and continuing teacher education. With the content of in-service provision dictated more and more by government priorities and generally restricted to more senior members of school staff, formal development opportunities for classroom teachers in areas of general concern to them are very limited. At the same time, the incidence of informal professional development as a result of involvement in collegial activity has been constrained by the changes in the patterns of association between teachers described in Chapter 6. Despite the unfavourable circumstances, however, some groups of teachers have been able to exploit the opportunity for curriculum review and planning offered by recent reforms in order to develop themselves professionally.

Teacher agency and teacher culture

The imposed structural changes to the education system described above would seem to suggest a transformation of teachers' work and a mutation of their role from semi-autonomous professional to managed and expendable employee. As their discretion to take curricular decisions in the best interest of their students is curtailed by central prescription, codification and surveillance, the bases of their claims to special expertise are undermined and their tasks are redefined away from the exercise of professional judgement and towards the routine application of standardized procedures. The combined forces of marketization and managerialism place further pressures upon them to conform to external requirements whilst their new terms and conditions of service and increased accountability create a more directed and insecure workforce. Finally, the intensification of their work and the diminished opportunities for professional development reduce not only the time available for adopting a more proactive approach to the reforms but also the skills, capacities and confidence so to do.

Despite all of the above, however, it is clear from the evidence that some teachers do indeed manage to be proactive and to assert a professional interpretation of their role. In such cases, the structural constraints are viewed as problems to be overcome – or even in some cases ignored – rather than as insoluble blockages. As long as governments remain dependent upon teachers to translate their policies into practice, then teachers will retain a degree of freedom in their day-to-day work. As yet, no government has been able to reduce education to a machine-deliverable process or to devise a teacher-proof curriculum. Accordingly, the human element will always tend to interfere with even the most carefully designed system and prevent it working in entirely predictable ways. Thus teachers do continue to have some choice over how they respond to policy initiatives, although they may react in varying ways. Whilst some may experience strong feelings of dis-empowerment and therefore adopt a passive approach to what is asked of them, others may deliberately refuse to view policy texts as operational pre-scriptions and instead see them as possible courses of action to be considered and amended as appropriate.

A key factor in determining teachers' responses to imposed reforms is the level of their 'professional confidence'. Teachers who are professionally con-fident have a strong belief not only in their *capacity* but also in their *auth-ority* to make important decisions about the conduct of their work (Helsby 1995). When faced with a problem, they do not defer to others or wait to be told what to do but instead move immediately to solve the problem through the exercise of their own professional judgement. In order to be able to do this, the teacher needs to feel 'in control' of the work situation. Thus pro-fessional confidence also implies that the teacher is not overwhelmed by excessive work demands that can never be properly met: the confident teacher has a sense of being able to manage the tasks in hand rather than being driven by them. Instead of crisis management, corner-cutting and ill-considered coping strategies, they are able to reflect upon, and make con-scious choices between, alternative courses of action and can feel that they are doing 'a good job'.

To some extent the level of professional confidence may be affected by the personal characteristics and predispositions of individuals and by their previous experiences. However, it is more importantly a collective attribute which is highly dependent upon a number of cultural and contextual factors. For example, a sense of being trusted and respected as a responsible and caring professional may well boost professional confidence, whilst public discourses about 'failing teachers', punitive inspection and accountability procedures and top-down management systems are likely to have the oppo-site effect. Similarly, it is more difficult to retain a sense of professional con-fidence when responsibility for what teachers perceive as core areas of their work is reduced in favour of external prescription, when resources are lack-ing and when compliance is required rather than creativity. Other factors potentially affecting teachers' confidence include the amount and quality of professional support available to them and, as indicated above, the weight of their workloads.

As can be seen from the above list, it might be reasonable to expect that the recent educational reforms in England would have had a largely adverse effect upon the levels of teachers' professional confidence, thereby making them more amenable to external direction. However, whilst it is easy to find examples of demoralized and unmotivated teachers, it is also possible to find examples of teachers who have come through the reform period with a renewed sense of professionalism (see, for example, Campbell and Neill 1994a; Woods *et al.* 1997). Evidence from the Professional Culture of Teachers study suggests that a key factor in this respect is the local culture within which a teacher works and, in particular, the existence of a strongly collaborative culture within a subject department or other small grouping (Helsby 1996a). Despite the drawbacks of some forms of collegiality mentioned in Chapter 6, membership of a vibrant 'professional community' (Talbert and McLaughlin 1994) can offer the reassurance that others face similar dilemmas and can enhance teachers' willingness to innovate. It can also broaden horizons by providing exposure to new ideas and new ways of doing things, especially when the collaboration extends beyond departmental or institutional limits.

In some schools small groups of teachers have made deliberate efforts to collaborate in developing creative responses to imposed changes and, in so doing, have developed both their professional skills and their professional confidence. In many cases, however, such efforts have been constrained by a lack of resources and by the general intensification of working life. Yet, as Tyack and Cuban (1995) remind us, reform is a cyclical process. In England, the system of 'payment by results' was succeeded by a lengthy period of 'legitimated professionalism' (Grace 1987). Despite the recent tendency to characterize teachers as 'failing' and to seek to control them, the current crisis in the recruitment and retention of teachers has already begun to have a significant effect upon public discourses, which are now characterized by a greater emphasis upon the 'professionalism' of teachers. The clear need to do more to attract able young graduates into teaching may demand not only higher salary levels but also greater freedom in work and more scope for creativity.

Professional confidence is something that may take a considerable amount of time to build up but that can be all too easily destroyed by intemperate discourses and ill-advised policy changes. Given the crucial role of teachers in improving education, a confident and motivated workforce would seem to be a prerequisite of any attempt to 'reform' schooling or 'raise standards'. Policy-makers would do well to heed traditional educational wisdom about the often debilitating and anxiety-producing effects of negative reinforcement and punishment (Stones 1966), whilst giving careful thought to what might be positively reinforced. Currently, it is rational management, systems-based approaches and efficiency that are being rewarded, whilst traditionally feminine qualities and values such as intuition, caring and people-based orientations are often belittled or ignored. Whilst this may accord well with a Taylorist view of the role of teachers as skilled but compliant technicians, it is at odds with a broader and more humanistic conception of them as independent moral agents, entrusted by society to reconcile the conflicting demands of education within their classrooms and to best meet the needs of their students, often in unpredictable ways.

The data presented in this book offer a snapshot view of some of the effects of educational change upon teachers' work over the last 10–15 years. Over this time, there have been a number of apparent 'ups' and 'downs' for teachers, most of which have been characterized by inconsistent and unpredictable responses. Like Acker (1999, forthcoming), who offers a detailed and evocative ethnographic account of teaching in an English primary school over a similar period of time, I would make no blanket claims on the basis of these findings: indeed their very diversity precludes any unqualified conclusions. Moreover, it remains to be seen what educational policies will emerge and how the system of schooling will be changed in the future. The only thing that can be said with any certainty is that teachers themselves will continue to play a key role in any developments, since teaching can never be regulated and supervised like labour on a production line. Accordingly, the future nature of teachers' work will be shaped not only by imposed structures but also by the accumulation of choices made by individual teachers working in a variety of cultures and contexts. It is this balance of power and influence which provides a safeguard against the dangers of domination of schooling by fashionable dogmas or autocratic prescription and which gives hope for the future education of young people.

REFERENCES

Acker, S. (1997) Primary school teachers' work: the response to educational reform, in G. Helsby and G. McCulloch (eds) *Teachers and the National Curriculum*. London: Cassell.

Acker, S. (1999) *The Realities of Teachers' Work: Never a Dull Moment*. London: Cassell.

Adelman, C. and Alexander, R. (1982) *The Self-Evaluating Institution: Practice and Principles in the Management of Educational Change*. London: Methuen.

Alexander, R.J. (1991) *Policy and Practice in Primary Education*. London: Routledge.

Alexander, R.J., Rose, J. and Woodhead, C. (1992) *Curriculum Organisation and Classroom Practice in Primary Schools: A Discussion Paper*. London: DES.

Althusser, L. (1971) *Lenin and Philosophy*, trans. Ben Brewster. London: New Left Books.

Angus, L. (1994) Sociological analysis and education management: the social context of the self-managing school, *British Journal of Sociology of Education*, 15(1): 79–91.

Apple, M.W. (1986) *Teachers and Texts: A Political Economy of Class and Gender Relations in Education*. New York: Routledge.

Apple, M.W. (1989) Critical introduction: ideology and the State in educational policy, in R. Dale *The State and Education Policy*, pp. 1–20. Milton Keynes: Open University Press.

Apple, M.W. (1996) *Cultural Politics and Education*. New York: Teachers College Press.

Archer, M.S. (1979) *The Social Origins of Education Systems*. London: Sage Publications.

Archer, M.S. and Vaughan, M.E.F. (1971) *Social Conflict and Educational Change in England and France, 1789–1848*. London: Cambridge University Press.

Auld, R. (1976) *William Tyndale Junior and Infants School Public Inquiry: A Report to the Inner London Education Authority*. London: ILEA.

Ball, S.J. (1990a) *Politics and Policy Making in Education.* London: Routledge.

Ball, S.J. (1990b) Education, inequality and school reform: values in crisis! Inaugural lecture, Centre for Educational Studies, King's College, London, 15 October.

Ball, S.J. (1994) *Education Reform: A Critical and Post-Structural Approach.* Buckingham: Open University Press.

Barnes, D., Johnson, G., Jordan, S., Layton, D., Medway, P. and Yeomans, D. (1987a) *The TVEI Curriculum 14–16. An Interim Report Based on Case Studies in Twelve Schools.* London: MSC.

Barnes, D., Johnson, G., Jordan, S., Layton, D., Medway, P. and Yeomans, D. (1987b) *A Second Report on the TVEI Curriculum: Courses for 14–16 Year Olds in Twenty-six Schools.* Sheffield: Training Agency.

Batteson, C. (1997) A review of education in the 'moment of 1976', *British Journal of Educational Studies,* 45(4): 363–77.

Beattie, J. (1986) Organisation and management: some theoretical considerations, in C. McCabe (ed.) *The Organisation of the Early Years of the Technical and Vocational Education Initiative.* Clevedon: Multilingual Matters.

Beresford, J. (1995) Teacher union perspectives on the management of professionals, in H. Busher and R. Saran (eds) *Managing Teachers as Professionals in Schools.* London: Kogan Page.

Bernstein, B. (1971) On the classification and framing of educational knowledge, in M.F.D. Young (ed.) *Knowledge and Control: New Directions for the Sociology of Education.* London: Collier-Macmillan.

Bichard, M. (1995) Quality in education and training. Address before the CBI Conference on Achieving Quality in Education and Training, London, 3 November.

Blackler, F. (1995) Knowledge, knowledge workers and organizations: an overview and interpretation, *Organization Studies,* 16(6): 1021–46.

Blackmore, J., Bigum, C., Hodgens, J. and Laskey, L. (1996) Managed change and self-management in Schools of the Future, *Leading and Managing,* 2(3): 195–220.

Bottery, M. (1996) The challenge to professionals from the New Public Management: implications for the teaching profession, *Oxford Review of Education,* 22(2): 179–97.

Bowe, R. and Ball, S. (1992) 'Doing what should come naturally': an exploration of LMS in one secondary school, in G. Wallace (ed.) *Local Management of Schools: Research and Experience.* Clevedon: Multilingual Matters.

Bowe, R. and Ball, S.J. with Gold, A. (1992) *Reforming Education and Changing Schools: Case Studies in Policy Sociology.* London: Routledge.

Bowles, S. and Gintis, H. (1976) *Schooling in Capitalist America.* London: Routledge & Kegan Paul.

Bridges, D. and Husbands, C. (eds) (1996) *Consorting and Collaborating in the Educational Marketplace.* London: Falmer Press.

Bridgwood, A. (1989) *Working Together: Consortium Links in TVEI.* Sheffield: Training Agency.

Bridgwood, A. (1996) Consortium collaboration: the experience of TVEI, in D. Bridges and C. Husbands (eds) *Consorting and Collaborating in the Education Marketplace.* London: Falmer Press.

Bullock, A. and Thomas, H. (1997) *Schools at the Centre? A Study of Decentralisation.* London: Routledge.

Bullough, R.V. and Gitlin, A.D. (1994) Challenging teacher education as training: four propositions, *Journal of Education for Teaching*, 20(1): 30–8.

Busher, H. and Saran, R. (1990) Teacher morale and their conditions of service: a report on field work. Paper presented to the Annual Conference of the British Educational Management and Administration Society, University of Reading, 14–16 September.

Busher, H. and Saran, R. (1995) Schools for the future, in H. Busher and R. Saran (eds) *Managing Teachers as Professionals in Schools*. London: Kogan Page.

Campbell, R.J. and Neill, S.R.St.J. (1994a) *Primary Teachers at Work*. London: Routledge.

Campbell, R.J. and Neill, S.R.St.J. (1994b) *Secondary Teachers at Work*. London: Routledge.

Carlgren, I. (1993) Professional cultures in Swedish teacher education. Paper presented to the meeting of the Professional Actions and Cultures of Teaching research network, London, Ontario, 25–27 September.

Carlgren, I. (1996) Professionalism and teachers as designers, in M. Kompf, W.R. Bond, D. Dworet and R.T. Boak (eds) *Changing Research and Practice: Teachers' Professionalism, Identities and Knowledge*. London: Falmer Press.

CCCS Education Group (1981) *Unpopular Education: Schooling and Social Democracy in England since 1944*. London: Hutchinson/Centre for Contemporary Cultural Studies, Birmingham.

Central Advisory Council for Education (1967) *Children and Their Primary Schools*. London: HMSO.

Champy, J. (1995) *Reengineering Management: The Mandate for New Leadership*. New York: Harper Business.

Chitty, C. (1989) *Towards a New Education System: The Victory of the New Right?* London: Falmer Press.

Chitty, C. and Lawn, M. (1995) Redefining the teacher and the curriculum, *Educational Review*, 47(2): 139–42.

Chubb, J.E. and Moe, T.M. (1990) *Politics, Markets and America's Schools*. Washington, DC: The Brookings Institute.

Chubb, J.E. and Moe, T.M. (1992a) Educational choice: why it is needed and how it will work, in C.E. Finn and T. Rebarber (eds) *Education Reform in the '90s*. New York: Macmillan.

Chubb, J.E. and Moe, T.M. (1992b) *A Lesson in School Reform from Great Britain*. Washington, DC: The Brookings Institute.

Clarke, J., Cochrane, A. and McLaughlin, E. (1994a) Why management matters, in J. Clarke, A. Cochrane and E. McLaughlin (eds) *Managing Social Policy*. London: Sage Publications.

Clarke, J., Cochrane, A. and McLaughlin, E. (1994b) Mission accomplished or unfinished business? The impact of managerialization, in J. Clarke, A. Cochrane and E. McLaughlin (eds) *Managing Social Policy*. London: Sage Publications.

Codd, J.A. (1996) Professionalism versus managerialism in New Zealand schools: educational leadership and the politics of teachers' work. Paper presented to the Annual Conference of the British Educational Research Association, Lancaster, 12–15 September.

Connell, R.W. (1985) *Teachers' Work*. London: George Allen & Unwin.

Court, M.R. (1997a) Reconstructing 'the principal' in Aotearoa/New Zealand: from professional leader to manager. Paper presented at the Norwegian National Conference in Educational Research, Oslo, 20–22 May.

Court, M.R. (1997b) Reconstructing 'the principal' in Aotearoa/New Zealand: professional/parent partnerships and 'devolution' dilemmas. Paper presented at the Norwegian National Conference in Educational Research, Oslo, 20–22 May.

Croll, P., Abbott, D., Broadfoot, P., Osborn, M. and Pollard, A. (1994) Teachers and educational policy: roles and models, *British Journal of Educational Studies*, 42(2): 333–47.

Cubberly, E.P. (1934) *Public Education in the United States*. Boston: Houghton Mifflin.

Dale, R. (1989) *The State and Education Policy*. Milton Keynes: Open University Press.

Dale, R. (1992) National reform, economic crisis and 'New Right' theory: a New Zealand perspective. Paper presented to the Annual Meeting of the American Educational Research Association, San Francisco, April.

Dale, R. (1998) Conflicting local and global influences on New Zealand education. Paper presented to the Annual Meeting of the American Educational Research Association, San Diego, CA, 13–17 April.

Davidson, G. and Parsons, C. (1990) Evaluating teaching and learning styles in TVEI, in D. Hopkins (ed.) *TVEI at the Change of Life*. Clevedon: Multilingual Matters.

Dearing, R. (1993) *The National Curriculum and its Assessment: Final Report*. London: SCAA.

Deem, R. (1994) Free marketeers or good citizens? Educational policy and lay participation in the administration of schools, *British Journal of Educational Studies*, 42(1): 23–37.

Department for Education and Employment (1997) *Teaching: High Status, High Standards*, Circular 10/97. London: DfEE.

Department of Education and Science (1977) *Education in Schools: A Consultative Document*, Cmnd 6869. London: HMSO.

Department of Education and Science (1985) *Better Schools*. London: HMSO.

Department of Education and Science (1987) *The National Curriculum 5–16: A Consultation Document*. London: DES.

Department of Education and Science (1989) *National Curriculum: From Policy to Practice*. London: HMSO.

Department for Education and Welsh Office (1992) *Choice and Diversity: A New Framework for Schools*, Cmnd 2021. London: HMSO.

Doyle, W. and Ponder, G. (1977) The practicality ethic in teacher decision-making, *Interchange*, 8(3): 1–12.

Drucker, P.F. (1993) *Post-capitalist Society*. New York: Harper.

Education Review Office (1996) *Professional Leadership in Primary Schools*, Education Evaluation Report No.7. Wellington: ERO.

Edwards, R. (1993) The inevitable future? Post-Fordism in work and learning, in R. Edwards, S. Sieminski and D. Zeldin (eds) *Adult Learners, Education and Training*. London: Routledge in association with The Open University.

Englund, T. (1996) Are professional teachers a good thing? in I.F. Goodson and A. Hargreaves (eds) *Teachers' Professional Lives.* London: Falmer Press.

Evans, J. and Davies, B. (1987) The social context of educational opportunities in new vocational educational initiatives, in D. Gleeson (ed.) *TVEI and Secondary Education: A Critical Appraisal.* Milton Keynes: Open University Press.

Evetts, J. (1994a) The new headteacher: the changing work culture of secondary headship, *School Organisation,* 14(1): 37–47.

Evetts, J. (1994b) *Becoming a Secondary Head Teacher.* London: Cassell.

Fergusson, R. (1994) Managerialism in education, in J. Clarke, A. Cochrane and E. McLaughlin (eds) *Managing Social Policy.* London: Sage Publications.

Fink, D. (1998) A retrospective, longitudinal ethnographic study: the attrition of change. Paper presented to the Annual Meeting of the American Educational Research Association, San Diego, CA, 13–17 April.

Finn, C.E. and Rebarber, T. (eds) (1992) *Education Reform in the '90s.* New York: Macmillan.

Fowler, F.C., Boyd, W.L. and Plank, D.N. (1993) International school reform: political considerations, in S.L. Jacobson and R. Berne (eds) *Reforming Education: The Emerging Systemic Approach.* Newbury Park, CA: Corwin Press.

Fullan, M. (1993) *Change Forces: Probing the Depths of Educational Reform.* London: Falmer Press.

Furlong, J. (1992) Reconstructing professionalism: ideological struggle in initial teacher education, in M. Arnot and L. Barton (eds) *Voicing Concerns: Sociological Perspectives on Contemporary Education Reforms.* Wallingford: Triangle Books.

Gee, J.P., Hull, G. and Lankshear, C. (1996) *The New Work Order: Behind the Language of the New Capitalism.* St Leonards, NSW: Allen & Unwin.

Gewirtz, S. (1997) Post-welfarism and the reconstruction of teachers' work in the UK, *Journal of Education Policy,* 12(4): 217–31.

Gewirtz, S., Ball, S.J. and Bowe, R. (1995) *Markets, Choice and Equity in Education.* Buckingham: Open University Press.

Giddens, A. (1981) Agency, institution and time-space analysis, in K. Knorr-Cetina and A.V. Cicourel (eds) *Advances in Social Theory and Methodology.* London: Routledge & Kegan Paul.

Giddens, A. (1984) *The Constitution of Society.* Cambridge: Polity Press.

Giddens, A. (1991) *Modernity and Self-Identity.* Cambridge: Polity Press.

Gipps, C.V. (1993) Policy-making and the use and misuse of evidence, in B. Simon and C. Chitty (eds) *Education Answers Back.* London: Lawrence and Wishart.

Giroux, H. (1984) Ideology, agency and the process of schooling, in L. Barton and S. Walker (eds) *Social Crisis and Educational Research.* London: Croom Helm.

Gleeson, D. (ed.) (1987a) *TVEI and Secondary Education: A Critical Appraisal.* Milton Keynes: Open University Press.

Gleeson, D. (1987b) General introduction: TVEI and secondary education, in D. Gleeson (ed.) *TVEI and Secondary Education: A Critical Appraisal.* Milton Keynes: Open University Press.

Goodson, I. (1994) *Studying Curriculum: Cases and Methods.* Buckingham: Open University Press.

Grace, G. (1987) Teachers and the state in Britain: a changing relation, in M. Lawn and G. Grace (eds) *Teachers: The Culture and Politics of Work*. Lewes: Falmer Press.

Grace, G. (1995) *School Leadership: Beyond Education Management*. London: Falmer Press.

Green, A. (1990) *Education and State Formation*. New York: St. Martin's Press.

Green, A. (1994) Postmodernism and state education, *Journal of Education Policy*, 9(1): 67–83.

Grundy, S. and Bonser, S. (1997) A new work order in Australian schools? Investigations from down under. Paper presented at the Norwegian National Conference in Educational Research, Oslo, 20–22 May.

Hargreaves, A. (1992) Cultures of teaching: a focus for change, in A. Hargreaves and M.G. Fullan (eds) *Understanding Teacher Development*. London: Cassell.

Hargreaves, A. (1993) Individualism and individuality: reinterpreting the teacher culture, in J.W. Little and M.W. McLaughlin (eds) *Teachers' Work: Individuals, Colleagues and Contexts*. New York: Teachers College Press.

Hargreaves, A. (1994) *Changing Teachers, Changing Times: Teachers' Work and Culture in the Postmodern Age*. London: Cassell.

Hargreaves, A. (1995) Beyond collaboration: critical teacher development in the postmodern age, in J. Smyth (ed.) *Critical Discourses on Teacher Development*. Toronto: OISE Press.

Hargreaves, A. and Dawe, R. (1990) Paths of professional development: contrived collegiality, collaborative culture, and the case of peer coaching, *Teaching and Teacher Education*, 6(3): 227–41.

Hargreaves, A. and Goodson, I. (1996) Teachers' professional lives: aspirations and actualities, in I.F. Goodson and A. Hargreaves (eds) *Teachers' Professional Lives*. London: Falmer Press.

Harland, J. (1987) The TVEI experience: issues of control, response and the professional role of teachers, in D. Gleeson (ed.) *TVEI and Secondary Education: A Critical Appraisal*. Milton Keynes: Open University Press.

Harris, K. (1994) *Teachers: Constructing the Future*. London: Falmer Press.

Hartley, D. (1994) Devolved school management: the 'new deal' in Scottish education, *Journal of Education Policy*, 9(2): 129–40.

Hartley, D. (1997a) *Re-schooling Society*. London: Falmer Press.

Hartley, D. (1997b) The new managerialism in education: a mission impossible? *Cambridge Journal of Education*, 27(1): 47–57.

Hartley, D. (1998) Repeat prescription: the National Curriculum for initial teacher training, *British Journal of Educational Studies*, 46(1): 68–83.

Hatcher, R. (1994) Market relationships and the management of teachers, *British Journal of Sociology of Education*, 15(1): 41–61.

Helsby, G. (1989) Central control and grassroots creativity: the paradox at the heart of TVEI, in A. Harrison and J. Gretton (eds) *Education and Training UK 1989: An Economic, Social and Policy Audit*. Newbury: Policy Journals.

Helsby, G. (1993) Creating the autonomous professional or the trained technician? Current directions in in-service teacher support, in G. Helsby (ed.) *The Influence and Legacy of TVEI*, special issue of *Evaluation and Research in Education*, 7(2).

Helsby, G. (1995) Teachers' construction of professionalism in England in the 1990s, *Journal of Education for Teaching*, 21(3): 317–32.

Helsby, G. (1996a) Defining and developing professionalism in English secondary schools, *Journal of Education for Teaching*, 22(2): 135–48.

Helsby, G. (1996b) Constraint or opportunity? Learning to live with the National Curriculum. Paper presented at the Annual Conference of the British Educational Research Association, Lancaster, 12–15 September.

Helsby, G. (1997) Multiple truths and contested realities: the changing face of teacher professionalism in England. Paper presented at the Norwegian National Conference in Educational Research, Oslo, 20–22 May.

Helsby, G. (1998) Changing teachers' work: the impact of two curriculum initiatives in England. Paper presented to the Annual Meeting of the American Educational Research Association, San Diego, CA, 13–17 April.

Helsby, G. and Bagguley, P. (1990) *TVEI: Student Outcomes in Twelve Pilot LEAs*. Sheffield: Training Agency.

Helsby, G. and Knight, P. (1997) Continuing professional development and the National Curriculum, in G. Helsby and G. McCulloch (eds) *Teachers and the National Curriculum*. London: Cassell.

Helsby, G. and Knight, P. (1998) Classroom management in England: times of turmoil – the impact of recent curriculum reforms, in N.K. Shimahara (ed.) *Politics of Classroom Life: Classroom Management in International Perspective*. New York: Garland Publishing.

Helsby, G. and McCulloch, G. (1996) Teacher professionalism and curriculum control, in I.F. Goodson and A. Hargreaves (eds) *Teachers' Professional Lives*. London: Falmer Press.

Helsby, G. and McCulloch, G. (1997) Introduction: teachers and the National Curriculum, in G. Helsby and G. McCulloch (eds) *Teachers and the National Curriculum*. London: Cassell.

Helsby, G. and McHugh, G. (1990) *Teacher Support and Curriculum Change: An Evaluation of Joint Support Activities*. Lancaster: Institute for Research and Development in Post-Compulsory Education/Training Agency.

Helsby, G., Knight, P. and Saunders, M. (1998) Preparing students for the new work order: the case of Advanced GNVQs, *British Educational Research Journal*, 24(1): 63–78.

Her Majestry's Inspectorate (1985) *Education Observed 3: Good Teachers*. London: HMSO.

Hesketh, A.J. and Knight, P.T. (1998) Secondary school prospectuses and educational markets, *Cambridge Journal of Education*, 28(1): 21–35.

Hickox, M.S.H. (1982) The Marxist sociology of education: a critique, *British Journal of Sociology*, 33(4): 563–78.

Hilsum, S. and Strong, C. (1978) *The Secondary Teacher's Day*. Windsor, NFER.

Hinckley, S. (1987) Implementing TVEI: some teacher-related issues, in S.M. Hinckley, C.J. Pole, D. Sims and S.M. Stoney, *The TVEI Experience: Views from Teachers and Students*. Sheffield: MSC.

Hirschman, A.O. (1970) *Exit, Voice and Loyalty: Response to Decline in Firms, Organizations and States*. Cambridge, MA: Harvard University Press.

Holly, P. (1987) *The Dilemmas of Low Attainment*. London: Further Education Unit.

Hood, C. (1991) A public management for all seasons? *Public Administration*, 69: 3–19.

Hopkins, D. (ed.) (1990) *TVEI at the Change of Life*. Clevedon: Multilingual Matters.

Hoyle, E. (1974) Professionality, professionalism and control in teaching, *London Educational Review*, 3: 13–19.

Hoyle, E. (1995) Changing conceptions of a profession, in H. Busher and R. Saran (eds) *Managing Teachers as Professionals in Schools*. London: Kogan Page.

Hoyle, E. and John, P. (1995) *Professional Knowledge and Professional Practice*. London: Cassell.

Huberman, M. (1993) The model of the independent artisan in teachers' professional relations, in J.W. Little, and M.W. McLaughlin (eds) *Teachers' Work: Individuals, Colleagues and Contexts*. New York: Teachers College Press.

Hutton, W. (1996) *The State We're In*. London: Vintage.

Inglis, F. (1989) Managerialism and morality: the corporate and the republican school, in W. Carr (ed.) *Quality in Teaching: Arguments for a Reflective Profession*. London: Falmer Press.

International Labour Office (1991) *Teachers: Challenges of the 1990s: Second Joint Meeting on Conditions of Work of Teachers*. Geneva: ILO.

Jenkins, E. (1997) Legislating philosophy and practice: teaching and assessing scientific investigation, in G. Helsby and G. McCulloch (eds) *Teachers and the National Curriculum*. London: Cassell.

Jesson, J. (1995) Curriculum in New Zealand: is it policy by dodgems? *Educational Review*, 47(2): 143–55.

Jones, K. (1994) *The Making of Social Policy in Britain 1830–1990*. London: Athlone Press.

Klette, K. (1998) Working time blues: on how Norwegian teachers experience restructuring in education. Paper presented to the Annual Meeting of the American Educational Research Association, San Diego, CA, 13–17 April.

Kogan, M. (1989) Accountability and teacher professionalism, in W. Carr (ed.) *Quality in Teaching: Arguments for a Reflective Profession*. Lewes: Falmer Press.

Lawn, M. (1987a) The spur and the bridle: changing the mode of curriculum control, *Journal of Curriculum Studies*, 19(3): 227–36.

Lawn, M. (1987b) What is the teacher's job? Work and welfare in elementary teaching, 1940–1945, in M. Lawn and G. Grace (eds) *Teachers: The Culture and Politics of Work*. Lewes: Falmer Press.

Lawn, M. (1995) Restructuring teaching in the USA and England: moving towards the differentiated, flexible teacher, *Journal of Education Policy*, 10(4): 347–60.

Lawn, M. (1996) *Modern Times? Work, Professionalism and Citizenship in Teaching*. London: Falmer Press.

Lawn, M. and Ozga, J. (1986) Unequal partners: teachers under indirect rule, *British Journal of Sociology of Education*, 7(2): 225–38.

Lawton, D. (1980) *The Politics of the School Curriculum*. London: Routledge & Kegan Paul.

Lester Smith, W.O. (1966) *Education: An Introductory Survey*. Harmondsworth: Penguin Books.

Levačić, R. (1992) The LEA and its schools: the decentralised organisation and the internal market, in Wallace, G. (ed.) *Local Management of Schools: Research and Experience*. Clevedon: Multilingual Matters.

Levačić, R. (1995) *Local Management of Schools: Analysis and Practice*. Bucking-ham: Open University Press.

Lieberman, A. (1993) Foreword, in J.W. Little, and M.W. McLaughlin (eds) *Teachers' Work: Individuals, Colleagues and Contexts*. New York: Teachers College Press.

Lima, J. Ávila de (1998) Improving the study of teacher collegiality. Paper presented to the Annual Meeting of the American Educational Research Association, San Diego, CA, 13–17 April.

Lines, A. and Stoney, S. (1989) *Managing TVEI in Schools: Four Years On*. Sheffield: NFER/Training Agency.

Lipsky, M. (1980) *Street-Level Bureaucracy: Dilemmas of the Individual in Public Services*. Russell Sage Foundation.

Little, J.W. (1990) The persistence of privacy: autonomy and initiative in teachers' professional relations, *Teachers College Record*, 91(4): 509–36.

Little, J.W. and McLaughlin, M.W. (1993) Perspectives on cultures and contexts of teaching, in J.W. Little and M.W. McLaughlin (eds) *Teachers' Work: Individuals, Colleagues and Contexts*. New York: Teachers College Press.

MacIntyre, A. (1981) *After Virtue*. London: Duckworth.

Mahony, P. and Hextall, I. (1997) Problems of accountability in reinvented government: a case study of the Teacher Training Agency, *Journal of Education Policy*, 12(4): 267–83.

Manpower Services Commission (1984) *TVEI Review 1984*. London: MSC.

Mayntz, R. (1979) Public bureaucracies and policy implementation, *International Social Science Journal*, 31(4): 633–45.

McCabe, C. (ed.) (1986) *The Organisation of the Early Years of the Technical and Vocational Education Initiative*. Clevedon: Multilingual Matters.

McCulloch, G. (1997a) Teachers and the National Curriculum in England and Wales: socio-historical frameworks, in G. Helsby and G. McCulloch (eds) *Teachers and the National Curriculum*. London: Cassell.

McCulloch, G. (1997b) Teachers, myth and memory. Paper presented to a meeting of the Professional Actions and Cultures of Teaching network, Oslo, 19–20 May.

McGovern, R. (1992) A view from the front, in G. Wallace (ed.) *Local Management of Schools: Research and Experience*. Clevedon: Multilingual Matters.

McHugh, M. and McMullan, L. (1995) Headteacher or manager? Implications for training and development, *School Organisation*, 15(1): 23–34.

McKeown, P. and Byrne, G. (1996) Competing in a selective system: the experiences of Northern Ireland. Paper presented at the annual conference of the British Educational Research Association, Lancaster, 12–15 September.

McLaughlin, M.W. (1993) What matters most in teachers' workplace context? in J.W. Little and M.W. McLaughlin (eds) *Teachers' Work: Individuals, Colleagues and Contexts*. New York: Teachers College Press.

McLaughlin, M.W. (1995) Rebuilding teacher professionalism in the United States. Keynote address to the international conference on Rethinking UK Education: What Next? London, 5–6 April.

Menter, I. with Muschamp, Y., Nicholls, P., Pollard, A. and Ozga, J (1995) Still carrying the can: primary-school headship in the 1990s, *School Organisation*, 15(3): 301–12.

Menter, I., Muschamp, Y., Nicholls, P., Ozga, J. and Pollard, A. (1997) *Work and Identity in the Primary School: A Post-Fordist Analysis*. Buckingham: Open University Press.

Merson, M. (1990) The problem of teaching style in TVEI, in D. Hopkins (ed.) *TVEI at the Change of Life*. Clevedon: Multilingual Matters.

Merson, M. (1992) The four ages of TVEI: a review of policy, *British Journal of Education and Work*, 5(2): 5–18.

Merson, M. (1996) Education, training and the flexible labour market, *British Journal of Education and Work*, 9(2): 17–29.

Millett, A. (1996) Pedagogy – the last corner of the secret garden. Third Annual Education Lecture, King's College, London, July.

Moore, R. (1990) TVEI, education and industry, in R. Dale, R. Bowe, D. Harris, M. Loveys, R. Moore, C. Shilling, P. Sikes, J. Trevitt and V. Valsecchi, *The TVEI Story: Policy, Practice and Preparation for the Workforce*. Milton Keynes: Open University Press.

Munn, P. (1992) Devolved management of schools: a victory for the producer over the consumer? in L. Paterson and D. McCrone (eds) *Scottish Government Year Book*. Edinburgh: Edinburgh University Press.

Murphy, J. (1992) Restructuring America's schools: an overview, in C.E. Finn and T. Rebarber (eds) *Education Reform in the '90s*. New York: Macmillan.

Murphy, J. (1998) New consumerism: evolving market dynamics in the institutional dimension of schooling, in J. Murphy and K.S. Louis (eds) *The Handbook on Research on Educational Administration*. San Francisco: Jossey-Bass.

National Commission on Excellence in Education (1983) *A Nation at Risk: The Imperative for Educational Reform*. Washington, DC: US Government Printing Office.

Office for Standards in Education and Teacher Training Agency (1996) *Assessment of Quality and Standards in Initial Teacher Training 1996/97*. London: Ofsted.

Organization for Economic Cooperation and Development (1987) *Quality of Schooling: A Clarifying Report*. Paris: OECD.

Osborn, M. (1997) Policy into practice into policy: creative mediation in the primary classroom, in G. Helsby and G. McCulloch (eds) *Teachers and the National Curriculum*. London: Cassell.

Ozga, J. (1992) Teacher professionalism. Paper presented to the Annual Conference of the British Educational Management and Administration Society, Bristol.

Ozga, J. (1995) Deskilling a profession: professionalism, deprofessionalisation and the new managerialism, in H. Busher and R. Saran (eds) *Managing Teachers as Professionals in Schools*. London: Kogan Page.

Ozga, J. (1996) Teacher professionalism: an overview rooted in current concerns. Paper presented to the Inaugural Conference of the Professional Studies Forum, Leeds, 10–11 January.

Peters, T.J. (1988) *Thriving on Chaos: Handbook for a Management Revolution*. London: Macmillan.

Peters, T.J. (1992) *Liberation Management: Necessary Disorganization for the Nanosecond Nineties*. New York: Fawcett.

Peters, T. and Waterman, R. (1982) *In Search of Excellence: Lessons from America's Best-run Companies*. New York: Harper and Row.

Pfeffer, N. and Coote, A. (1991) *Is Quality Good for You? A Critical Review of Quality Assurance in Welfare Services.* London: Institute for Public Policy Research.

Pollard, A., Broadfoot, P., Croll, P., Osborn, M. and Abbott, D. (1994) *Changing English Primary Schools? The Impact of the Education Reform Act at Key Stage 2.* London: Tyrell Press.

Poulson, L. (1996) Accountability: a key-word in the discourse of educational reform, *Journal of Education Policy,* 11(5): 579–92.

Power, S., Halpin, D. and Whitty, G. (1997) Managing the state and the market: 'new' education management in five countries, *British Journal of Educational Studies,* 45(4): 342–62.

Quicke, J. (1996) Work, education and democratic identity, *International Studies in Sociology of Education,* 6(1): 49–66.

Reay, D. (1998) Micro-politics in the 1990s: staff relationships in secondary schooling, *Journal of Education Policy,* 13(2): 179–96.

Reich, R.B. (1993) *The Work of Nations: Preparing Ourselves for 21st Century Capitalism.* London: Simon & Schuster.

Reynolds, D. (1984) Relative autonomy reconstructed, in L. Barton and S. Walker (eds) *Social Crisis and Educational Research.* London: Croom Helm.

Rizvi, F. (1989) Bureaucratic rationality and the promise of democratic schooling, in W. Carr (ed.) *Quality in Teaching: Arguments for a Reflective Profession.* London: Falmer Press.

Robertson, S.L. (1996) Teachers' work, restructuring and postfordism: constructing the new 'professionalism', in I.F. Goodson and A. Hargreaves (eds) *Teachers' Professional Lives.* London: Falmer Press.

Robertson, S.L. (1998) Strip away the bark. Expose the heartwood. Get to the heart of the matter: Restructuring and reregulating teachers' labour in New Zealand. Paper presented to the Annual Meeting of the American Educational Research Association, San Diego, CA, 13–17 April.

Rosenholtz, S.J. (1989) *Teachers' Workplace: The Social Organization of Schools.* New York: Teachers College Press.

Sachs, J. (1997) Reclaiming teacher professionalism: an Australian perspective. Paper presented at the Norwegian National Conference in Educational Research, Oslo, 20–22 May.

Saunders, L., Stradling, B., Morris, M. and Murray, K. (1991) *Clusters and Consortia: Co-ordinating Educational Change in the 1990s.* Sheffield: Employment Department.

Schön, D.A. (1983) *The Reflective Practitioner: How Professionals Think in Action.* London: Temple Smith.

Senge, P.M. (1991) *The Fifth Discipline: The Art and Practice of the Learning Organization.* New York: Doubleday.

Sharpe, F.G. (1996) Towards a research paradigm on devolution, *Journal of Educational Administration,* 34(1): 4–23.

Shulman, L.S. (1983) Autonomy and obligation: the remote control of teaching, in L.S. Shulman and G. Sykes (eds) *Handbook of Teaching and Policy.* New York: Longman.

Sikes, P. and Taylor, M. (1987) Some problems with defining, interpreting and communicating vocational education, in D. Gleeson (ed.) *TVEI and Secondary Education: A Critical Appraisal.* Milton Keynes: Open University Press.

Siskin, L.S. (1994) *Realms of Knowledge: Academic Departments in Secondary Schools.* London: Falmer Press.

Smyth, J. (1995) What's happening to teachers' work in Australia? *Educational Review,* 47(2): 189–98.

Stenhouse, L. (1975) *An Introduction to Curriculum Research and Development.* London: Heinemann.

Stones, E. (1966) *An Introduction to Educational Psychology.* London: Methuen.

Stronach, I. and Morris, B. (1994) Polemical notes on educational evaluation in the age of 'policy hysteria', *Evaluation and Research in Education,* 8(1–2): 5–19.

Talbert, J.E. and McLaughlin, M.W. (1994) Teacher professionalism in local school contexts, *American Journal of Education,* 102: 123–53.

Taylor, W. (1994) Teacher education: backstage to centre stage, in T. Becher (ed.) *Governments and Professional Education.* Buckingham: Society for Research into Higher Education and Open University Press.

Teacher Training Agency (1997) *Consultation: Training Curriculum and Standards for New Teachers.* London: TTA.

Trow, M. (1994) *Managerialism and the Academic Profession: Quality and Control.* London: Quality Support Centre.

Tyack, D. and Cuban, L. (1995) *Tinkering toward Utopia: A Century of Public School Reform.* Cambridge, MA: Harvard University Press.

van Zanten, A. (1995) Market trends in the French school system: overt policy, hidden strategies, actual changes. Paper presented to the European Conference on Educational Research, University of Bath, September.

Vulliamy, G. and Webb, R. (1991) Teacher research and educational change: an empirical study, *British Educational Research Journal,* 17(3): 219–36.

Wallace, G. (1992) The organisation and the teacher, in G. Wallace (ed.) *Local Management of Schools: Research and Experience.* Clevedon: Multilingual Matters.

Wallace, M. (1998) A counter-policy to subvert education reform? Collaboration among schools and colleges in a competitive climate, *British Educational Research Journal,* 24(2): 195–215.

Walsh, K. (1987) The politics of teacher appraisal, in M. Lawn and G. Grace (eds) *Teachers: The Culture and Politics of Work.* Lewes: Falmer Press.

Warnock, M. (1988) *A Common Policy for Education.* Oxford: Oxford University Press.

Watts, A.G. (1983) *Education, Unemployment and the Future of Work.* Milton Keynes: Open University Press.

Webb, R. and Vulliamy, G. (1996) A deluge of directives: conflict between collegiality and managerialism in the post-ERA primary school, *British Educational Research Journal,* 22(4): 441–58.

Westheimer, J. (1998) *Among School Teachers: Community Autonomy and Ideology in Teachers' Work.* New York: Teachers College Press.

Williams, R. (1961) *The Long Revolution.* London: Chatto and Windus.

Wilmott, H. (1993) Strength is ignorance; slavery is freedom: managing culture in modern organisations, *Journal of Management Studies,* 30(4): 515–52.

Woodhead, C. (1995) *A Question of Standards: Finding the Balance*. London: Politeia.

Woods, P. and Jeffrey, B. (1997) Creative teaching in the primary National Curriculum, in G. Helsby and G. McCulloch (eds) *Teachers and the National Curriculum*. London: Cassell.

Woods, P., Jeffrey, B., Troman, G. and Boyle, M. (1997) *Restructuring Schools, Reconstructing Teachers*. Buckingham: Open University Press.

Young, M. (1998) Rethinking teacher education for a global future: lessons from the English, *Journal of Education for Teaching*, 24(1): 51–62.

AUTHOR INDEX

SUBJECT INDEX